SNAP SHOT

ALSO BY

DAN KOREM

The Art of Profiling
READING PEOPLE
RIGHT THE FIRST TIME
EXPANDED, 2ND ED.

Rage of the Random Actor
DISARMING CATASTROPHIC ACTS
AND RESTORING LIVES

Suburban Gangs
THE AFFLUENT REBELS

READING AND TREATING PEOPLE RIGHT THE FIRST TIME

FROM NEIGHBORS ACROSS THE STREET, TO CLASSROOMS, TO NEGOTIATION TABLES, TO THE FACE OF A NATION

DAN KOREM

INTERNATIONAL FOCUS PRESS
RICHARDSON, TEXAS

International Focus Press
P.O. Box 831587, Richardson, Texas 75083-1587
www.ifpinc.com

The author is grateful for permission to use the following copyrighted material: Chapter 6: Jim Borgman's ZITS 2006 cartoon, © 2006 Zits Partnership, Dist. By King Features; Chapter 16: illustrations from Monty Roberts's book, *From My Hands to Yours, 2nd ed.*, © 2007, Monty Roberts, Inc., Solvang, CA; Chapter 17: Dr. Kenneth Libbrecht generously provided photographs of snow crystals, many of which are published in his books, including *The Art of the Snowflake,* 2007; Chapter 25: Bottomliners 2011 cartoon by Eric and Bill Teitelbaum, © Tribune Content Agency, LLC.

ISBN 978-0-9893358-1-2
Library of Congress Catalog Number: 2015930224

Printed in the United States of America
First Printing March 2015.

Book designed by Jen Adams-Maki
Jacket Designed by Todd Hart Design

For my Sandy,
More than a snapshot in time,
you captivated my heart for the ages.

For Carrie, Erik, and Luke,
Your lives have been this life's greatest treasure,
Your contributions inspire me to stay the path until it's finished.

CONTENTS

CHAPTER ONE

They Saw It...

Four Short Stories

[Ever had to quickly figure out something about someone? They did.]

An entrepreneur in his twenties, Josh had to quickly solve a puzzle: A major player wanted to do business with his start-up company, but he couldn't get the VP to sign the contract. The negotiations just seemed to drag on without a specific reason. They wanted his services, could afford it, and there wasn't another competitor interfering. Frustrated, he called his friend David for input because David knew how to profile people and read specific human traits.

David immediately asked, "Is the VP conventional or unconventional?"

"Definitely unconventional."

"How do you know that?"

"He's always talking about pushing the envelope with new ideas."

"What's more important to him, innovation or seeing his ideas implemented?"

"Seeing his ideas implemented," Josh fired back.

"Has he ever dragged his feet when following through on details?"

"Yes."

"OK. Send him an email that you are concerned that if the contract isn't wrapped up soon, some of his key ideas might not be implemented."

The email went out. The deal closed that day based upon one behavioral read made in seconds.

This is a real case in which David, a young professional, knew how to rapid-fire profile people on the spot using the *Korem Profiling System*™ (*KPS*). I developed the *KPS* in the early 1990s, and it was published in my 1997 book *The Art of Profiling—Reading People Right the First Time.*

Making snapshot reads is one component of the *KPS*. A snapshot read isn't a multipage comprehensive profile, which the *KPS* delivers, but a smaller slice of insight. For example: does a person prefer to be conventional or unconventional?

David had learned to identify the comprehensive profile of any company or player in a company, and quickly identify if a behavioral tendency needed to be addressed. In this case, he used just one snapshot read and figured out that the VP preferred to be unconventional in how he approached his work. A benefit of this human trait was that the VP liked change, innovation, and was open-minded. A potential drawback was that he might not follow-up on day-to-day details, like signing a contract, which for him was tedious.

Because of David's skill, Josh closed the deal.

Trevor, in the next case, put his skill to work at home with his wife.

Profiling at Home—Even Better Than Closing Deals

"Snapshot reads improved how I meet my wife's needs and understand her. Before I learned to profile, I wasn't the best."

Trevor is the owner of one of the most successful companies of its kind in North America, and while he uses the *KPS* in his business, he said the most valuable impact was one snapshot read he made in his marriage.

"I realized that my wife prefers to be assertive when she communicates, even when there isn't a conflict. She just has a more commanding tone, while I'm less assertive. Neither is good or bad. We're just different.

"Before I learned to profile, if we had a disagreement, I assumed that her assertiveness was a call for a verbal fight. Now I realize that all she wants from me is to be just a little bit more assertive, rather than fight, because for her it shows her that I am engaged and listening. And, I can do that. Boy, things are better.

"Thinking about profiling her has also made me pay closer attention to other things, like what she wants—such as keeping the house just a little bit cleaner.

"She's told me, 'I just want someone to notice the mess and signify some kind of intent to do something about it.'

"That's an easy one. I just put up the dishes without prompting and it pays huge dividends. And yes, I've gotten my teenage boys on the page with me.

"And, this all started by learning to profile for my business, and then making the common sense applications with my wife."

Like Trevor's boys, teenagers can also learn to profile like Amber figured out how to work with a teacher.

Student Raises the Bar

Amber thought her science teacher, Ms. Dominguez, didn't like her. No matter how hard Amber tried, Ms. Dominguez never showed any emotion. Amber thought her teacher didn't care about her. Then Amber learned to make snapshot reads and realized Ms. Dominguez had the CONTROL trait (when you see all caps, it's a specific term for making snapshot reads in the *KPS*). She realized that Ms. Dominquez rarely showed much emotion in any positive or negative situation or with anyone. For the first time, Amber learned that some people don't have to show emotion to show that they are pleased with you. Once she learned to profile, Amber noticed Ms. Dominguez's kind words and the occasional pat on the back to assure Amber that she was doing well. Once she understood Ms. Dominguez, Amber worked harder and her grades went up.

A few weeks later, Amber and several students were asked to speak to a group of school administrators from surrounding districts about how they used their new profiling skills to raise the bar on their campus.

"At the beginning of the year, I didn't quite get along with my AP chemistry teacher. But since I learned to profile, I've used a lot of my skills to change a little bit of how I do things because I realized it really wasn't her that had a problem, but me," Amber explained.

"She understates her relationship with her chemistry teacher," interjected her principal. "It was bad!"

"You say your grade in science went up. How much did it go up?" asked one of the skeptical administrators.

"I had an 87 and right now it's sitting at 98."

Think Amber had an idyllic life? A few years earlier, a RANDOM ACTOR drifter (a profile you'll learn about in Chapter 22) came through Amber's small town and randomly slaughtered her entire family. She survived by hiding.

Amber was diligent and kindhearted; you'd never know this was part of her background. Can you understand why it was important that she thought her teacher cared for her personally? She lost her family. She was a good student and person. She just needed someone to read and treat her right the first time. Not much to ask for. For Amber, learning to profile filled in the gap for understanding others that her parents might have provided if they were still alive.

While snapshot reads are best put to use elevating the lives of others, they can also be a lifesaver.

Just weeks before, Amber's principal used the *KPS* to identify a troubled student who, if triggered, might do something irrational when a former First Lady came to give a speech at the school. The Secret Service, when doing their security sweep, never asked her about students on her campus who have the RANDOM ACTOR traits. In effect, Amber's principal outperformed the Secret Service. She reached out to that student and mitigated his paranoia, while the special agents didn't even know he could be identified as someone that should be "on the radar."

Here's another example where a potentially bad day was averted by other school administrators:

Find One Student Out of 1,500 in 30 Minutes...Tick, Tick, Tick

Her voice was steady, but pointedly alarmed.

"Dan, I need your help. Can you be here at 7:00 a.m. tomorrow morning?"

Dr. Childers, the superintendent of a large suburban school district that bordered a major military contractor, had reason to be concerned. Bomb threats had been escalating at the high school for several months, and it was near the end of spring, when stressors are the highest.

A month before, she heard me give a speech about why the needle was at "10" for potential school massacre attacks in her area, like the 1999 massacre at Columbine High School in Littleton, Colorado.

Calls like Dr. Childers's were frequent. A year before, the head of intelligence of a major police department had a serious threat in another suburb near Dr. Childers. He asked me to train one of his intel officers *on the phone* in how to identify the RANDOM ACTOR profile—the profile of almost every mass school shooter/bomber, as well as most suicide bombers, postal and company shooters, and serial killers. Within two hours of arriving at a 3,000-student, upscale suburban high school, the officer found not one but two school massacre plots—and the threats were successfully mitigated.

When I arrived the next morning to meet with Dr. Childers's administrators, they were huddled around the table in the high school principal's conference room.

They immediately began the meeting by telling me about a half a dozen students who might be making the threats.

"If this isn't a prank, and if the threats truly are escalating, it will probably be one of about 90 students in your school," I started.

"About 6% of your students have the RANDOM ACTOR profile, which is consistent for school districts like yours across the country," I explained.

"And, most who are committing attacks have this profile and usually aren't on anyone's radar. They haven't been arrested or regularly in trouble, like the students you described," I added.

"Here are the two traits in the RANDOM ACTOR profile:

"First, they're extremely unconventional. They like to be *different*. This by itself doesn't mean someone will blow up a school.

"Second, they are *extremely fearful* in their day-to-day decisions. They may be very bright and confident in their competency, but otherwise, most decisions are made out of extreme fear.

"Do any of these students you've just mentioned have these two traits?" I asked. None of them did, but they had been in fights.

"Where is the wall where the threats were written?" I asked.

They described the location on the second floor and, because of the location of the threat, they knew during which period they were scrawled on the wall. The threats were left several times in the same proximity.

"Which classes on the hall are more structured disciplines like history, math, or language arts?" I asked. "Classes that are more conventional can alienate a person with the RANDOM ACTOR profile, who is extremely UNCONVENTIONAL. In other words, theater, video production, shop, and classes that are more UNCONVENTIONAL usually won't set them off."

They rattled off three classes.

"Get the rolls from those classes," I instructed, "and tell me which students have the RANDOM ACTOR traits *and* if they did something that was off. You might not have considered it to be important, but it showed paranoia and/or was a comment about harming others—even if it seemed flip."

"Yeah, Jeremy has that profile, and I remember him making a joke about shooting up the school a couple of years ago, but didn't think much of it at the time," one of the administers remembered. Jeremy wasn't on anyone's list for special attention, let alone a suspect for RANDOM ACTOR violence.

"Can we get some papers he's written in a composition class?" I asked.

We got lucky. He was in a composition class, and within 10 minutes we were poring over his papers, which were filled with despair, isolation, anger, and more.

"If Jeremy is the student, I want Mr. Velka [the principal] to bring him down and talk to him. Mr. Velka, I need about another 15 minutes to give you some do's and don'ts of what to say and how to say it."

It was 7:30 a.m.

By 8:00 a.m., Jeremy was in Mr. Velka's office. As instructed, using nonthreatening open-ended questions, Mr. Velka asked Jeremy for his insight about the threats. He explained that he heard Jeremy was astute and might be able to shed light from a student's perspective.

"Well, he's not Hispanic," Jeremy jumped in. "He's going to be white, pretty smart, and his parents probably work at the plant [the military contractor nearby]. He's had problems with them and he's angry, but I don't think he's going to do anything right now." In effect, Jeremy was describing himself and, in an odd way, was letting Mr. Velka know he wasn't going to act now—without admitting he was guilty. He trusted Mr. Velka and his approach.

"Jeremy, I've done a lot reaching out to various student leaders. Is there anyone else you think I should get to help me to make sure that all students feel a part of our school?"

"Well, who did you talk to?" Jeremy asked.

"You know, student council leaders, class leaders, and others," Mr. Velka explained.

"Yeah, but what about us students *in the middle*? Who aren't the tops but also aren't always in trouble?" he added.

"About how many students are we talking about?" Mr. Velka asked.

"About 70 or 80," Jeremy said firmly. Mr. Velka was stunned. It was approximately the same number of students with the RANDOM ACTOR profile I told the administrators were in Mr. Velka's school—and Jeremy knew it without sophisticated training or mentoring.

That day, the threats stopped. Jeremy became part of Mr. Velka's team to reach all students, and he did well the rest of the year.

Out of 1,500 students, Jeremy was identified by administrators equipped with only thirty minutes of training. The result: a threat was mitigated, and a young teen's life was restored. Not all students have to go to jail to make a turn for the good. They just need someone to profile them and *treat and lead them right the first time.*

Making and Using Snapshot Reads

David, Trevor, Amber and her principal, and Dr. Childers are some of over 40,000 people I've taught how to make snapshot reads using the *KPS*. For me, nothing is more valuable or rewarding than investing in others.

If these four stories have you thinking, *I'd sure like to do that or help someone I know*, you won't be disappointed.

As you learn how to make and use snapshot reads using the *KPS*, use the following three questions to help stimulate yourself to find ways to use your new skill. Be sure to read them again *after* each chapter while the chapter concepts and examples are fresh in your mind, and you'll be surprised what you come up with.

1. **Did it, but don't know how I did it:** When did you intuitively "profile" someone (or a group/company/etc.) in a way that enabled you to produce a significant result and wish you had a system so:
    - You can do it again and produce the same results?
    - You can transfer the skill and teach others how to do it?

2. **Didn't do it, but wished I could have:** When did you wish you could have profiled someone (or a group/company/etc.) in the past so that you could have:
    - Produced a positive result?
    - Solved a problem?
    - Avoided a difficult situation?

3. **Will need to do it, don't know how:** When will you need to profile someone (or a group/company/etc.) in the future so that you can:
    - Produce a positive result?
    - Solve a problem?
    - Avoid a difficult situation?

What you'll learn is pretty straightforward. First, you'll briefly learn how I developed the *KPS*. Next, you'll learn how it works—with theory kept to a minimum—so you can immediately start making snapshot reads. And then, the rest of the book shows you how others have used their new insight to do amazing things in every area of life, gain remarkable insights, and solve perplexing people puzzles.

Everything that is presented is guided by one goal and philosophy:

I know who you are.
Good for me. Better for you.
It's the art of treating people right the first time.

This isn't just a clever saying. It's an attitude about life that's the heartbeat of the best profilers and what you'll learn in this book.

CHAPTER TWO

Reading People...
A Natural Reaction

[We all do it.
We're just not very good at it.]

Reading people is a natural reaction when we first meet someone. It's a natural tendency to size people up and look for patterns that tell us if we'll like or dislike someone, or the best way to communicate, mentor, lead, or work with someone. The problem is that most of us aren't very good at it. Reading the human factor for most people is difficult and inexact. Not only do they not know what to read, they can't do it with systematic accuracy. Stuck, they resort to educated guesses, gut feel, and reactions. That's when trouble and confusion take over. Sound familiar?

Like Josh, who was trying to close a contract, people can usually read *nonbehavioral situational* factors such as knowledge, skill, ability, and experience—or find someone else who can.

If our child is struggling with math concepts, we can talk to a teacher or school counselor. If we're stymied by a problem at work, we find someone who can fill in the facts about the *situation*. If a head coach needs data on a player, he can go to a player's position coach for a report. If we need a doctor who is a specialist, we can ask friends who have had positive outcomes for referrals. But what do you do when you need to know a specific *human factor*?

For Josh, figuring out how the VP liked to operate between his ears was the deal-closing factor; it was the *human factor* he needed to know. He already knew the key *situational* factors: they wanted and could afford his services, and there wasn't another competitor. But, Josh didn't know how to motivate the VP to move forward because he couldn't identify the VP's profile and how to uniquely motivate him. David, who could profile, did connect the dots and the deal closed.

Before Amber learned to make snapshot reads, she couldn't understand that her teacher *didn't* need to show emotion to show that she cared. Once Amber made just one snapshot read, resistance to her teacher instantly diminished and her grade went up.

The need for making accurate snapshot reads presents itself daily. For example, what if you need a doctor who is not only competent, but who is also open to new ideas and innovation? A doctor who is extremely conventional and isn't inquisitive probably isn't the right one to trust with a shoulder injury that requires a creative approach to rehab.

Believe it or not, in most situations—both personal and professional—accurately reading a person's behavioral traits is usually the easiest part of successfully interacting with someone...if you can rapid-fire profile and make snapshot reads with systematic accuracy.

And, that's what you're going to learn.

First: How to consistently make accurate on-the-spot snapshot reads without stereotyping—even without meeting someone, as David did—*or even if you can't speak their language.*

Second: How to *apply* your new insight and *treat someone right the first time.*

For you teenage and college students, what you're going to learn will not only help you understand your peers and the adults around you, it will separate you from the competition in whatever you're going to do in life. (And yes, it will give you more insight into people you date and even marry!)

Third: You'll be able to profile yourself and consider how others perceive you and how you would prefer to be treated.

Profiling Lite

"Please, I need just one read...today."

"Look," Stephanie, an exec, prodded, "I'll get *The Art of Profiling*, but can you help me with just one quick read? I won't have time to learn your whole system on the plane."

That's how this book started.

She wanted to know how to make one *KPS* snapshot read to select a team leader. She had to be sure that a highly skilled candidate for a team leadership position was a confident decision maker. She thought I could help because one of the *KPS* snapshot reads identifies whether or not a person is confident, cautious, or high fearful.

She had been burned in the past by credentials and experience. She needed someone who was experienced *and* confident to lead a team.

I met Stephanie in 2005 while signing copies of *The Art of Profiling* at the busiest bookstore at Dallas-Fort Worth International Airport. It's one of the only places I do signings because the world walks past your table. Literally.

Once a week, for a few hours a day for several months in a busy terminal, I met thousands on their way to work with top-of-the-mind problems to solve. Hundreds of Stephanies asked me the same question: *Can you show me how to make just one quick read? I'll learn your system later, but I need help now.*

The Stephanies who stopped by had deals to close, critical hires to complete, negotiations in foreign countries, family and personal relationships to enhance or repair, children to guide, and even professional and collegiate athletic teams to coach.

None had the ability to rapid-fire profile.

In the full-blown *KPS*, you make four different on-the-spot snapshot reads, combine them, and you get a two-page comprehensive profile that identifies how a person is likely to communicate, perform tasks, and make decisions...and how to successfully interact with a person or team order to sell, lead, motivate, confront, and more. It's like a hip-pocket hostage-negotiator's guide. You're in a dynamic situation; you have to make an accurate on-the-spot read, and then take appropriate action. (An example of a COMPREHENSIVE profile is provided in Chapter 16, which also acts as one of two safety checks to confirm the accuracy of your reads.)

This book is profiling "lite." It's a primer to get you up and running. You'll learn the four snapshot reads and how to immediately put them to use. Later, you can decide whether or not you want to learn the full system. Some issues, though, like those in Chapters 11–14, are explored in more detail because of their significance in our lives.

Throughout the book, a "snapshot read" means you're making rapid-fire, on-the-spot observations of a person's *actions*. The *KPS* shows you where and how to make your reads and how to do it quickly, in seconds or minutes, to ensure accuracy. The read is in effect a two-part call to action: first we observe and then we act based upon the read.

Mastery Doesn't Require 10,000 Hours...Just Days or Weeks

A current competency theory is that we have to invest 10,000 or more hours to become the best in a profession, from music to sports science to running a company. This may be true in some disciplines, but not rapid-fire profiling. In fact, rapid-fire profiling is a more attainable and accessible skill than most of the core disciplines taught in high school and college.

My company, Korem & Associates, has trained over 40,000 people from dozens of countries how to rapid-fire profile. We baseline everyone's accuracy by having them make snapshot reads of video clips of real people in real situations. They have ten seconds to make a snapshot read and enter their responses on an interactive keypad. These are tracked by our computer.

Seventeen years of collecting data shows that globally, the average person who hasn't been trained to profile only has 25–35% accuracy. This means people are typically ineffective when interacting with others up to 65–75% of the time, which is brutally apparent when video of their everyday interactions is reviewed.

In a two-day training environment, where they learn the whole *KPS*, average accuracy increases to 75–80%. For those who self-tutor using *The Art of Profiling*, high levels of accuracy are attained in two to three months, as demonstrated by Lieutenant General Peter Devlin.

A former deputy commanding general at Fort Hood, and later the chief over all Canadian land forces, Devlin sent me an email when he was earlier deployed to Afghanistan as a colonel in the Canadian army. He explained how he used the *KPS* for leadership and diplomatic interactions.

> Thank you for your book—The Art of Profiling!
> My name is Colonel Peter Devlin, a Canadian Infantry Officer who commands the 2 Canadian Mechanized Brigade Group and commanded the Kabul Multi-National Brigade in Kabul, Afghanistan, from July 2003 to January 2004. There were 22 different nations that provided troops to the brigade and I interacted with their national and tactical commanders on a regular basis. I also dealt with Afghan authorities daily, including government officials (federal, provincial and municipal), military leadership, elders, religious leaders, nomads and more. Your book assisted me in preparing strategies for the many people I interacted with every day. The job of a leader is to influence people for mission success and your book assisted me in successfully accomplishing my mission. Thanks.
>
> –Peter Devlin, Colonel, Commander 2 CMBG

Yes, some of us have an intuitive gift. About 5–15% of the population has an intuitive ability to profile people accurately.[1] Some are born with an innate gift, others learn it from a parent, relative, or an adult mentor, while others cultivate the skill to survive. The problem is they don't know how they do it, how to correct a misread, or what they need to do to take it to the next level and increase accuracy. And, most important, they can't transfer their skill to their colleagues, friends, spouses, or children, like David did when he helped Josh close a contract.

They Needed to Negotiate Without Stereotyping

Since the early 1980s, working as an investigative journalist, reading people accurately across all cultures without stereotyping was a daily necessity for me.

For example, in 1981, three years after the 1978 Jonestown suicidal massacre, which claimed over 900 lives and was the largest in recent history, a famous athlete had fallen into a cultlike group led by a man who used clever deceptions to convince his followers he had powers. The athlete's family asked me to investigate the group, which had similar markings to other suicidal cult groups, though it was in its embryonic stage. That's when I formed a production company and hired one of Dan Rather's former producers at *60 Minutes*, and Hugh Aynesworth, the Pulitzer Prize nominee who had just finished writing *The Only Living Witness*, in which he obtained the confession of serial killer, Ted Bundy.

The result was the 1983 documentary, *Psychic Confession*,[2] which contains the first confession of a cultlike figure who made homicidal-suicidal threats and who also claimed to have powers using sleight of hand. Law enforcement credited my accurate reads and interactions with the leader and his followers as a strategic factor that helped avert catastrophe.

Other investigations have followed across more than thirty countries: those at war, those in transition from communism to democracy, newly developing countries, and countries at peace. I spent seven years uncovering why gangs were forming in affluent suburbs and small towns in the U.S. and Europe. I even found an antidote that stops gang formation and suicide ideation, which resulted in my book, *Suburban Gangs—The Affluent Rebels* (1995) and a book for parents on at-risk youth trends, *Streetwise Parents—Fool-Proof Kids* (1992). I've not only tried to uncover the finest, thinnest wires of what makes us tick for good and evil, but I've also looked for and have applied solutions on a large scale.

Throughout, reading people accurately in all cultures was critical for successful interviews, investigations, consoling victims of crime, and obtaining confessions.

Today, when most people think of profiling, they think of criminal profiling, where behavioral patterns are identified to apprehend a suspect, defuse a hostile situation, and so on. Criminal profiling, however, is just one small corner of behavioral profiling.

A dramatic turn. My life took a dramatic turn when I was asked to use profiling for a very different application.

In the late 1980s, members of the Young Presidents Organization (YPO) asked me if I could develop a rapid-fire on-the-spot profiling system they could use for foreign negotiations, to quickly understand others without succumbing to cultural or ethnic stereotyping. (Members are all presidents of major companies before they're 40 and can remain a member until they're 50.) I had spoken at a number of their conferences in several countries, and they were intrigued with the video clips I showed in which I was able to quickly establish rapport with complete strangers and obtain transparent interviews that revealed lifesaving insights. I had also used my skills when negotiating media contracts, so the YPO members' request didn't seem far-fetched.

After some initial digging, I found that a comprehensive system like they wanted didn't exist. So I recruited behavioral experts from major companies, law enforcement, and psychologists from academia to help me develop and refine what is now known as the *Korem Profiling System*™. Once it was developed, in 1995, I presented the *KPS* to more than ninety leading North American and European police psychologists at the FBI's Behavioral Sciences Unit. They agreed that the *KPS* concepts were sound, and the results produced over the years have demonstrated its effectiveness.

On a personal level. Once it was developed, I started to use the *KPS* in all interactions in my personal life. My wife, Sandy, and I used it when working with hundreds of inner-city youths through an outreach at our church, to more quickly connect with the kids without stereotyping. Sandy, a former labor and delivery nurse, also used her insight as she built a leading catering establishment and gourmet takeaway shops, especially when working with clients and hiring and leading staff—which created lots of pillow talk late into the night. (She also patiently agreed to role-play five different guys' wives during my undercover days of investigating bad guys.) And, we showed our three kids how to use the skill to even help a struggling teacher. Today, all three have become remarkably successful at young ages and trailblazers in their individual fields—each applying their insight into others, a skill they learned while growing up with Mom and Dad.

Is This Like...?

SNAPSHOT READ
Rapid-fire, on-the-spot observations of a person's actions.

Snapshot reads used for on-the-spot behavioral profiling aren't to be confused with racial or ethnic stereotyping (which government officials *incorrectly* call profiling). Behavioral profiling is based upon reading a person's *actions*, and *never* race or ethnicity.[3] In fact, *if you can't rapid-fire profile, you'll racially or ethnically stereotype out of ignorance* (more on this throughout the book and in Chapter 23).

Snapshot reads and rapid-fire profiling are also only slightly similar to a written behavioral self-assessment test you might have filled out when applying for employment, where you answered questions such as: *Are you more expressive or are you more controlled?* These tests are also used for career development, counseling, marriage-prep courses, and so on.

Making rapid-fire snapshot reads is different. Rapid-fire profiling is reading people on the fly *without* a test.

The biggest drawback to tests is that they have limitations and can produce inaccuracies without providing a way to check accuracy. First, because people have to agree to take a test and fill it out truthfully. Inaccuracy occurs because not everyone tests well, or maybe they just had a bad day. Others may give dodgy answers to be perceived a certain way,[4] and some tests are just poorly constructed.

In other "profiling" methods, people verbally answer a battery of questions. Using the *KPS* to make snapshot reads doesn't use tests or batteries of questions; to do so in most cases would be intrusive and offensive. Imagine meeting someone professionally or personally for the first time and asking them to take a test or answer a battery of questions so you can better understand them. Not a smart play and unlikely to promote trust.

Inaccurate reads and avoiding disastrous results. In the early 1990s, executive officers of the Chicago and Los Angeles chapters of the Society for Human Resource Management (SHRM), contacted me and said that the *KPS* was the first practical check on written tests they had encountered, and as a result we trained over 2,000 SHRM professionals. Their consensus was not to discard assessment tests, but rather balance them with rapid-fire reads to check the accuracy of the tests.

Sometimes clients ask us to review a key executive hire or promotion. While not in the placement business, they want us to kick the tires on reads from a test. We regularly find important reads are completely off.

A common example is when a candidate's test identifies them as having high innovator tendencies, which means he or she has the UNCONVENTIONAL trait. When we meet the candidate, though, in minutes it is apparent the candidate is CONVENTIONAL. They don't like to innovate, but they can sustain and lead a situation. In other words, the candidate is *adaptable* and can *adjust* to a new situation. This is completely different from innovating and creating a new situation or solution. Imagine placing a new leader into a situation where you expect innovation but what you get is adapting to current or new situations. The results can be disastrous.

Or, what if a school counselor makes the same misread based on a standardized test and tells you that your child is an innovator, but it never shows up in his schoolwork? Now agonizing efforts are focused on solving a "lack-of-creativity problem" when the real issue is an inaccurate read. The reality is that your child isn't hardwired to be exceptionally creative—and there is nothing wrong with that. Teachers have shared with me the misery of trying to solve the unsolvable before they learned to make accurate snapshot reads.

In short, snapshot reads are used when you have to understand someone now, *without* tests or batteries of questions. Another significant difference between the rapid-fire *KPS* and tests and lists of questions is that *KPS* has two quick safety checks to ensure your accuracy, if you choose to learn them.

Additionally, on-the-spot profiling is also a powerful tool to *rule out* the human factor. For example, what if the VP Josh was trying to close a deal with demonstrated that he *was* a follow-through guy who didn't drop the ball? Then Josh could quickly eliminate a behavioral pothole and look at nonbehavioral factors, such as the possibility that: the company had other priorities, couldn't afford the project, etc.

How Are You Going to Use Your New Skill?

Will you use snapshot reads for professional needs, to improve a personal relationship, or to mentor a teen or child? Or are you a teenager trying to figure out how to navigate your parents, a teacher, or a friend? (Be sure to *reread* the three questions in Chapter 1 *after* you finish each chapter to stimulate your imagination and bring something to mind you might have missed.)

Remember, you'll even be able to profile people *before* you meet them—even if you *can't speak their language*, which is invaluable if you travel abroad for business or pleasure, or interact with diverse cultures for any reason. You'll also learn how to make reads *separate* from cultural customs, to avoid racial and ethnic stereotyping (Chapter 23).

Don't make the most common mistake. Most people first focus on using snapshot reads to avert or diminish difficult or disastrous situations. You may have been harmed in the past or are afraid of trouble in the future. I've written quite a bit on that subject, and we'll look at some important reads you can make to prevent catastrophic events.

It's far better, though, to first focus on reading others for positive reasons. This will help you resist the temptation to only profile others when there is trouble.

Most of the examples you'll learn focus on positive ways to elevate performance, improve relationships, and assist people who are struggling. You'll even be able to teach young teens how to make snapshot reads and use them. All my kids could rapid-fire profile by the time they were 14, and you'll learn amazing things kids have accomplished with their new insight.

The case examples I've selected are from people I've mentored or consulted, some of whom were trained by us, and others who simply read *The Art of Profiling*. As a courtesy, names and places have been changed when appropriate. Here are some examples:

Sales. Only one life insurance agent in the entire industry was trained to make one snapshot read when setting appointments. Using the read and one slight modification, in just three weeks, cancellations dropped 13%, and he became the number two first-year-out-of-college performer for one of the top North American companies (Chapter 8).

Leadership. With one snapshot read, you'll learn how to identify a true leader separate from his or her expertise, an invaluable skill for team environments (Chapter 20). You'll also learn how a coach made a snapshot read and applied a slight modification that enabled a team with one predominant profile to follow a leader who had a completely different profile, producing their best results in years (Chapter 8).

Kids and education. A high school student made one snapshot read of a struggling first-year calculus teacher, suggested one small change, and her class took off (Chapter 8).

Teachers solve the ADHD riddle. Teachers, who could profile, made one read that solved the riddle of why most of their students were misdiagnosed as ADHD and what the teachers did (without medication) that immediately restored classroom performance (Chapter 12).

Increasing capacity to make CONFIDENT decisions. Parents and kids, in 30 minutes, learned how to increase their capacity to make confident decisions *separate* from their giftedness or training and do some amazing stuff (Chapter 19).

Develop trust. Learn a simple technique to quickly develop trust when first meeting someone. The former VP of one of the world's largest property-management firms reduced the time it took to establish rapport with a person she met for the first time, from 15 minutes to just five (Chapter 4).

Golfers, news broadcasters, lawyers, and others who suddenly can't perform something they've done all their lives. One of the most celebrated pitchers in collegiate history suddenly couldn't throw to first base. Coaches call it the "thang," and it became a national sports story. With one snapshot read, an adjustment was made *off the field* that had nothing to do with the mechanics of throwing a ball, and overnight the pitcher could throw to first base. A similar phenomenon, called the yips, afflicts professional and amateur golfers and is also corrected off the course. This same phenomenon also suddenly afflicts news broadcasters who can't read the news, lawyers who suddenly can't write technical briefs, and others (Chapter 13).

Identify why a teacher is gifted so that quality/skill can be immediately transferred to another teacher. One read identified why one of the world's elite golf coaches can shorten the time for comprehension, retention, and ability to execute—a concept any teacher can apply (Chapter 7).

Getting a job. A graduating law student profiled the law firms and partners where he applied, wrote letters, and conducted his interviews based upon their profiles. He received more offers at a higher dollar than any other graduating law student in his class (Chapter 8).

Stronger families. Throughout the book you'll pick up insights on how to better nurture, discipline, guide, and direct kids and teens.

Travels to distant lands. As you'll learn through many examples in many chapters, snapshot reads can peel back the surface of a culture and the fascinating people you meet and places you visit for business and pleasure. For example, I uncovered an extraordinary story while on holiday in Normandy, France—all because I made a snapshot read of someone in a painting (Chapters 23 and 24).

Predicting the collapse of a giant. I addressed the partners of one of the nation's leading firms, made one snapshot read, and predicted the company's collapse several years before the demise. Few believed it when I said that Andersen, the cash-flush accounting giant with 100,000 employees and generating nine billion dollars a year, would collapse (Chapter 9).

Law enforcement. In seconds, a police chief made just two quick reads and averted the first mass attack of 2008 on U.S. soil by a former military professional. Six previous agencies that couldn't make snapshot reads had engaged the suspect and saw nothing suspicious. These same two reads have been used to mitigate many school rampage attacks and threats, and homicide-suicide terrorist attacks (Chapter 22).

One snapshot read that increases your ability to detect lying. A little known read that anyone can make (Chapter 15).

The tectonic shift in the Earth's behavioral profile. You'll learn how the Earth's behavioral profile has shifted almost overnight in the last 30 years and the dramatic impact this shift will continue to have on your personal and professional life (Chapter 8).

In addition to practical ways you can use snapshot reads, your new insight will give you a bigger, more complete picture of the world—things in life you'd completely miss unless you could profile.

Other Tools

This book is the companion to *The Art of Profiling*, the expanded second edition of which contains over 70 pages of additional profiles and strategies. I recommend that you read *Snapshot* first, as it quickly presents core concepts you can immediately use. As already noted, *The Art of Profiling* teaches the complete *KPS*. If you choose to learn the *KPS*, I recommend referring back to *Snapshot* for ways to use your four reads, as most of the application examples are different. *Snapshot* is also a useful quick refresher of the core concepts.

While I've written this book as an entry point to learn how to make and use snapshot reads, please read the "Source Notes" if you like more details, insights, and historical perspectives. Regarding stylistic conventions: as this book is written for an international audience, the male pronoun will be applied when appropriate, as it is the current standard. Also, specific terms are provided in all-caps format to avoid confusion. The term ASSERTIVE, for example, only designates someone who is assertive when communicating, rather than the broader dictionary definition. I've also added chapter reference "reminders" throughout the book to make it easier to locate concepts you have or will read.

Another valuable tool is the **Pocket PeopleReader™**, which can be loaded onto your cell phone. It automates the *KPS* and provides all 20 comprehensive profiles. Four taps on your app and up pops a person's profile, with guidance how to lead, motivate, sell/present, defuse a confrontation, and more. (Details on the Korem Associates website: koremassociates.com.)

As needed, updated examples and *KPS* developments are provided on the "Live Addendum" update for this book on the IFP website: ifpinc.com.

So here you are at "my table." What do you have on your mind today? Business, repairing a personal relationship, leading a team, coaching an athlete? Maybe you're just curious, or perhaps you're a teenager just trying to figure others out. It doesn't matter. In about the time it takes to fly from Dallas to Los Angeles or New York, you'll put a couple of quick snapshot reads in your pocket that you can use when you land. Promise. I know you have a plane to catch, homework to finish, or kids to put to sleep, so let's get started.

CHAPTER THREE

Wired to Read

It's in all of us

[Reading someone to close a deal is important.
Reading someone to save lives is another matter.]

Valentine's Day. February 2008. Peaceful DeKalb, Illinois. That's when a 22-year-old former student, Steven Kazmierczak opened fire on classmates in a lecture hall at Northern Illinois University, killing 6 and wounding 16 before killing himself. Like most private citizens, the media was unable to profile, and it showed in their coverage—like this observation from an Associated Press reporter: *If there is such a thing as a profile of a mass murderer, Steven Kazmierczak didn't fit it.*[1]

In fact, there was nothing remarkable about his case and he should have been on a high-risk watch list since high school, as you'll learn in Chapter 22.

Jim Thomas, a nationally recognized criminal-justice scholar, who also couldn't rapid-fire profile, had Kazmierczak in his introductory sociology course and said he never recognized the life-threatening threat in front of him. He said: *In this large class he stood out. So I tried to use him as an unpaid assistant. He stood out because he was hardworking, he was bright, he would come up and* ***talk*** *about ideas behind what I'd taught.... He seemed as normal as you or I.* [2]

What did Thomas focus on? He focused on how Kazmierczak *talked* to him about his ideas.

How many times after a school rampage do we hear something like *he seemed like such a nice guy*...or...*he was quiet and pleasant*. That's how many people described Tamerlan and Dzhokhar Tsarnaev, the brothers who committed the Boston Marathon bombing on April 15, 2013. In Kazmierczak's case, people described him as "gentle" and "happy,"[3] and those who knew Dzhokhar described his as a "sweet boy...always smiling, friendly, happy."[4]

Why are so many fooled by these individuals?

Because they focused on how they communicated—their communication actions or their *talk*—and not on how they performed tasks and made decisions—their *walk*.

Think about it. Logically, which part of a killer's profile will kill you? The talk or walk?

The obvious answer is the *walk*: how someone performs actions and makes decisions.

As a counterpoint, since 1997, we've trained over 20,000 educators how to identify the mass school-rampage killer. The result? Many attacks have been averted *and* without a single call to our office where someone misidentified a student as a threat who wasn't (more in Chapter 22).

Statistically, from the thousands of those whose snapshot reads we've tracked, the number one reason for misreads in any situation—not just mass killers—is that a person's communication actions are confused with how they will *act*.

In other words, *talk* is confused with the *walk*.

When I was investigating cases, making *talk* and *walk* reads separately was paramount or lives would be put at risk. Someone may seem pleasant when they talked to you, but it was more important to know what they would *do* and how they made *decisions*—how they would *perform*.

Four Wires in All of Us

We've all heard the expression, *he's wired a certain way*, or *she's wired differently*. It's a way we recognize and respect that people are different. It also alerts us that we should respect this uniqueness and treat people based on their profile. The four snapshot reads you'll use in the *KPS* are four of the finest, thinnest wires of human behavior found in everyone. They were selected to help the YPO presidents who asked me to develop a system they could use for negotiations.

The corporate leaders related to me negotiation after negotiation in which someone with whom they were negotiating *talked* confidently but never *performed* or made *decisions* confidently. Their misreads were frustrating, costly, and often promoted needless distrust.

When I surveyed the YPO presidents, I asked what specifically they wanted to know and in what order. Here is what they said:

First, how does a person prefer to communicate? Obviously, this is a priority, as this is how negotiations begin. They gave me many examples where they didn't begin appropriately and the problems and mistrust it caused, which necessitated spending valuable time repairing damage.

Second, how does a person prefer to operate or perform? This is important so they could do business appropriately.

Third, how does a person prefer to make decisions? This is a logical need because all negotiations have the goal of reaching a decision.

The behavioral experts I recruited helped me identify four behavioral wires found in everyone that could deliver this information. Over time, I refined the wires so anyone could make rapid-fire snapshot reads. [5]

Two wires, which we'll also refer to as *gauges* or *traits*, identify how a person communicates. We call these the communication or *talk* wires and they are shown below:

Wire 1: Does a person prefer to CONTROL or EXPRESS emotions when he/she communicates? (CONTROL–EXPRESS wire)

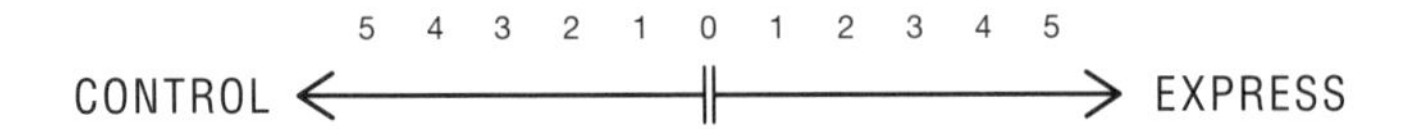

Wire 2: Does a person prefer to be ASSERTIVE or NONASSERTIVE when he/she communicates? (ASSERTIVE–NONASSERTIVE wire)

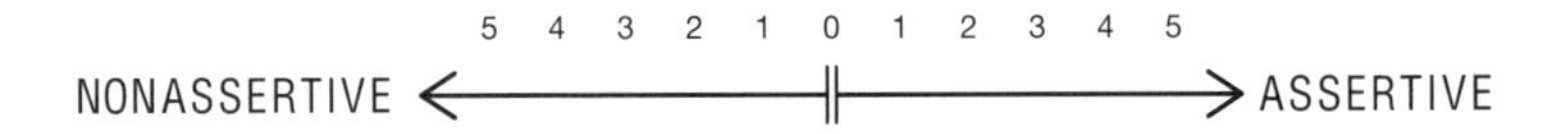

For example, if we make a snapshot read and observe that a person is on the ASSERTIVE side of the wire, we say this person has an ASSERTIVE trait.

Each wire is depicted with a 0 to 5 scale to identify the strength of someone's trait, and it reminds us that some of us are a little CONTROL or EXPRESS (about 1), others are moderate (about 3), and some of us have a stronger trait (4 or higher).

If you think about it, everyone displays these actions. We usually prefer to either control or express our emotions, or be assertive or nonassertive when we communicate. Yes, we can vary some, but we usually tilt in one direction or the other in most situations. This is true globally across cultures, which is why the *KPS* can be used in any country.

The other two wires/gauges/traits identify how people like to operate and make decisions—what we call the performance or *walk* wires.

Wire 3: Does a person prefer to be CONVENTIONAL or UNCONVENTIONAL? (CONVENTIONAL–UNCONVENTIONAL wire)

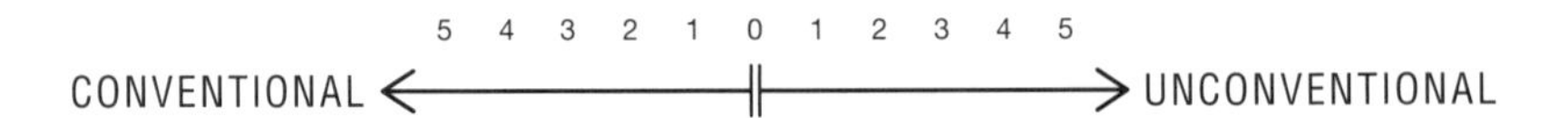

Wire 4: Does a person make decisions *confidently, cautiously,* or out of *extreme fear?* (CONFIDENT–CAUTIOUS/FEARFUL wire)

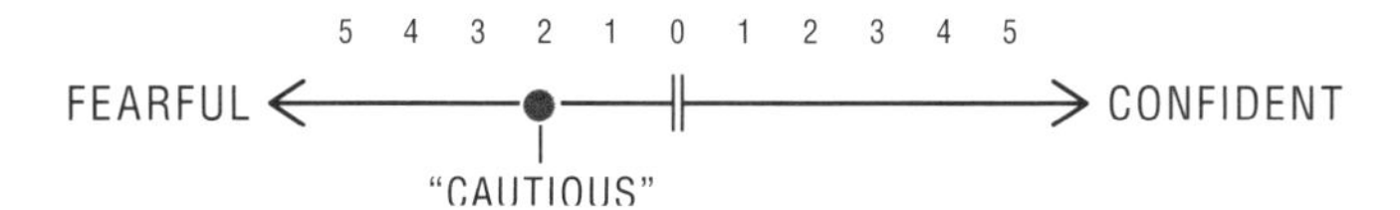

The fourth wire has *three* points so we can distinguish between CONFIDENT, CAUTIOUS, and extreme FEARFUL, which is paranoia and is inherently destructive.

People who are 5 FEARFUL might just be extremely fearful or they may have a diagnosable fear such as paranoid schizophrenia. For this reason, we want to be able to distinguish between people who are CAUTIOUS and people who are extremely FEARFUL (more in Chapter 15).

When making snapshot reads, we read the wires/gauges/traits *separately.* This minimizes misreading a person's *talk* for his or her *walk*, the mistake that plagued the YPO presidents during negotiations. For example, a person may be quiet and nonassertive, but it won't tell you how he or she makes decisions, where you need the CONFIDENT–CAUTIOUS/FEARFUL wire.

At this point, you may have a question, like:

- How do I know if a read is correct?
- How do I read someone that has on a game face (whether deliberately or not deliberately)?
- Do I read facial expressions?

We'll fill in these blanks as we progress. For now, you only need a mental picture of the four behavioral wires we all have.

A Simple Refinement That Instantly Increases Accuracy by 20% or Higher

There is a simple technique you'll use that will immediately increase your rapid-fire profiling accuracy by 20% or higher. (Remember, almost everything you're going to learn is based upon data, and isn't just an opinion. Every group in the world that has applied the following technique has seen increases accuracy without additional instruction.)

It works like this:

Imagine you meet Cheryl for the first time, and she tells you what she does and doesn't like about her work. You want to know if she's CONVENTIONAL or UNCONVENTIONAL, similar to David's read based upon Josh's observations. Your read will determine whether or not she's a good fit for a specific assignment on a team, in a contract negotiation, to take on a particular responsibility, and so on.

While interacting with her, if you ask yourself, "Does Cheryl seem to tilt towards being CONVENTIONAL or UNCONVENTIONAL?" your accuracy will be impaired. Why? Because you're relying upon your intuition, gut feeling, how you feel or don't feel that day, and so on. It's too subjective when comparing her to two descriptive words: CONVENTIONAL and UNCONVENTIONAL. Instead, here is how you are going to make your reads:

At the end of each wire, you'll put a famous person who will represent the extremes. For CONVENTIONAL, for example, you might put Queen Elizabeth II, as she is extremely conventional and traditional in almost everything she does. For the UNCONVENTIONAL end of the wire, you might use Jim Carrey, the zany actor.

The key is that you will select people you can relate to and can immediately visualize.

So while you're talking to Cheryl, you're asking yourself, "Does she seem more like Jim or the Queen?" (or QE2 as she is affectionately called by the Brits). This doesn't mean that Cheryl is as *extreme* as the Queen or Jim Carrey. You're just making a read of which side Cheryl *tilts* toward. That's it.

A young Dutch professional said he imagines playing a mental video game in his mind. There is a picture of Queen Elizabeth II on his left and Jim Carrey on his right. The person he is reading is in the middle and there is a slider beneath the person. As he interacts or observes someone, he mentally moves the slider so Queen Elizabeth II or Jim Carey is over the person's head, and he quickly answers: *Who is he/she more like?*

You'll customize your wires by selecting people you want to represent the extremes. You'll be given lots of options. (Additional options will be provided on the Live Addendum for this book on the IFP website.) You can even choose someone you know, like your Aunt Margaret, as long as she is as extreme as the examples that are provided. If she isn't as extreme, your whole gauge will be off. The key is that you can visualize and mentally call these people up quickly, anytime, anywhere.

The reason this works is you *aren't* making subjective intuitive reads using descriptive words like CONVENTIONAL and UNCONVENTIONAL. Rather, you're comparing someone to people that represent the extremes of each wire. And, you'll use this gauge for everyone.

This is the first technique that will immediately increase your accuracy. Here's the second refinement:

Ten-Second Reads

When you make your rapid-fire snapshot reads, you'll do it quickly—within 10 seconds. If you don't, I've found that people overthink and second-guess their read, and accuracy drops. When we monitor people making reads, accuracy drops 5–10% every ten seconds because people talk themselves out of their accurate read.[6] The lesson: Overthink it and accuracy drops.

So here is how you'll make a snapshot read:

You're interacting with Cheryl. After a few minutes, you see she is more like Queen Elizabeth II. She's likes to do things that are CONVENTIONAL. Within 10 seconds of *observing* she is more like the queen, you make your read. Most of us do this naturally. We meet people and we immediately start sizing them up. The difference is that your current process is subjective and relies on intuition. Using the wire with extremes in 10 seconds enables you to make reads with clarity and increased accuracy, regardless of your native ability.

Making reads quickly, though, doesn't mean you won't make another snapshot read to check your first read. In some cases you will, but you'll also make those additional reads quickly. And, there are two safety checks you'll be introduced to later.

Make your read in ten seconds.

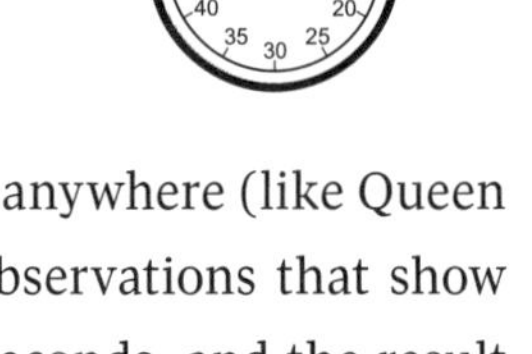

To sum it up: You make rapid-fire snapshot reads by comparing someone to two visual extremes that you can recall in your mind anytime, anywhere (like Queen Elizabeth II and Jim Carrey). Once you've made observations that show which way they tilt, you finalize your read in ten seconds, and the result will be increased accuracy.

What if I Make a Mistake?

You *will* make mistakes...but, you'll make *fewer* mistakes using the technique I've just described. Remember, the average accuracy is only 25–35% for those who haven't learned to rapid-fire profile. So don't let making a mistake hold you back. *You already are making mistakes.*

By making ten-second reads and comparing someone to the extremes of a gauge, your *inaccuracy* will immediately *decrease*. It's a statistical fact that tens of thousands have demonstrated to themselves.

I've given hundreds of speeches across dozens of countries, and audiences in as little as 10 minutes demonstrate this remarkable increase in accuracy. After an audience views a video clip of someone in an everyday situation, they profile that person using interactive keypads.

In the photo on the left, you see that 100+ professionals from over a dozen Fortune 500 companies demonstrated 28% accuracy *without* using the refinements. Then, after a few minutes of instruction, they rapid-fire profiled an equally difficult clip using the two refinements and their accuracy jumped to 50% or higher. This happens every time. Across cultures.

Even teenagers see the same jump in accuracy. During a talk to over 50 first- and second-generation Taiwanese high school students, they hit 63% accuracy (photo on the right) within minutes of learning to make reads in 10 seconds using the extremes of each wire.

Before

After

For More Advanced Needs

You may need to make more complex reads, like combining two or three snapshot reads at the same time to gain greater insight into someone. This can be done, but it will require more effort. To get a picture of how much information is available, quickly scan the ARTIST–LOYALIST comprehensive profile in Chapter 16. Comprehensive profiles, along with the list of type actions explained in that chapter, can also be used as "safety checks" to ensure the accuracy of your snapshot reads.

Using the refinements and suggestions throughout the book, your accuracy should double to 50% or higher. If you need a higher degree of accuracy, 80% or higher, you can learn the entire *KPS*, which also provides increased guidance on how to interact with someone.

For now, though, there are plenty of singular snapshot reads that you can put to immediate use, and by the time you finish the book, you'll know if you want more.

Visual Recap

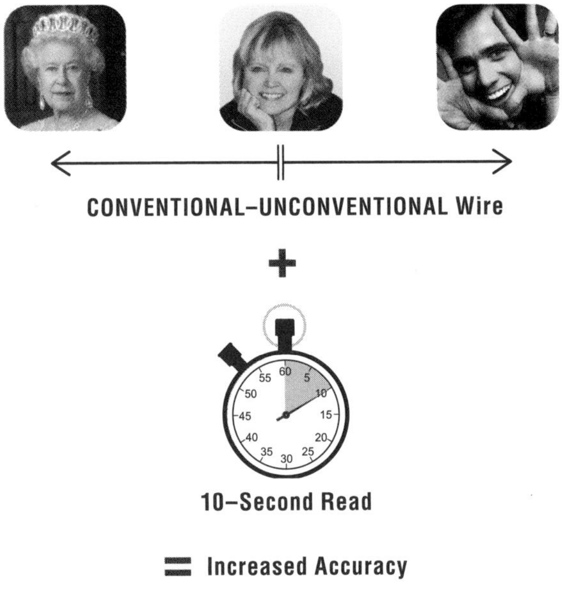

CONVENTIONAL–UNCONVENTIONAL Wire

+

10–Second Read

= Increased Accuracy

Now that you have your bearings, let's learn how to make snapshot reads with the ASSERTIVE–NONASSERTIVE communication wire.

CHAPTER FOUR

ASSERTIVE-NONASSERTIVE

Your First Wire

[Ever known someone who had trouble being assertive when they needed to be and it cost them?]

That was Henry. He owned a high-tech service company with over a hundred employees. Most people did business with Henry because he was attentive to details, listened well, and was extremely thorough. But Henry had a problem.

Even when he could provide better service, with better terms, and at a better price, he didn't close deals with about 20% of the companies he called on. He thought there might be a behavioral disconnect between himself and these clients. He was frustrated and wanted to close the gap, so he called me for assistance.

After a short consult, it was clear to me that Henry was right: There was a behavioral disconnect.

Henry profiled himself as being extremely NONASSERTIVE and laid-back when he *communicates* (5 on the wire), and his trait was clearly evident when I met with him. He said that he perceived his role was to listen carefully, deliver every detail, without surprises, and at a fair price. He refrained from being strongly persuasive with a client, but rather let his reputation and his team's performance speak for themselves. This was his philosophy and it worked for securing contracts with most clients.

Then we profiled those deals he didn't close, and there was a pattern. He had a much lower closing ratio in one-on-one meetings with people who were ASSERTIVE—his opposite.

Here was the root of Henry's closing ratio: Some ASSERTIVE people stereotype a NONASSERTIVE person as someone who won't perform—even though talk isn't walk.

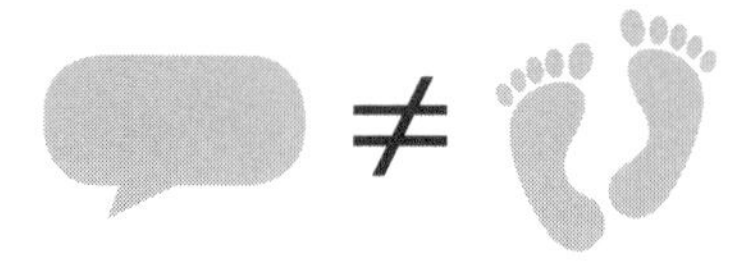

His potential clients confused a lack of assertiveness when communicating with a lack of commitment to deliver. Henry was battling a similar situation like the YPO presidents who wanted a rapid-fire system for negotiations to avoid stereotyping. In this case, people who were ASSERTIVE were stereotyping Henry that he wouldn't perform.

The Solution: We agreed that Henry had to become more ASSERTIVE in a way that fit him so he could connect with his potential ASSERTIVE clients. There are three ways people show assertiveness when they talk to others:

- Nonverbals (such as body position, use of hands, and facial expressions)
- Tone of voice
- Choice of words

So I had Henry role-play being a little more forceful during a presentation using each of these elements. When he tried to be more forceful with his choice of words and tone of voice, it didn't work. It looked affected—contrived and forced. It wasn't natural. In part, this was because in the Asian country where he was born, assertiveness—even positive assertiveness—when communicating can be construed as rude or disrespectful.

This caused him to have a mental block.

I noticed, though, that he used a mechanical pencil to make notes in his portfolio. This conveyed precision. For Henry, his full communication package told you he didn't miss a detail and was very precise with each word he recorded on his pad. So we tried two slight nonverbal modifications.

First, we changed his body position. When reviewing a contract, Henry usually sat with his shoulders open—his right shoulder slanted away from the client. Instead, I had him turn and face the client more directly as he approached the closing stages of the presentation, as this subtly conveys a bit more assertiveness. Henry was comfortable with this modification and it looked natural.

Second, as he reviewed each point of the contract on his pad, I told him to make a careful, deliberate check mark next to each point, and then look at the client after each check for acknowledgement that this is what he or she wanted. The emphatic check mark conveyed assertiveness and that Henry was on top of delivering each detail.

Together, these slight communication modifications conveyed that Henry would assertively deliver—that he was in control. What Henry did might not work for another person with the same profile as his, but it worked for quiet, thoughtful Henry.

The Result: Henry's behavioral disconnect didn't cost him any more clients. He not only increased his client base, but he also learned how to explore making subtle adjustments that, for him, were natural and comfortable.

The Lesson: If you are NONASSERTIVE and dealing with someone who is ASSERTIVE and you must be more ASSERTIVE, find something that you can do using your nonverbals, choice of words, or tone of voice to convey being a little more ASSERTIVE. A nonverbal is the easiest, like straightening your head and squaring your shoulders. In Henry's case, he squared his shoulders and added emphatic check marks. Using more ASSERTIVE words or phrases is the next easiest, such as: show, give, tell, provide, watch, look, and so on. For Henry, this was better than NONASSERTIVE words and phrases, like: perhaps, could we, seems like, etc. For a NONASSERTIVE person, modifying one's tone of voice is often the hardest technique to apply to appear more ASSERTIVE, and if not done well, often appears affected and strained.

Personalize Your ASSERTIVE–NONASSERTIVE Wire

Below is a list of famous people who represent the extremes of being ASSERTIVE and NONASSERTIVE when they communicate. Select one person from each list whom you will use to represent each extreme. The only qualification is that you can instantly recall and visualize this person. You can also choose someone you know, but they must be as extreme as the examples provided or your whole gauge will be off.

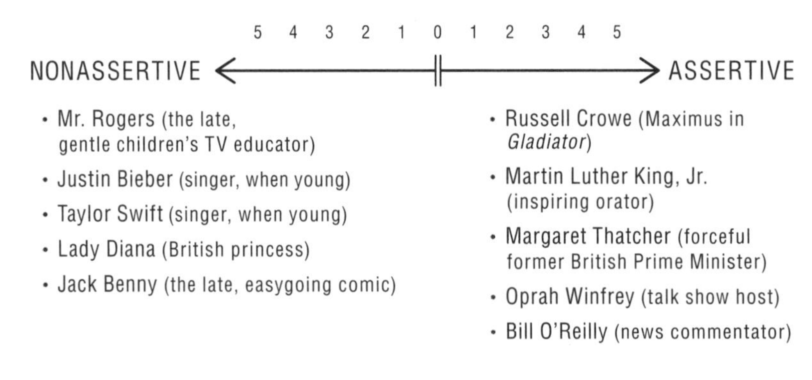

You might also want to view video clips on the Internet of the examples provided if you're uncertain what an extreme example looks like. However, if you are viewing an actor, like Russell Crowe, do so in the movie noted, and not another role where he might portray someone with a different trait. (Currently it's difficult to identify famous people who are *extremely* NONASSERTIVE because media doesn't typically promote people with this trait. The examples provided, though, will help you get started.)

Once you've finalized your extremes for your wire, when interacting with someone, you'll ask yourself: *Is this person more like Russell Crowe or Taylor Swift?*

As you'll recall, each side of the wire/gauge is calibrated from 0–5 as a reminder that some people will be just a little ASSERTIVE or extremely ASSERTIVE, or a little NONASSERTIVE or extremely NONASSERTIVE.

Here are possible positive and negative actions for each side of the wire. Remember, these are only *communication* actions.

> **People who are ASSERTIVE:** Strong, confident, overbearing, unsympathetic, aggressive, lead conversation, egotistical, directive, blunt, and forceful

> **People who are NONASSERTIVE:** Inquisitive, attentive, curious, appear uninformed or naive, agreeable, altruistic, weak, nonaggressive, indirect, and laid-back

Your Plot Point and the Concept of Range

To help you get your bearings, identify your approximate plot point on the ASSERTIVE–NONASSERTIVE wire. Let's assume you plotted yourself at 3 ASSERTIVE (Point A).

The average person's range usually extends 1/2 to 1 full point in each direction as we don't use our trait with exactly the same strength each day or in specific situations. So with a plot point of 3, we know your range is about 2–4 ASSERTIVE.[1]

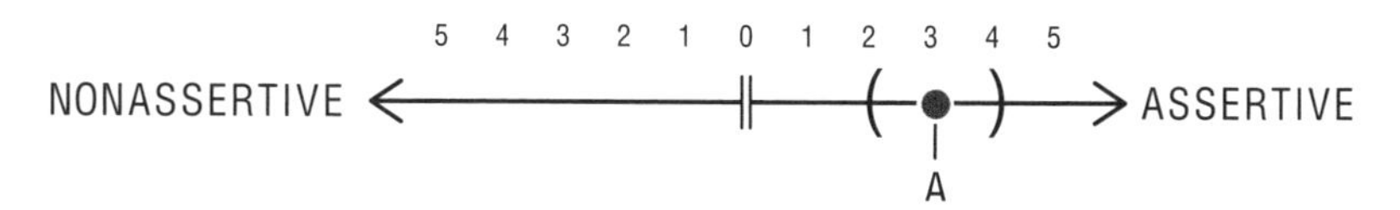

Acknowledging the concept of range reduces stereotyping. It restrains us from assuming, "She always does that," because people don't always act or react with the same degree of intensity. For example, at work you may tilt in one direction and at home another.

Recognizing we have a range also reminds us that we can naturally be a little more or less ASSERTIVE or NONASSERTIVE when required. We can use a nonverbal, tone of voice, or choice of words that is a little more in either direction when necessary. While this natural tendency works in most situations, sometimes a more deliberate action is required, as in Henry's case. He had to adjust for his extreme 5 NONASSERTIVE trait, and a slight movement to 4 NONASSERTIVE alone wouldn't work, so he used the techniques we identified.

Quick!

Which journalist tilts more towards Russell Crowe and appears more ASSERTIVE and forceful? Urs or Anita? Don't over think it. Make your snapshot read now.

Urs Gehriger
Die Weltewoche, Switzerland

Anita Blaszczak
Rzeczpospolita, Warsaw, Poland

If you thought it was Urs, you're correct. His head is more vertical, his eye contact is stronger, and he's leaning in. Anita is a bit more relaxed, easygoing, and her head is tilted to her right—a more laid-back, NONASSERTIVE posture.

Both journalists interviewed me for two different articles on how people use rapid-fire profiling in the workplace. Urs was a journalist for *Die Weltewoche*, one of Switzerland's leading newspapers. Anita was an editor at *Rzeczpospolita*, which is like the *Wall Street Journal* in Poland. In the middle of each interview, both asked me if I could profile them. It's a common question posed during interviews. I asked them to freeze and I took their photos with my cellphone—two of Urs and three of Anita. In both sets of photos their trait changed from NONASSERTIVE to ASSERTIVE. It's an example of people unconsciously putting on a "game face." But, it's still possible to read their actual trait. Here is what happened:

Urs. Before my interview with Urs at the Hotel Schweizerhof in Lucerne, Switzerland, I observed him in the hotel lobby talking to the concierge. My snapshot read was that he communicated more like Russell Crowe and not Taylor Swift or Mr. Rogers. Even though he spoke Swiss German, which I don't, you could see his commanding presence and hear an ASSERTIVE tone of voice. (One simple technique to profile someone in a foreign country is to profile another person first. In this case, I profiled the concierge the day before, when I asked for directions, then compared Urs to the concierge the next day.)

Although naturally ASSERTIVE, when Urs interviewed me he used a technique we teach for interviewing, and he did it intuitively, without training. It's a technique where an ASSERTIVE person can be more NONASSERTIVE, which is effective when asking questions, allowing people to more freely express themselves without unintentional pressure.

As you can see in the first photograph on the next page, Urs appears NONASSERTIVE. He sat with his right shoulder open to me, his head in a nice relaxed tilt, and he kept his hands in his lap and never used them as a

Interviewing me – open, inquiring, NONASSERTIVE posture

Urs actual trait—telling me about his dissertation

"pointer" for emphasis, which some ASSERTIVE people do.

Together, these three nonverbals convey openness and an inquiring presence, which is ideal for a fact-gathering, nonconfrontational interview. He also refrained from using an aggressive tone of voice, although his questions were probing and well thought out. Collectively, his actions conveyed restraint, which is usually more effective to put someone at ease and collect information quickly and with greater transparency. However, I knew I could be a little more ASSERTIVE and add emphasis with Urs, if it seemed appropriate, because that was his actual trait and it wouldn't make him uncomfortable.

Right after I snapped the first photo, I asked Urs to tell me about his doctorate in history. This took him out of his reporter mindset. I was now the journalist interviewing Urs, which brought out his actual trait. He explained that his dissertation focused on how water was a strategic factor that contributed to the formation of the state of Israel.

In the middle of his fascinating explanation, his ASSERTIVE trait kicked in. He squared his shoulders, straightened his head, and leaned in a bit more to me—all ASSERTIVE communication actions. His tone of voice also became more ASSERTIVE. He was no longer the interviewer, he was the teacher and expositor, and his actual ASSERTIVE trait appeared.

When Urs interviewed me he didn't deliberately put on a game face and appear more NONASSERTIVE, but in fact, that is what happened. However, because I took a moment to observe him talking with the concierge *before* the interview and it was apparent he was more like Russell Crowe, I made a snapshot read in 10 seconds that he was ASSERTIVE. This allowed me to be prepared for our interview. It didn't take me by surprise nor did I inaccurately assume that his assertiveness meant he was trying to convince me of his paper's position. I just read it for what it was. Urs was an ASSERTIVE person who also learned the art of restraint during an interview, out of respect for others.

I showed Urs the two photos and counseled him that for interviews, where he wanted to be open and inquiring, to resist adopting the posture in the second photo and watch his tone of voice. He immediately saw the value of our short "coaching session" and was genuinely thankful.

In effect, Urs learned the *opposite* technique used by Henry, who needed to be more assertive. Urs opened his posture to better make himself accessible to those he's interviewing, while Henry squared his shoulders to convey he could get the job done with ASSERTIVE clients.

Anita. Like Urs, Anita was also at the top of her craft—well prepared and genuinely interested in finding unique perspectives for her readers. When she asked me to profile her during our Warsaw interview, I asked her to freeze and shot three photos in rapid succession. When you look at the sequence, in the first photo you see her actual trait, which is NONASSERTIVE. She looks relaxed, agreeable, and inviting—her head is tilted to the side and her shoulders are *softly* squared to the table.

While no two people display their trait exactly the same way, you can see Anita's NONASSERTIVE trait and that she looks more like Taylor Swift/Mr. Rogers than Russell Crowe/Margaret Thatcher.

Seconds after the first photo, you can see Anita start to morph into her game face and appear more ASSERTIVE in the last photo. Her head is more erect and she's pulled her shoulders back slightly—a position she intuitively adopts when in a managerial role as an editor at the table. Being more ASSERTIVE wasn't her actual trait, but it was an intuitive action she learned in order to be taken seriously.

Anita's actual NONASSERTIVE trait...she is changing...Anita's ASSERTIVE game face

Before we started the interview, my snapshot read was that she was NONASSERTIVE. This was based on how I saw her interact with her assistant. So I made sure to restrain my ASSERTIVE trait just a bit, which put her at ease. The result was that it made her job easier and allowed for a more efficient, time-saving interview, and provided her more time for follow-up questions.

Here's one more example of a female executive who needed to use the kinds of techniques just reviewed to establish trust.

Establishing Trust. The former VP of one of the nation's largest commercial management firms retired. She was now donating time to raise funds for a new science center and wanted to learn how to profile. She explained to me that she wanted to reduce the time it took for her to establish trust with a potential contributor. With a little coaching, she realized that her ASSERTIVE trait sometimes created an unintentional barrier when establishing trust. People tended to tense up, even though she always conveyed that she was a "servant leader." With a little coaching, she found that being a little more like Urs immediately reduced the amount of time it took her to establish trust with new contributors—from fifteen to just five minutes.

Tips and Lessons

As this is your first wire, we'll spend a little more time here than on the other wires. To help you, here are some useful tips when first learning to use your snapshot reads:

Your first reads. When using a wire/gauge for the first time, it's sometimes best to profile people other than family or close friends. Emotional attachments can cause confusion; it's common. That's why for the first few days, it's best to read people with whom there isn't a lot at stake. Then try those closest to you.

Interacting with people who have a game face. Urs and Anita are examples of people who unknowingly put on a game face. Still, it's possible to profile people by making more than one read. Yes, there will be times you'll be fooled at first, but if you can make a couple of reads of someone when they are interacting with others (like I did when I observed Urs and the concierge), it will further reduce inaccuracy.

Thoughtful interactions reduce stereotyping. While profiling is about finding patterns, there is an infinite variety in those patterns. When we observe people who are ASSERTIVE, one may be ASSERTIVE only with their choice of words, while another with their choice of words *and* tone of voice, and so on. Added to this, people have different plot points on their gauge. One person may be 1 NONASSERTIVE and another 4 NONASSERTIVE. One person may only show the positives of being NONASSERTIVE, like agreeable and attentive, while another person may show mainly the negatives, like weak and naive. So we can't put people in boxes and stereotype that all who have a specific trait are exactly the same.

We can, however, identify that they *do* have a specific trait and they would appreciate it if we would respect their trait, as I did with Anita. It's the anchor of our profiling philosophy:

I know who you are.
Good for me. Better for you.
It's the art of treating people right the first time.

Use your range to promote empathy. Using the side of our range that tilts toward a person's trait is called *empathy*, and it's a thoughtful thing to do. While the other person might not be able to articulate what you're doing, it's always appreciated.

When I purposefully restrained my ASSERTIVE trait to put Anita at ease, it allowed her to quickly and efficiently ask her questions. I didn't allow my assertiveness to cause a needless disconnect.

Similarly, if you're a NONASSERTIVE person talking to an ASSERTIVE person, who prefers that you be a *little* more direct and forceful, you can do it because of your natural range. You can move a point or so in that direction.

Empathy, though, is different from sympathy.

Sympathy is when we connect with a person *emotionally*, like being enthusiastic, caring, concerned, supportive, and so on. Being sympathetic is a positive, but one or more of traits may or may not come into play. For example, you can be concerned about someone regardless of whether you are ASSERTIVE or NONASSERTIVE.

When making accurate snapshot reads and improving interactions, empathy will rarely get you in trouble. If, however, your emotions dominate an interaction, this can cause misreads and miscommunication. This doesn't mean emotions are inherently destructive, because they aren't.

Emotions are a natural part of being human. Just be sure you don't confuse empathy for sympathy when trying to make accurate reads.

A good axiom when engaged in an important first-time interaction with someone is to first identify a person's trait, then decide whether you need to be more empathetic, and then convey sympathy appropriately.

Remember, rapid-fire profiling as taught in the *KPS* isn't about manipulation, but about attuning yourself to others and making adjustments that improve lives.

Be natural, don't mimic. While you don't always have to modify how you interact with someone, it's useful to know that you can in a way that naturally fits you. Don't, however, try to mimic someone's behavior—what some call "modeling"—like crossing your arms when someone crosses his arms and so on. My experience is that when people do that, it looks contrived at best, especially when a person has a completely different profile. This is often evident when viewing video recordings of people modeling someone else's behavior. Far better to just slightly tilt toward the side of your natural range when it's appropriate, like I did with Anita, and Henry did with his ASSERTIVE clients.

Be prepared. When people interview or are quizzing you, it's your responsibility to read their assertiveness trait and slightly modify to help that person effectively do their job. If you don't know exactly how you display your trait, ask a friend to shoot photos and video of you in a typical daily situation. Then study them and practice making small modifications to your nonverbals, choice of words, and tone of voice until you find what combination works best for you.

There's no turning back the NONASSERTIVE guy. If people are going to be hesitant, resistant, or put off when they first engage someone, it's usually with an ASSERTIVE person. If you're getting mixed signals and have difficulty making a read, tilt toward the NONASSERTIVE side of your range if you are ASSERTIVE. If you're NONASSERTIVE, don't worry. Just do the best you can until you can make a read.

It's easier to restrain what you have than create what you don't have. A common cause for misreads is when a person restrains a trait, like Urs, who restrained his ASSERTIVE trait. If I hadn't made a read of Urs when he talked to the concierge, I might have thought he was NONASSERTIVE. It happens. But now that you know that someone can restrain a trait, you can correct your read. If, for example, I saw that Urs was ASSERTIVE with the concierge *after* the interview, I would realize that he restrained his trait during the interview.

For Anita, though, trying to be ASSERTIVE doesn't work so well, which is why her expression is a bit affected in the third photo and she doesn't look as natural as Urs, who was restraining his trait.

So the lesson here is that it's easier for people to restrain a trait they have (like Urs) than to create what they don't have (like Anita). We'll get to another practical application of this principle shortly.

Beware: Don't Overuse Facial Reads

As already noted, when people communicate they use their nonverbals (tilt of the head, use of hands, facial expression, etc.), choice of words, or tone of voice. These are the three basic sources for making reads of the two communication wires. For this reason, don't over focus on facial expressions as taught in many profiling systems. Why? Because many people *never show a facial expression* when they show their trait. They might only show their trait with the tone of voice or choice of words.

In the case of Urs, what if he only showed his assertiveness with the tone of his voice, choice of words, and a nonverbal when he squared his body? If you tried to make a read looking for a facial expression, you'd fail. That's why taking in a person's *full persona* and not focusing on facial expressions is a more accurate and reliable method.

And there's another factor: I have shown facial-expression examples (like those below) from various well-known facial recognition systems to thousands of people, and there is always significant discrepancy in how people interpret specific expressions. This is because many expressions can have more than one meaning and have different cultural interpretations.

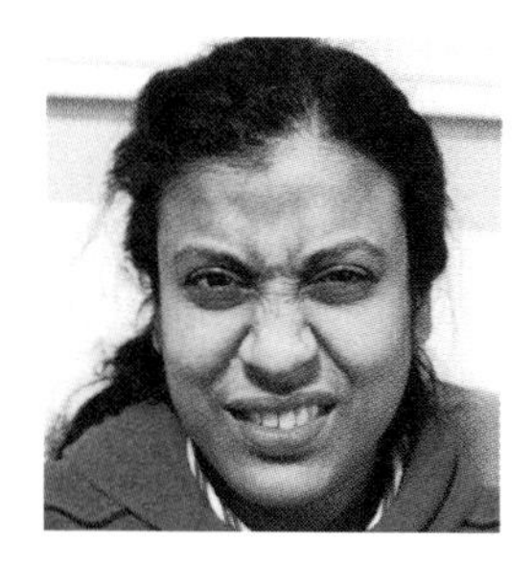

The left facial expression is interpreted in some popular systems as "disgust" that can relate to a person's character, but it might also be a visceral reaction to something that just smells or is nasty.

The right facial expression is often presented as holding someone in "contempt," but it can also represent annoyance or impatience.

Misinterpretation of facial expressions is another reason why the most reliable course of action is to interact with someone for a minute or two, take in their *full persona*, make a read in 10 seconds (Russell Crowe or Taylor Swift), and don't over think it. When you do, accuracy usually jumps 20–30%.

Overcoming Stereotypes to Get the Job

As I shared, all my kids could rapid-fire profile by the age of 14. I viewed it as a life skill everyone should acquire.

When my oldest son, Erik, was a junior in high school, he felt he was passed over for the starting job at right tackle in his division 5-A high school football team. He genuinely thought he was the better athlete than the fellow chosen and wanted some advice. Here is a shortened version of our dialogue and the action that he took to get the job.

"Why didn't you get the job?" I asked.

"The coach doesn't think I'm tough. He's ASSERTIVE and the guy who got the job is also ASSERTIVE. I'm not as ASSERTIVE as the other guy. So the coach assumed I couldn't perform. But I always get more pancake blocks, and I'm faster."

Erik recognized that the coach was misreading his talk for his walk and physicality. Erik was correct in his read in that he was low NONASSERTIVE, about 1 on the of 0–5 scale. Because of his range, Erik could easily move to low ASSERTIVE. About 15% of the population is what we call a combination type: they can operate on both sides of the gauge. The benchmark is that a person is just a little ASSERTIVE or a little NONASSERTIVE. You can't be high ASSERTIVE and high NONASSERTIVE. (If you are, you might need counseling!)

"So, what's the fix?" I probed.

He thought about it, and said, "I just need to act and talk more assertively. I'm not going to cuss, but I need to meet his comfort level."

Going forward, Erik tilted toward the assertive side of his natural range anytime he was on the field or around the coach. The coach interpreted this change as Erik becoming tougher, more committed over the year. As a result, when Erik was a senior, he was elevated to first-string, made all-city and runner-up all-district. It was probably a tipping point for Erik. That opportunity led to his playing collegiate ball as a 12th Man walk-on at Texas A&M. By the time he was 25, he was a Division I head coach. He has since coached on championship football teams, like Florida State University, and is recognized as a premier "high-performance" coach, including coaching Olympic champions.

As a father, I've thought about how his life might be different if he hadn't accurately made that one simple snapshot read and modified his interaction with his coach. Today, Erik easily shifts between being ASSERTIVE and NONASSERTIVE, respecting the many men he must lead and coaches and administrators he supports.

Profiling a Message to Stop Bullying

It's also possible to make snapshot reads of messages to see if they will connect with an intended audience. Look at this antibullying poster and reflect on what you've learned in this chapter. Now identify why the poster, which was posted in schools, won't behaviorally work for some students, especially those most likely to be targeted by bullies.

Answer: This poster was in a hallway at a school where I was training educators and counselors. I took the group to the poster and asked them to profile who the poster *wouldn't* connect with. Immediately they said: A *NONASSERTIVE student*. They pointed out that the poster starts out with phrases that appeal to the ASSERTIVE trait.

They said that if you ask a NONASSERTIVE student, especially one who is high NONASSERTIVE, to be ASSERTIVE, *make eye contact, tell the bully to stop*, some of these kids would freeze. They wouldn't be able to do it. They aren't naturally assertive or aggressive when they communicate—the first three directives on the poster. Yes, some might be able to do it for self-preservation, but others wouldn't. It's not natural for NONASSERTIVE kids to use their communication trait to take command of a situation.

The educators pointed out that some NONASSERTIVE kids might be able to take *action* to avoid or neutralize the bully, but standing toe-to-toe verbally isn't a recommended option unless they've demonstrated the ability to do it.

The poster is well intentioned, but the creators didn't profile their target audience. They didn't take into consideration whether or not kids with different traits could apply the prescriptive actions. Kids who are ASSERTIVE communicators might be able to follow through, but how do we modify the poster for those who are NONASSERTIVE? And, NONASSERTIVE students are *more* likely to be the bully's target, especially if they are insecure.

Based upon their experience, the educators agreed that it would be better to ask the student to *do* something rather than to *communicate* something, especially the higher his NONASSERTIVE trait. Their suggestion was: *Go get help.*

You're not asking the student to communicate with the bully, but rather take action to get help.

What messages would you use on this poster to reach all kids—both ASSERTIVE and NONASSERTIVE?

When crafting messages, first profile the target audience, then profile the message itself. Next, evaluate if they match. (Another observation: the poster assumes that the person is a CONFIDENT decision maker—another trait to be considered and explained in Chapter 15.)

A Game-Saver in Marriage

This last suggestion is especially directed at those with the ASSERTIVE trait tilting toward the higher end. It helps us understand the principle we covered earlier.

> It is easier to restrain something you have,
> than to create and do something you don't have.

In marriage, let's assume that you're ASSERTIVE and your spouse is

NONASSERTIVE. It is easier for you to *restrain* your assertiveness than to expect your spouse to be *more* ASSERTIVE. That's because it's easier for you to restrain what you do have—assertiveness—than to expect your mate to be more ASSERTIVE, something they *don't* have, a concept you learned earlier in the chapter. Don't ask them to do it. It's unlikely they'll be able to do it with any consistency.

When there is a disagreement, deliberately restrain your assertiveness. This won't happen overnight. It's like a muscle you exercise as an act of your will. Over time, as a couple, you will find yourselves navigating even the most difficult situations with greater ease—reducing stress and the length of the "conflict."

No, it isn't easy.

Yes, it is worth every ounce of effort to commit yourself to *strengthening* your restraint.

This same principle is applicable in any interaction between ASSERTIVE opposites, but it especially pays great dividends in close relationships like marriage.

Regarding asking your NONASSERTIVE mate to be more ASSERTIVE: the rule of thumb is he or she must make the decision to practice being more ASSERTIVE, as in the following humbling example.

In the early years of our marriage, my wife, Sandy, did the scheduling for my speaking engagements. I couldn't afford an assistant. Sandy, who is NONASSERTIVE, never told me at the time that she absolutely didn't like talking on the phone, particularly when she had to negotiate a point in a contract. Years later, she told me that before she made the calls for that day, she prayed a prayer from Psalms: *May the words of my mouth and the meditation of my heart be acceptable unto you, oh Lord, my Rock and my Redeemer.* When she shared this with me about 15 years ago, it was one of the most humbling moments for me in our 42 years of marriage. Her selfless act, silently performed with grace, later became an invaluable asset for her when 23 years ago she started her catering business and gourmet take-home shops, The Festive Kitchen. If she hadn't worked all those years for me, she may have never developed the critical skill of talking to clients by phone.

Grace under fire—elevated for the benefit of others.

In effect, Sandy learned to expand her *range* as an act of will. Just as ASSERTIVE people can restrain their trait for the benefit of others, NONASSERTIVE people can also expand and stretch their range, as did Sandy and Henry.

Reminders for Using the ASSERTIVE–NONASSERTIVE Wire

This is a short list of reminders for using the ASSERTIVE–NONASSERTIVE wire. Much more can, of course, be provided, but remember: This book is designed to show you how rapid-fire profiling works and give you concepts you can use today.

When it comes to restraining a trait:

ASSERTIVE: easier to restrain and be more NONASSERTIVE

NONASSERTIVE: harder to be more ASSERTIVE

If you are ASSERTIVE:

1. Practice restraining your trait.

   Nonverbals: open the position of your body/shoulders; don't lean in; slightly tilt your head; don't make assertive use of your hands

   Choice of words: refrain from using words or phrases such as tell/give/show me; soften choice of words and use phrases like perhaps, would you mind/provide, can you, etc.

   Tone of voice: restrain your assertiveness.
2. Best to start off using the NONASSERTIVE side of your range if unsure of a person's trait.
3. If a person is NONASSERTIVE, avoid the stereotype that they will also be NONASSERTIVE when they perform a task or make a decision.

If you are NONASSERTIVE:

1. Practice interacting with ASSERTIVE people using the ASSERTIVE side of your range as explained in this chapter.
2. Like Henry, develop a couple of actions you can use when you need to be ASSERTIVE; use the suggestions provided in the chapter to find the actions that fit you.
3. Resist stereotyping that people who are ASSERTIVE are all self-centered, egotistical, etc.
4. Resist the stereotype that if a person is ASSERTIVE, he or she will also be assertive when performing a task or making a decision.

We've taken some extra time with this first wire so you understand how to make a snapshot read with a wire and how to use your new insight. Now let's learn the second communication wire: CONTROL–EXPRESS. We use it to identify whether someone prefers to control or express emotions when they communicate.

CHAPTER FIVE

CONTROL-EXPRESS

Your Second Wire

[Do They Like Me?
Are They Telling the Truth?]

Cheery and full of life. That's Helena, a flight attendant for Finnair who hit a behavioral bump on a flight.

"I imagine that smiles communicate satisfaction. On one long-haul flight, though, a business class customer did not smile once during eight hours. OK, she did look me in the eye when I served her. But a smile? No. I was pretty sure she was dissatisfied with our service.

"Towards the end of the flight, she rang the call bell. I crept sheepishly toward her. The woman wanted me to know that this was the best flight ever! I broke out into a smile, but she didn't. Interpreting body language and reading thoughts are clearly best left to the professionals."

Helena's misread is what is called stereotyping. She linked satisfaction with a smile. Helena, who usually expresses emotions when she communicates, smiles to let others know when she likes something. The problem is that not everyone smiles or shows emotion when they're satisfied. If a person typically controls emotions, especially to the extreme, they may not smile. They may use words, a thoughtful pat on the back, or a written note.

The Lesson: You can't identify satisfaction solely by a display of emotion. You have to read the CONTROL–EXPRESS wire first. It's usually the easiest wire to read, but one that is easy to stereotype if you start with preconceived notions like Helena.

Here's another example.

An old friend, Michael Ammar, is one of the world's top sleight-of-hand magicians. He was with another famous magician, David Blaine, watching a third magician do an amazing trick. David said, "Wow, that's great."

Michael turned to David, and said, "Tell your face that!" David has the EXPRESS trait but *doesn't* show emotion with his face, only with words *and* a slight lilt in his tone of voice.

"His facial expression was completely deadpan, and it's always that way," Michael says with a laugh.

The CONTROL–EXPRESS wire helps us identify whether people prefer to CONTROL or EXPRESS emotions when they communicate. As you've already learned, Jim Carrey is an example of extreme EXPRESS and Queen Elizabeth is a standard for extreme CONTROL. Like the ASSERTIVE–NONASSERTIVE wire, people can display CONTROL and EXPRESS with nonverbals, choice of words (like Helena's passenger and David Blaine), or tone of voice. They may use only one of the three, or a combination. We can't assume that everyone will display or not display emotion as we do, which is why we profile them first to avoid stereotyping.

Importance of the CONTROL–EXPRESS Wire

This is the *emotive* connector wire. Making a successful read with this wire helps us quickly connect and communicate with people and avoid misinterpreting and second-guessing intent or interest. People who are EXPRESS, like Helena, often think that CONTROL people aren't interested, appreciative, or engaged because of a lack of emotion. Conversely, people who are CONTROL often stereotype and think that a person who shows emotion is weak, lacks substance, oversells, and is naïve. However, if you know your trait and someone else's trait, you can establish rapport and minimize misreads of them and them of you. Accurate reads also help us better determine truthfulness, which we'll look at later.

To get started, please customize your CONTROL–EXPRESS wire. Like you did for the ASSERTIVE–NONASSERTIVE trait, choose a person for each extreme from the list below—someone you can visualize quickly. If you want to use someone you know as an extreme, be sure he or she is as extreme as the examples or your whole gauge will be off.

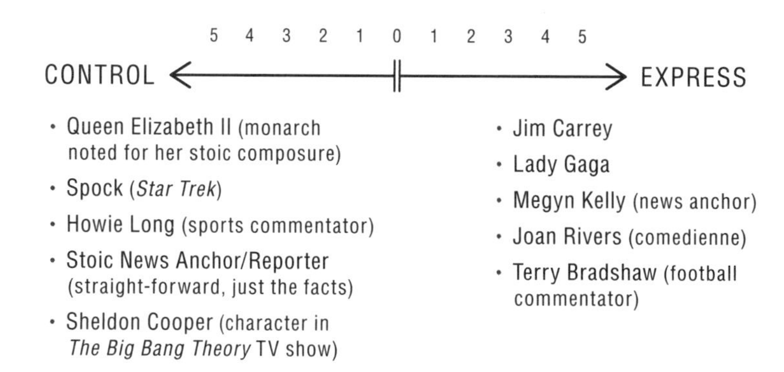

Here are possible positive and negative actions for each side of the wire. Remember, these are only *communication* actions.

People who CONTROL Emotions: Private, controlled, introverted, quiet, suspicious, introspective, indifferent, detailed, thoughtful, and pensive

People who EXPRESS Emotions: Outgoing, emotional, sensitive, fiery, explosive, passionate, short-fused, moody, dramatic, and expressive

Like the ASSERTIVE–NONASSERTIVE wire, make your read in 10 seconds by comparing them to the extremes. Don't overthink it. If you are a visual person, use your "mental slider," putting each extreme over the person's face and asking yourself: *More like Queen Elizabeth or Jim Carrey?*

Like you did with the first wire, start out making snapshot reads with people other than family or close friends, as emotional attachments can cause confusion. And remember, don't worry if you make a mistake. As already noted, most people misread others 65% or more of the time. The principles outlined will reduce your misreads.

A Noted Psychologist's Take on the Wires

"I'm probably not going to do real well at the start, am I?" Jacqui Stephens asked me. She's the director of behavioral health and social services at Parkland Memorial Hospital in Dallas, one of the nation's largest charity hospitals. (Parkland is famous because President John F. Kennedy was taken there right after he was shot by Lee Harvey Oswald.) Jacqui had a hunch that it might take a beat or two longer for her to learn the *KPS* than others who weren't trained in the behavioral sciences.

"Why do you say that?" I asked. Jacqui is sharp, so I didn't understand.

"Because those in my profession are trained to recognize deviancies, but there's not a lot of emphasis on reading healthy traits or testing our recognition skills like you're doing," she explained. She was right. Most behavioral science professionals take a day or so to get their bearings with the *KPS*, and once they do, they catch up to the rest of the group. After she learned the system, she explained why accurate snapshot reads are a powerful barrier to stereotyping.

"People use stereotyping as an end point. Profiling like you teach it is used as a beginning point," she adds.

In Helena's case, had she profiled her passenger as CONTROL, she wouldn't have stereotyped that the woman was dissatisfied and realized that words without an emotional tone of voice or nonverbals, like a soft pat on the arm, can be used to convey satisfaction.

"Profiling can also enhance what I would call 'mutuality' of application. It gives me a better understanding of someone, and that understanding can have an impact on *me* as well as the patient. The worst therapists want to *do* things to others, rather than assisting a person with what that person naturally has," Jacqui adds.

Don't Confuse Emotional Reactions with the EXPRESS Trait

There is a part of our brain that is called the amygdala. It's often referred to as the fight-or-flight part of our brain. If you see a rattlesnake, for example, the image bypasses the brain's cognitive reasoning process and goes straight to the amygdala, which evokes an emotional response. You don't think—you just act to protect yourself.[1] Or, someone sees something funny and laughs—an emotive reaction. Or, someone is just in a serendipitous mood, like Queen Elizabeth II in the photo below. We don't want to confuse these types of reactions with how people typically prefer to *communicate*.

We can't stereotype that people who have the CONTROL trait never show emotion. Here, Queen Elizabeth II shows emotion as she mugs for the camera with Kate by her side. Prince Phillip couldn't come so Kate came instead! (June 2012).

The Lesson: Both CONTROL and EXPRESS people can have an emotional reaction: laugh, cry, act surprised, and so on. When making rapid-fire reads of the CONTROL–EXPRESS trait, we read how people *typically* prefer to communicate.

Now let's look at some ways to use your CONTROL–EXPRESS reads.

If You're CONTROL, How to Connect with People Who Are EXPRESS

Let's imagine that we are coaching Helena's high-CONTROL passenger. The goal is to help her express satisfaction to an EXPRESS person like Helena.

There are several options, we just need to find one that is natural and comfortable for her that doesn't look staged or affected.

Insight: Like people who are high NONASSERTIVE, the stronger the CONTROL trait, the easier it is to use a nonverbal or choice of words rather than modifying the tone of the voice.

We could encourage Helena's passenger to try gently nodding her head (nonverbal) as she uses words to thank Helena. She could try adding a descriptive word or two for emphasis: *I really appreciate your splendid service.* She might tap Helena's hand or arm (nonverbal) as she conveys satisfaction. Or, she might write a short personal note.

People who are low CONTROL can try slightly modifying the tone of their voice to show more emotion, but this is difficult for those who are high CONTROL—4 or higher on the scale.

While these suggestions seem simple, the net result can be significant when interacting with people like Helena who are EXPRESS—especially the stronger the trait.

Remember, as explained in Chapter 4, you can restrain something you *have*, but it's difficult to create something you *don't* have. In the case of Helena's passenger, instead of asking her to show more emotion, it's better to ask her to *do* specific actions, as noted, that convey concern, appreciation, empathy, and so on.

Here's another example where EXPRESS elements are added to a high -CONTROL person's presentation:

CONTROL Presenter Uses Additional Elements to Convey EXPRESS

When assisting clients, we sometimes use subject-matter experts to review how they've used the *KPS* for a specific application. One particular adjunct faculty member was a high-CONTROL detective who prevented a school bombing in the affluent Dallas suburb of Plano, home to several Fortune

500 companies. The Plano case he was going to present was compelling, he knew his material, and the presentation was well paced. The challenge was that he was extreme (5) CONTROL. This can be a problem for people who are EXPRESS, and can put audiences to sleep. The work-around was to incorporate EXPRESS elements into his delivery.

First, video clips and slides were integrated into the presentation at least four times an hour, which added an element of EXPRESS and still moved the content forward. Second, we leveraged our interactive keypad technology by asking the audience to discuss a critical point and enter their responses. When CONTROL and EXPRESS people solve problems together, it creates an EXPRESS group environment, complementing the presenter. The little extra effort to inject a little more EXPRESS into the presentation paid off.

When his presenter ratings were evaluated, he rated 10 on a scale of 1–10. This is a typical outcome when there is a well-scripted and -paced presentation that complements a subject-matter expert's knowledge and ability to deliver content. If you're a student, this added touch can mean the difference between an "A" or a "B" when giving an oral presentation.

If you're high CONTROL, ask someone you trust who is perceptive and a good communicator for ideas of what you can add to your interactions that can seamlessly convey EXPRESS.

If You are EXPRESS, You Can Restrain Emotions to be Believed

Most people who are EXPRESS will use their trait when trying to convince others of something they believe in, whether it be a point of view or a product—especially if there is resistance. They do this because it's a comfortable, natural way to convey with emphasis that what they are saying is true, and they believe it.

When I was producing documentaries, I noticed in interviews that I video recorded that when some EXPRESS people want to be believed they'll restrain their EXPRESS trait. It's done intuitively to be believed—to convey that it's *just about the facts*. No embellishment. No emotional pleas. Just the facts. In effect, it's like a game face. They aren't trying to fool anyone, they've just learned over time to that it's easier to be taken seriously if they *restrain* their trait when talking about *facts*. If you have the EXPRESS trait, you can do the same.

If you are EXPRESS and in a critical discussion, a presentation where facts are important, or engaged in an interaction with someone who is CONTROL, restrain your EXPRESS trait just a notch or two. For example, if you are 3 EXPRESS, you restrain your trait to 2 or 1 EXPRESS. Even though you're still on the EXPRESS side of the wire, the downshift will be subconsciously noted and appreciated—and will usually reduce doubt and skepticism. If you're 1 EXPRESS, you might restrain your expressiveness to 1 CONTROL.

For interactions or presentations where there is a mix of CONTROL and EXPRESS people, your EXPRESS trait can communicate that you are engaged. When delivering points that directly point to facts, slightly restraining your trait will connect with listeners who are CONTROL, and subtly convey that you're after a smart, well-thought-out decision. This can be a turning point for those listening to you who are CONTROL and who may have struggled in the past relating to someone who is EXPRESS.

The Lesson: People who are EXPRESS can learn to restrain their trait, but in most cases it requires more attention and care to ask CONTROL people—especially high CONTROL—to show more emotion. It's best to have them convey appreciation, concern, empathy, etc., through their actions, like a hand-written note, nonverbals, and choice of words rather than through the tone of their voice.

Cross-Cultural Reads of CONTROL–EXPRESS

Anna was my translator when I lectured in Poland at the state police academy in Szczytno in the north about 100 km from Gdańsk. I noticed that the word "Terrorism" was misspelled as "Rerrorism" on one of the buildings, so I asked Anna to stand next to the amusing sign for a picture. When I took the shot, she was stoic. I then asked her to think of her children. Instantly, out popped her actual EXPRESS trait and she gently smiled. Her restraint was a holdover from the days of communism, when people tried not to attract attention when in public—by refraining from any display of emotion or direct eye contact.

When abroad, it's useful to know if there is a cultural trait that people display in public that may be different from their actual trait. For Anna, her actual trait was EXPRESS. Knowing this, when we were in a public setting, I communicated with her based upon her learned CONTROL trait. But, in a face-to-face setting, when she told me about her family, we conversed based upon her actual trait, which is EXPRESS—and she really appreciated it. (More on cross-cultural profiling in Chapter 23.)

The Lesson: In some countries EXPRESS people have learned to restrain their EXPRESS trait and appear CONTROL, and they appreciate it if you communicate with them based upon whether you are in a public or private situation.

Discerning Truth from Lies

The scene: Hundreds of experts at an international conference on fraud in Toronto viewed a video clip of a juror from the infamous 1995 O.J. Simpson trial. When I asked them if she was lying or telling the truth, more than 95% said she was lying, when in fact she was telling the truth.

O.J. trial juror telling the truth

Misreading how people use their CONTROL–EXPRESS trait is a major cause of getting false positives that someone is lying. That's what happened to the fraud experts. The witness showed a lot of emotion as she responded to questions from a *60 Minutes* correspondent, even looking away as she spoke. Because the experts couldn't profile the juror's CONTROL–EXPRESS trait, they were fooled.

Anyone can improve their ability to discern truth from lies if they can rapid-fire profile. The reason, though, isn't an obvious one. Here is how it works:

Contrary to popular myths and TV shows, the only thing people typically do when they lie is something *different* from when they tell the truth (except psychopaths, and that's another story). Most of us have been taught since childhood that if a person doesn't make steady eye contact, stutters, shows more emotion or doesn't show any emotion, says *I swear*, flushes around the neck, etc., these are indicators of lying. The fact is that there are people who do those things when they tell the truth.

To reduce false positives and improve your discernment, apply the following two principles:

First, study how people tell the truth. Know what it looks like when a person tells the truth in good times and in bad, under stress or when filled with joy, successful or struggling, etc. This will give you your first edge. If you can discern the truth, then any deviation is a deception. It's common sense, but not taught in police academies. The idea is to have a baseline and a familiarity with how people convey the truth in all kinds of life situations.

When my kids were young, I regularly asked them *"How do you know he's telling the truth?"* when I knew someone was telling the truth. They would then articulate in detail what they saw or heard. We rarely had similar discussions on how people lied and deceived. The focus was on their ability to discern truthfulness. Here were some typical teaching questions I used.

"How do you know he's telling the truth? You heard him clear his voice like he was nervous?"

"Right, Dad, but he has sinus problems."

"Why do you think she was telling the truth? Didn't you see how red she was around her neck?"

"Yes, but she's always nervous when she meets someone new."

"Why is Caroline avoiding eye contact?"

"She's just embarrassed."

"But Enrique wasn't embarrassed and he didn't make eye contact," I'd prod back.

"Yes, but he looks away to picture in his mind what he wants to tell you."

As a result of those mini-lessons, they learned the many complexities of how people tell the truth. Then, when confronted with someone who was off, they spotted it.

In one instance, an assistant who worked for me came to the house to get some papers. My boys were 8 and 10. She complained that she was late because she got a ticket.

"Why did you get a ticket?" the boys asked.

"I was just going five miles over the speed limit," she complained.

"Are you sure?" they asked cocking their heads, sensing something *wasn't the truth.*

"Well, it probably was ten miles over...."

"Are you sure?" they politely interrupted.

"OK. It was 15 miles over," she admitted, her face now flush red.

Lesson learned. They had received instruction and guidance on detecting the truth, and what they saw didn't match.

The second principle. Identify whether a person is CONTROL or EXPRESS and how they use their trait before you ask a question that involves truthfulness. There are several reasons why this is necessary.

First, we know that when people lie, they usually do something different from when they tell the truth.

Also, it's a well-known principle that under pressure, people usually use their actual trait because that's what feels the most natural.

Baselining how someone uses his trait helps us avoid false positives for lying. For example, someone who is low EXPRESS may naturally restrain his trait when first talking to you. If you jump right into a question where there is some pressure, he might show EXPRESS—his actual trait—to add emphasis in order to be believed. Then you interpret this as lying because he is communicating *differently* than he was a few minutes before. I've watched many seasoned investigators fall prey to this misread.

Or, some people who are CONTROL prefer to avoid eye contact, provoking the false assumption that they are lying, when, in fact, this is what they do when pressed with a difficult question—even when answering truthfully.

To baseline the CONTROL–EXPRESS trait, first ask questions that have different degrees of personal/emotional attachment that you know they'll probably answer truthfully.

For example, you might ask about traffic they encountered on their way to work, which reflects a low level of personal/emotional attachment. Then ask about a moderately difficult relationship or situation, which reflects a higher level of personal/emotional attachment. After several questions, you should have an idea of how they use their trait, and you can ask your truth-seeking question(s).

There is obviously much more that could be written on this subject, but these two discernment principles will help you reduce false positives:

1. Study how people tell the truth.
2. After identifying the CONTROL–EXPRESS trait, observe how a person uses the trait when answering questions that have little or high personal/emotional attachment.

Transformational, Not Transactional Coaching

I think you'll agree that the concepts you're being coached to apply are at minimum critical for specific situations, and for some people will even be life-changing. Before we leave this chapter, I want to share with you one of the most eloquent statements I've ever read on coaching others, which directly applies to teaching others how to make and use rapid-fire profiling with snapshot reads.

It's from Joe Ehrmann, former NFL great turned pastor in the inner-city, turned communicator to the world, and the subject of the Pulitzer Prize winning book, *Season of Life* by Jeffrey Marx.[2] In his book, *InSideOut Coaching*, Joe, who was called "The most important coach in America" by *Parade Magazine*, writes that he's not a transaction coach, but a transformational coach.

> I saw the transactional coaches: the kind of coaches who use players as tools to meet their personal needs for validation, status, and identity. They held their power over us to elicit the response they wanted. I obeyed these coaches out of necessity but I never accepted their belief systems or bought into their programs. Coach first, team second, and player's growth and needs last, if at all, were their modus operandi....
>
> They operated on a quid pro quo basis to incentivize us to perform better; they looked for what they could get out of coaching and not what they could give; they ignored athletes' developmental needs and often manipulated and distorted the values of winning and losing....
>
> I also saw the transformational coaches, who used their coaching platform to impart life-changing messages that I began to understand

> only decades later. Coach-power, like all forms of power, can be used for good or for bad, for self or for others. Transformational coaches are others-centered. They use their power and platform to nurture and transform players. I followed these coaches because I sensed their authenticity; they have affected me for a lifetime. Players first, team second, coach's needs met by meeting the needs of players.[3]

You do this for me and I'll do that for you. I've watched many trudge that path and its end is lonely and hollow. After I developed the *KPS*, a criterion I used before taking on a client was this: Does this person value other people? If not, I usually passed. If discussions tilted towards *leveraging human capital*, instead of *elevating people* as a part of the process, I politely declined.

The ideas in Joe's book have changed many lives. And the most rewarding part of the journey is people who have shared with me how they've helped shape someone else's life by sharing what they learned.

Don't compromise. Use what you're learning for the benefit of others first. You won't regret it. (You'll also find a surprise bonus in the next chapter when you do.)

Summary for Using the CONTROL–EXPRESS Wire

Remember: It is easier to restrain something you have, than to create and do something you don't have.

EXPRESS: easier to restrain and be less expressive

CONTROL: harder to be more EXPRESS

If you are CONTROL:

1. To convey a bit more EXPRESS, you can use:
   Actions: illustrations, hand-written notes, etc.
   Nonverbals: such as a pat on the back or arm

Choice of words: carefully select words that reflect who you are and how you think

Tone of voice: this may be harder to modulate the higher your CONTROL trait

2. Your CONTROL trait can convey sincerity and calm.
3. Avoid stereotyping that all EXPRESS people exaggerate or can't be taken seriously.

If you are EXPRESS:

1. You can restrain your trait if needed.
2. Restrain if talking about facts.
3. Avoid stereotyping that all CONTROL people are heartless, dissatisfied, etc.

Before we learn how to use the two performance wires, we're going to make a short stop and look at fascinating insights into who rapid-fire profiles with the highest accuracy and why. This will help you adopt the same thought processes and mindsets when making and using snapshot reads.

SNAPSHOT REMINDER

Be sure to reread the three questions at the end of Chapter 1 to stimulate how you can use the CONTROL–EXPRESS wire.

CHAPTER SIX

Who Sees It First... the Quickest?

[Ever been amazed at how ordinary people do the most extraordinary things?]

Now you can become one of "them."

We're going to look at who learns to rapid-fire profile the quickest and why. There are patterns in profiling, and the quicker you can embrace them, the faster you'll increase your accuracy.

The answers to the following questions connect the dots of who learns to profile the fastest *and why.*

- Which professionals in an organization are the fastest learners...*and why?*
- What age group learns the fastest...*and why?*
- Which culture has the potential for learning the quickest...*and why?*
- Which educators start out with the highest accuracy...*and why?*
- What character quality is most important...*and why?*
- Who has the highest accuracy, men or women...*and why?* (This last one takes us into dangerous territory and be prepared for a *big* surprise!)

The *why* part of the equation is where you can connect the dots to shorten your learning curve. The goal is to immediately use what you have in common with the top performers and learn to adopt other characteristics they have that you don't.

About 10 years ago, the patterns emerged to me after training 20,000-plus professionals and college and high school students the *KPS*. We used the data captured by our interactive system (explained in Chapter 2) to accelerate accuracy to as high as 90% in just a day of instruction. In fact, we can now predict who will usually achieve 90% accuracy *before* we begin training.

As I introduce you to various groups of people, try and pick out who you think would be the top performer and *why*. Use a piece of paper, a wallet, credit card, or any other small object to cover the answers that follow the list of options for each group. Wrestle with your personal answers before reading the actual answer. You may even want to read them with a group of colleagues or friends. Be prepared for some significant misconceptions and "aha" moments.

Which Group of Professionals has the Highest Accuracy After One Day of Instruction?

(Mothers get an honorary first place but aren't included on the list!)

- Sales
- Homicide detectives
- Priests/Pastors
- Senior management
- Auditors
- Athletic coaches
- Screen writers
- Engineers
- Lawyers
- Marketing professionals
- Human resources
- Security
- Graphic designers
- Financial officers
- Politicians
- Actors
- IT
- Restaurateurs

We've shown variations of this list to thousands of people and most assume that homicide detectives have the highest accuracy because of their interrogation skills. The second most common response is human resource professionals who do hiring interviews. Others assume it is salesmen because they have to size people up quickly. Others select politicians and actors because they have to read their audience.

The correct answer, though, by a landslide is *auditors*!

I stumbled across this in 1997, when I trained the audit unit at American Airlines. They were the first professionals as a group to achieve 90% accuracy in just two days. It was baffling. They even easily profiled clips of people who put on a game face and concealed their actual traits, like the journalists Anita and Urs in Chapter 4. After just three hours of instruction, they were hitting 75% accuracy.

The stereotype of auditors is that they are inept when reading people because they're only interested in crunching numbers, checking systems, and monitoring compliance with regulations. What happened at American Airlines, though, wasn't an anomaly. Since then, thousands of auditors have been trained, and virtually every group globally finishes at 90% accuracy. Auditors are the crack profilers right out of the gate. The question is, what do they do that the rest of us don't? Before the answer is revealed, let's look at two more groups (be sure to cover the answers).

Which age group learns to profile the fastest?

- 14–18
- 19–26
- 27–35
- 36–45
- 46–55
- 56–75

Who did you pick? Those with age and experience, those who are younger and have a clean slate, or those in the middle with experience and open minds?

Answer: 19–26.

The question is why. Or, put another way: *What is it that auditors and 19–26-year-olds have in common*? Yes, there is linkage! Now, consider this next group.

People From Which Two Countries or Regions Have the Highest Accuracy When First Learning to Profile?

- Americans
- Asians
- Brazilians
- Poles
- Israelis
- Swedes
- Kenyans
- Germans
- British
- Canadians
- Turks
- New Zealanders

Make your selection before reading further.

Globally, most people assume Israelis are the quickest learners because of their intense security needs. After Israelis, people just guess, but the answer is Asians and Poles (remember this is based on data and not a theory). Like auditors and 19–26-year-olds, they usually attain 90% accuracy. (For the sake of diplomacy, we won't disclose who has the lowest accuracy and struggles to reach 75%.)

Now let's connect the dots and reveal the *why* behind the first three high-performing groups. As you discover the common thread in these three very different clusters of people, make a mental inventory of what you have in common with how they think so you can put it to work for you.

Dot 1: Why Auditors Have the Highest Accuracy

Surprised by the American Airlines audit unit's accuracy, I assumed someone had seen the clips in another workshop and tipped them off. So I asked them, "Why are you doing so well? No group has ever scored this high."

They said that once they were convinced the *system* was logical *and* reliable, they just followed it. They used the *KPS* wires and made their reads in ten seconds. By trusting the system, they resisted intuitive reads based on their experience or intuition—their gut instinct.

This made sense. An auditor's natural tendency is to trust reliable systems. It's reflective of what they do: test systems to be sure they are operating within compliance. For them, following the *KPS* was a natural instinct once they saw it worked, even though they often aren't naturally gifted with people reading skills.

The Lesson: Teach a group of people who will trust a proven and reliable *system*, and they will rapid-profile people with a high degree of accuracy because they resist the natural tendency to make intuitive or experienced-based reads. Are you the type of person who will follow a logical, proven system? If so, that's one asset in your corner when using the *KPS*.

Dot 2: Who Doesn't Do as Well and Why?

Groups of professionals that operate out of a show of force, experience, or that just try to wing it, usually level out at about 75% accuracy after a day or two of instruction. Now 75% accuracy isn't bad; that's about a 300% jump from where they start—25–35% accuracy. But it's not the highest.

So who has the poorest performance after a couple of days of instruction? *Salesmen and lawyers.* As a group, they typically lead with their communication skills and are confident that they can improvise and wing it. When they are video recorded making presentations, you can see that they are effective at sensing when they are *off* and how they quickly modify to compensate. The interaction disconnect followed by a modification, though, can promote distrust with a client or jury. When clients sense the shift, it can become a momentary distraction and raise questions: *Why did Maria change? What's Jack up to?* However, when sales and legal professionals make disciplined reads, they do better.

Law enforcement (including homicide detectives), senior management, and athletic coaches are typical examples of those who peak at 75–80% (during two days of instruction) and take longer to reach higher accuracy levels. Officers are used to operating out of a show of force. Senior management and coaches are often accustomed to operating from a show of power and moving human markers on a board. In both instances, it's often about reading a *situation first and not a person.* Sometimes this is appropriate, for example, if someone draws a weapon on an officer. We don't want officers in immediate danger profiling, but rather using their training to subdue the attacker. Once these professionals, however, learn to trust a system where they read the person *first*, their accurate read becomes a force multiplier, increasing the effectiveness of their interactions with others.

A clever application. Over time, we found ways to deploy pockets of people within an organization who naturally trust systems—such as engineers, technicians, and so on—to lead the way and encourage others to do the same.

A clever application of this "trusting a reliable-system principle first" was discovered by Dave Sullivan, the sales manager at a high-end financial software company. Each of his account managers made calls with a technician. Dave directed that both his account managers and technicians profile their clients using the *KPS*, and if there was a difference of opinions, the team went with the read of the technician, unless the account manager had been tested to have higher accuracy. The result: Dave's team broke all sales records.

"It was about getting our human factor interactions right—from the first meeting, to contracting, to follow-up service," Dave said.

Dot 3: What Do 19–26-year-olds and Auditors Have in Common?

Answer: Both will trust a reliable system when making rapid-fire reads.

The mistaken impression is that young adults and older teens have the highest accuracy because they are a clean slate and don't start with preconceived ideas about how to read people. While this sounds logical, it isn't the reason young people almost always reach 90% accuracy or higher in a day or so of instruction. The actual reason is *they don't know how to read people and have no other choice except to trust the system—as long as they see it works.*

That's it.

Like auditors, they will trust a system *because they don't have a system.* They don't know how to read people and don't have enough life experiences to form a secure opinion. So, if you tell them to *make a read with the wire in ten seconds* and don't look at anything else, as a group they'll do it!

I first observed this in 2002 and 2003 with students at two very different universities: Texas A&M, a state campus of over 40,000; and Lehigh University, an Ivy League school. At Texas A&M, I trained about 90 undergraduate student leaders, and at Lehigh, I was an executive-in-residence in the MBA program working with about 40 MBA candidates. In both cases, professors wanted students to have rapid-fire profiling skills for leadership roles on campus and for a competitive advantage when they entered the workplace.

Both groups of students hit 90% accuracy within four hours of instruction. At the breaks, I asked students why they thought their accuracy was so high. The typical response was, "Using the wires makes sense and works better than what I usually do when I meet someone."

Joasia, my "adopted" bratanica, which means niece (the "c" is pronounced "tz").

Teens produce dynamic results. Teaching teens and mature middle school students how to profile is always a lot of fun, especially when they are trained with their parents, teachers, or leaders from their community. Like Joasia, they always perform as well as, if not better, than adults.

She was the equivalent of a junior in high school in Poland when she learned to profile. She and her mother, a brilliant translator, and father, a

Polish scholar, stay with us on their visits to America. When she was with us in 2010, I took Joasia to a workshop for educators. At the beginning of the workshop, I announced to the 50-plus high school teachers that Joasia would have the highest profiling accuracy in the class. At the end of the day, she was the top performer, tied with another teacher. The teachers were stunned. First, they were amazed that a teen would outperform them, and second, that it was possible to predict performance before we started—which was what they would like to do in their classrooms.

Why Asians and Poles Have the Highest Accuracy

This one is a stumper. Applying what you've learned, why do you think Asians and Poles attain 90% accuracy in a day or two, regardless of their profession? Please take a moment and reflect on this before reading further.

Answer: Like auditors and 19–26-year-olds, these diverse cultures like to follow systems.

This isn't to stereotype every person who is Asian or Polish, especially in Asia, where there are many countries and cultures. But collectively, they will tell you they don't mind following systems. In Poland, they are quick to point out, however, that they will trust a *good system* but *not* a destructive system like communism, which dominated their lives for a generation. Additionally, Poles highly cherish personal relationships, which, when combined with trusting a system, produces exceptional rapid-fire profiling results.

In 2009, Mrs. Irena Koźmińska, the wife of the former Polish ambassador to the U.S., asked if I would train the staff at Pope John Paul II High School (*gymnasium* in Polish) in Warsaw while I was in the country. I did, and they attained over 90% accuracy.

On the same trip, I also trained Polish airport security and state law enforcement in one of Poland's major cities. Over 90% of the over 100 security professionals couldn't speak English and all instruction was conducted through a translator. Yet, they also produced 90% accuracy.

In both trainings, all video clips were Americans speaking English, which made their collective performance even more impressive because cultural nuances didn't stump them. They didn't make snapshot reads from the anchor point of their own culture, which can lead to stereotyping and misreads. Rather, they made their reads, just like you, by comparing people to the extremes of the four profiling wires.

Mrs. Irena Koźmińska, left, and educators at John Paul II Gymnasium (high school) learning to rapid-fire profile. (October 2009, Dan Korem)

Polish airport security learning to profile cross-culturally without stereotyping. (October 2009, Dan Korem)

The Lesson: Diverse professionals from different cultures with very different needs all trusted a reliable system and produced the same results, just like 19–26-year-olds and auditors. Now take a moment and consider what you do and how you like to handle situations. If you're willing to tilt toward trusting a proven system and making snapshot reads in ten seconds, your accuracy will increase.

Now let's look briefly at three other groups and what they reveal about reading others with elite accuracy.

Which Character Quality Produces the Best Rapid-Fire Profilers?

- Transparent and honest
- Quick on their feet
- Naturally good with people
- Shrewd
- Experienced
- Good communicator

When presented these options, the most common answers people choose are *shrewd* or *naturally good with people*. But, neither is correct.

The correct answer is: *Transparent and honest.*

After a day of training, we ask the person with the highest accuracy to stand and be recognized. The persistent character quality acknowledged in this person by his or her peers is *transparent and honest*. Why is this consistent for about 80% of the top first-day performers?

My take on this actually starts with the best investigators and interviewers I've trained, including those who obtain confessions more quickly than their colleagues; make the best selections for hiring staff; and obtain usable information the quickest.

Those who are the best are usually what-you-see-is-what-you-get individuals. They might not tell you all that they know, but you know whatever they tell you can be trusted. They are transparent and honest. Related to rapid-fire profiling, it works like this:

People can often sense a manipulator, an inveigler, a schemer. When they do, they shut down. However, when they sense a person is honest and transparent, they will reveal more hidden nooks and crannies in their life, experiences, and relationships. This means the honest, transparent person develops a greater inventory of human-factor information and connections. Before they learn to profile, they start out with more insight—more data points. This person also doesn't have self-imposed blinders, like the manipulator, who may ignore the dark side in others because it reminds them of themselves.

Regularly, I'm asked, "Aren't you afraid that the bad guys will use this profiling stuff?"

My response from experience is that there is an insulating barrier that prevents the self-centered person from developing elite profiling skills. They never develop the depth of insight the "good guys" have who use their skill for a much broader and positive agenda: educating students, improving lives, lifting up those in need, reinforcing the basic philosophy—*I know who you are. Good for me. Better for you. It's the art of treating people right the first time.*

Which Educators are the Best Profilers in a School District/System?

- Principals
- Counselors
- Coaches
- Elementary school teachers
- High school teachers
- School secretaries

Don't you think this is an important question to answer and leverage in order to elevate teachers working with our kids?

The answer has significant implications because students spend an average of 1,150 hours each year with educators who have a profound influence on their development as individuals and their performance in the classroom.

So who are the best when it comes to reading kids and instructing them based upon their profile?

Answer: *Elementary school teachers!*

Most of us would assume school counselors, but data from training over 15,000 educators tells a different story. The question is: *why elementary school teachers?*

This answer was explained to me by Estralee Michaelson, the former school-safety coordinator for the Farmington Public Schools (12,000 students) in the Detroit suburb of Farmington, Michigan. She explicitly directed me to include specific instructions during a profiling workshop for more than 100 high school teachers and principals, who were to apply profiling to promote safety and improve classroom instruction.

"I want you to tell them to stand at the door of their classroom for the first two weeks of the school year and greet each student by name."

"Why?" I asked.

"Because secondary teachers are notorious for teaching the text but not the student," was her feisty reply.

"I've had students who were absent because of illness for up to two weeks and a teacher never noticed. We need to turn this around."

Her insight helped solve another riddle that puzzled me for about a year. In the dozens of school systems where K–12 educators were trained together (usually several hundred at a time), the elementary school teachers usually outperformed their junior high, middle school, and high school colleagues. They usually achieved 85% accuracy as a group, while secondary school teachers averaged 75%. It wasn't uncommon for the high school teams to bristle because they considered themselves an academic step above their elementary counterparts. But, it was clear: as a group, elementary school teachers were more focused on nurturing as well as educating their students, when compared to secondary school teachers.

One quick way I found to identify school districts that emphasized *students first* and *text and tests second* was to look at one statistic. When both elementary and secondary teachers have high profiling accuracy (80% or higher), administrators usually emphasize *students first* and text and tests second.[1] But, if elementary clearly outperforms secondary school teachers, secondary leadership was more likely impersonal, text/test-driven, or just complacent—and students suffered as a result.

What I learned from educators and transparent and honest people helped connect the fourth dot that promotes high profiling accuracy.

Dot 4: If You Care About People, You Will Rapid-fire Profile with Greater Accuracy...

This is especially true if you do it with honesty and transparency, trusting a reliable system, and making your reads in 10 seconds to avoid second-guessing and talking yourself out of an accurate read.

And now for a controversial question!

Who are the Better Profilers, Men or Women?

Yes, we are venturing into perilous territory, but this is a moment of truth that's not about being politically correct.

Statistically, when people from almost every type of demographic in the world are polled and asked this question, regardless of whether they are men or women, about 75% vote that women are the better profilers.

What do you think? Take a moment and reflect on this before reading the answer.

The actual answer is: Neither! *Men and women perform equally well but for very different reasons.* This is based upon profiling test data from more than 40,000 men and women.

The perception that women are better profilers probably starts at home. Maybe our moms read our inner thoughts better than dads because they paid closer attention and spent more time with us. But when moms and dads learn to rapid-fire profile, they demonstrate the same rate of accuracy. In fact, there is rarely more than a 5% variation. What's the story here?

To begin, men and women are obviously different. The question is: What is it in our *differences* that allow both to profile with equal accuracy? The answer is in how we are created.

It's a physical fact that has been demonstrated in the lab that women are better multitaskers than men.[2] According to current research, women have more estrogen in their brains when they are being formed in the womb, which allows for more connections in the brain and contributes to their multitasking skill. (Another theory is that women have a "thicker" corpus callosum—the pathway between the "left" and "right" side of the brain, and this is what contributes to enhanced multitasking.)[3] Related to profiling, this allows women to observe more disparate points of human actions and behavior more quickly than men. When you tell them to make a read using the two ends of the wire, like Jim Carrey and Queen Elizabeth, they do it...but they also notice all kinds of other data about the person as well. Here's an example:

What?! My wife, Sandy, and I were lying in bed watching an English cold-case detective show, "Waking the Dead", on PBS's *Masterpiece Mystery Theater.* During the show, the detective superintendent was talking to his psychologist over a quiet dinner and a glass of wine. The camera maintained a head and shoulder shot as it did a slow dolly move around the couple.

All of a sudden, Sandy says, "Look, her earring is missing!"

"What?" I replied, bewildered.

"Look, her earring is missing," she said emphatically.

"What do you mean her earring is missing?"

"Well, it looks like it fell off between scenes."

"Why are you looking at her earring? Aren't you listening to the dialogue?" I asked, stunned that she'd be zeroed in on earrings!

"I was listening, but I also saw that her earring was missing," she firmly retorted.

I rewound the show and, just like Sandy said, the earring was missing and had fallen off. I was flabbergasted because it wasn't a tiny stud earring, but about *three inches long!* Yes, I humbly apologized to Sandy, and yes, she justifiably pinched me for doubting her. Since then, I have shown this clip

Now you see it. Now you don't! At least I didn't!

to all kinds of groups in various countries, and the women always catch the missing earring and the men as a group rarely do.

So what do men have that enables them to profile accurately even though they may see less than women and are typically not robust multitaskers?

Men are mechanically wired to track moving objects better than women.[4] They are better at point-to-point exercises, like reading a map, where most women struggle. In fact, in combat, there's an unwritten code that you never give a woman a map or you die! (We're speaking of women and men as a group demographic, of course, and not individuals.) Similarly, professional women golfers have never been able to putt as well as men, even though it doesn't require strength. It's because putting is the most direct point-to-point part of the game. (There is a solution that we'll cover in Chapter 13.)

So when men are directed to rapid-fire profile, they do it well because for them it's a point-to-point exercise. Observe, look at a wire, and make a read.

That's why, for completely different reasons, men and women show no variance when it comes to rapid-fire profiling people with the *KPS*. For those who need a visual reference of this difference, the cartoon says it all.

Building teams. For team and family leaders, the wise leader recruits both men and women when profiling, to harness women's observing-disparate-dots and men's direct-read-the-wire tendencies. This combination allows for a more complete picture when developing strategies and making critical decisions and is compelling evidence for why both men and women deserve their place at the decision-making table.

One Last Mystery: The Pizza Caper

This last demographic stumped me for five years. I even offered a $100 reward to anyone who could solve it. Here's how it started:

At the beginning of a workshop at the University of Chicago in the spring of 2002, I asked participants, who were business professionals, to answer an "important" behavioral question on their keypads. The question was: "What would you like to eat for your last meal?" This was to add a bit of levity. Here were their menu options:

- Hamburger
- Steak
- Pizza
- Lemon meringue pie
- Green tomato

Later, after they profiled a few video clips, I put up the results showing which food group was in the lead. Those who chose pizza were ahead. The pizza eaters sustained their lead throughout the day and were the top performers to the end. The class liked the amusing twist and the resultant banter: *They won because they're crusty!...What's in their pepperoni that isn't in mine?!*

The next workshop, I added the same question. Pizza won. The next workshop: pizza won. *For five straight years pizza won almost every single workshop—that's thousands who were trained from every sort of profession.* It was baffling. What is it about pizza that makes great profilers? I even changed the focus of the list to:

- Like to watch football
- Phil Mickelson fan
- Eat pizza for my last meal
- Don't watch football
- Julia Roberts fan

It didn't matter. Pizza continued to dominate. You can imagine pizza franchises going nuts with this one, and pizza becoming the new food staple of potential FBI recruits.

It wasn't until March of 2007 in Canada, at the University of Windsor, while training Canadian law enforcement that someone stepped forward and cracked the pizza caper. Janet Hayes, an RCMP officer (Royal Canadian Mounted Police), figured it out. Before reading Janet's solution, what do you think the answer is? You've learned enough to connect the dots. The answer is buried in one of the top performing demographics.

Janet Hayes, RCMP, who cracked the pizza caper.

Janet's theory was that those who selected pizza were probably the younger members in the workshop, and those who eat pizza might be more social in their interactions, as it's a sharing food. The "social" part I wasn't quite sure about, but the young person part was spot on. When I compared age demographics to those who chose pizza, I found a match. Those who chose pizza were younger than those who selected the other options. Case closed. Now pass the pizza.

So Who are the Best Profilers?

The best profiler is, of course, an honest and transparent 19–26-year-old Asian or Polish auditor, who used to teach elementary school kids, cares about people, and eats pizza! Or, to put it in simpler terms, the best profilers are people who:

- Trust a reliable system instead of operating out of power, intuition, or shooting from the hip
- Are transparent and honest
- Care about people first

Now let's look at how one of the world's leading coaches used two snapshot reads to hand off "giftedness."

CHAPTER SEVEN

Handing Off Giftedness

[Ever known someone who was gifted and wished you could emulate what they do just a little bit?]

Meet Shawn Humphries. He's one of the world's foremost golf teachers and he likes a challenge. When PGA tour pro Brandt Jobe had a finger reattached after severing it in a freak accident, Shawn helped Jobe retool his swing with creative modifications so he could rejoin the tour.

Shawn is also the founder of an elite golf academy for promising kids, ages 10 through 18. What's amazing is that he always seems in control of the more than 125 students he works with in group and one-on-one settings. The kids and their parents love him. Most people say "he's gifted"—and he is.

As the school grew, Shawn decided to add instructors. He wanted to know, though, which parts of his "giftedness" (my term, not his) could be replicated by his new team members. When he found out I was an avid golfer, he said he thought rapid-fire profiling might help identify exactly what he was doing over and above the format of his system, and asked if I could help.

What follows is a powerful instructional technique we uncovered that can be used by anyone to lead or instruct others. Shawn developed it intuitively before he learned the *KPS*. In fact, he wasn't even aware he did it until I captured it on video and we looked at it through the lens of rapid-fire profiling. Here's what happened:

Shawn's students have a reputation for learning fast. This is due to his proven system and his earlier experience running legendary golfer Byron Nelson's golf academies.

Reviewing video I recorded of Shawn instructing students, I clocked how long it took a student to grasp and execute a new shot.

That's when I spotted the unique technique Shawn uses.

One student, Janie, who was NONASSERTIVE, struggled to internalize a fundamental concept for most golf shots: how to make solid contact with the ball on any surface—flat, uphill, downhill, and so on.

A five-foot-tall nationally ranked star striker in volleyball, Janie also quickly excelled on her high school golf team. She enlisted in Shawn's academy to accelerate her learning curve.

I observed that as Shawn, who is ASSERTIVE, worked her through his process for making solid contact, his six-foot-five-inch, lanky frame stood directly across from Janie—his shoulders square to hers.

Several minutes elapsed and Janie wasn't getting it. A competitor, she was frustrated.

Then the camera recorded Shawn's gifted touch.

It was just a slight modification that Shawn intuitively applied based on her profile, and within thirty seconds, she was executing with confidence.

What he did was similar to the case of Urs, the journalist in Chapter 4, who intuitively opened his shoulders and adopted a more NONASSERTIVE posture during interviews.

Like Urs, Shawn intuitively learned to be less ASSERTIVE, but he used a technique for one-on-one instruction with NONASSERTIVE students that is even more elegant and precise.

When Shawn stood squarely and directly in front of Janie, it shut her down. She needed physical space to process, something most NONASSERTIVE students need who are instructed by an ASSERTIVE teacher.

Sensing her frustration, Shawn moved to a position ten feet behind

Janie, crouched down, and continued to guide her through the process, as shown below.

Moving behind her created space, and crouching down minimized his towering height. His position, though, also allowed Shawn to observe the mechanics of Janie's swing. In the second view, notice Shawn's open shoulder position relative to Janie, slight tilt of the head, and open use of his hands, which he combines with a NONASSERTIVE tone of voice and choice of words. At a quick glance, without profiling, it might seem that the reason for Janie's immediate success was because Shawn crouched down so his large frame didn't loom over her. But that was only a part of the equation.

It was *how* Shawn crouched down behind Janie that was genius.

Notice that his body position is open and angled to his left. He isn't square on to Janie. Also, his head is slightly tilted (like Urs), his hands are in a relaxed position, and when in use his palms are up. Shawn also softened the tone of his voice and choice of words.

As a counterpoint to how Shawn positioned himself, notice on the next page that when Janie is asked to watch Shawn's swing, she is square to Shawn—which is the natural tendency for anyone, especially an athlete, trying to observe mechanics. Also notice that her natural way of using her hand is more directive and assertive, even though she is NONASSERTIVE, as she is pointing something out to Shawn.

Shawn, however, resisted a natural tendency used by most instructors: standing directly across from a student and adopting a square stance. The result is that he produces quicker results than most other teachers.

More importantly, Shawn's technique can immediately be taught to and applied by any instructor, regardless of that person's profile. All instructors have to know is if a student is NONASSERTIVE and if adopting an ASSERTIVE stance inhibits his or her ability to learn.

It's significant that, without a snapshot rapid-fire read, the nuances of Shawn's technique would have remained buried, and mastery would take longer for some students. It's unlikely that a battery of behavioral tests would have uncovered Shawn's technique.

The combination of two snapshot reads—identifying Shawn and Janie's trait—and observing how Shawn accommodated her trait allowed his technique to pop right out so it could be handed off to other instructors.

Absent this observation process, another ASSERTIVE teacher might try to emulate Shawn and position himself behind a student—but continue to use squared shoulders, ASSERTIVE choice of words and tone of voice, hand gestures, etc., producing substandard results.

It's Your Turn...

How can you use Shawn's concept for leading or teaching others? Are there times that you seem to disconnect and shut other people down while working with them? Maybe you know someone else who has this disconnect.

Now you have a starting point to turn this around.

Before I showed Shawn his profile disconnect with Janie and what he did to remove it and why it worked, he couldn't pass this insight along to other instructors.

Now, he can immediately teach any instructor the same down-the-line open-body position and palms-up use of hands—quickly without ambiguity. Then, over time, he can also help them restrain their tone of voice and choice of words.

Maybe you've watched someone who is able to seamlessly direct, offer suggestions, teach, mentor, or discipline others. Observe them. Make snapshot reads of all four of their traits. Identify the profiles of the people with whom they are interacting. See if you find an accommodation of a trait that you can emulate. Is there anything else they are doing that adds to the communication process, like Shawn's position in a direct line of sight to his students, which not only creates space but also allows him to observe a student's mechanics?

If people tell you that you are gifted when working with others, have someone shoot some video, review it, and see if there is a trait pattern, so that you can slice off your giftedness and hand it off to others.

And so the hunt begins!

Now let's learn how to use the first *performance/walk* wire: CONVENTIONAL–UNCONVENTIONAL.

CHAPTER EIGHT

CONVENTIONAL—UNCONVENTIONAL

Your Third Wire

[When the Earth Shifted Profiles]

It was a major disconnect. My youngest son, Luke, was a high school junior and frustrated with his AP calculus teacher—really frustrated.

"Dad, we were making all A's and B's in the first six weeks and now we're making B's and C's. It's not right!" he complained.

"What's the problem?" I asked.

"All Miss Higgins wants to do is see how many problems we can solve in a period. It's horrible."

"Well, what's her profile? Is she CONVENTIONAL or UNCONVENTIONAL?" When necessary, my kids would profile a teacher or peer and ask for advice if they couldn't figure out how to solve a situation.

"She's definitely CONVENTIONAL. She's really in the box. She's a five, (extreme on the 1–5 scale)."

"Is she a nice person?"

"Oh yeah, she'll do anything to help you, and she isn't moody."

"Well, what's the profile of the class?"

"We're pretty high UNCONVENTIONAL—about a 4."

"So, what's the solution?" I asked.

"I don't know. I mean, maybe if she could just give us problems that were different."

"What do you mean by that?" I probed.

"Well, the problems she gives us are all the same. Maybe she could give us problems from stuff that's really happening."

"You mean like in real life?" I asked.

"Yeah."

"Is she ASSERTIVE or laid back when she talks to you guys?"

"She's definitely laid back."

"So, what can you do?"

"Maybe I could tell her..."

"Tell her, or suggest to her? Remember, she's laid back," I emphasized.

"Right, I could suggest to her that we really appreciate that she wants us to increase our speed, but would she mind using problems from stories in the newspaper or business magazines? I could explain that I have my own business and that I appreciate that she wants me to work quickly, but could we use real live situations." (Luke started a video production business earlier that year.)

"You think that might work?" I asked.

"Yeah, I could try it."

Miss Higgins had no idea that a teenage student had made a snapshot read and saw her CONVENTIONAL trait disconnect with her UNCONVENTIONAL class. As a result Luke suggested that she lead her UNCONVENTIONAL "team" a little bit differently. Nor was she aware that he presented his suggestion in a low-key way based upon her NONASSERTIVE trait. The results: Class grades went back up to A's and B's over the next six weeks. Luke and his class were happy. And, Miss Higgins, a new teacher, was really happy.

It's what we call: *Start clean, finish clean!* A teacher was helped and she didn't even know it!

What Luke experienced is now commonplace in all walks of life—the disconnect of using CONVENTIONAL approaches with people who are UNCONVENTIONAL. It occurs daily because of the greatest behavioral shift in the history of the planet: the shift from the CONVENTIONAL to the UNCONVENTIONAL trait. Luke learned about this shift and used his new insight to help his teacher improve her performance. In Chapter 1 you saw how Josh encouraged an UNCONVENTIONAL executive to move forward when a contract was stalled.

So that you can produce similar positive results, let's prepare your CONVENTIONAL– UNCONVENTIONAL wire.

Personalize Your CONVENTIONAL–UNCONVENTIONAL Wire

The CONVENTIONAL–UNCONVENTIONAL wire helps identify how a person prefers to perform tasks. Please select who you want to represent the extremes of your gauge like you did with the first two wires. Be certain you can quickly recall and visualize your selections. If you elect to use someone you know, they must be as extreme as the examples provided.

You'll notice in the examples below there aren't any examples of young famous people who have the *extreme* CONVENTIONAL trait. That's because UNCONVENTIONAL people are promoted in the media and not CONVENTIONAL—similar to ASSERTIVE people being promoted and not NONASSERTIVE (Chapter 4). So you may need to use someone that you know personally, such as: a family accountant, a math teacher, an engineer, someone who works in government, or a politician. (If you read the 1st edition of *The Art of Profiling*, PREDICTABLE–UNPREDICTABLE has been replaced with this wire.)[1]

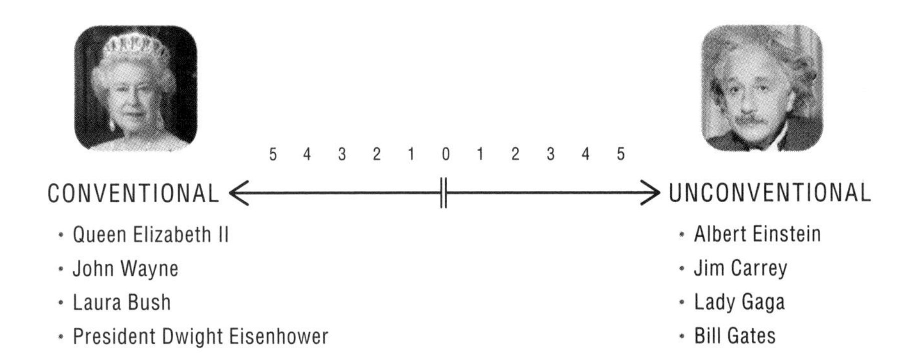

Here are the possible positive and negative actions for each side of the wire:

> **CONVENTIONAL:** Organized, reliable, stiff, dependable, staid, unimaginative, unbending, precise, persistent, logical, industrious, orderly, self-disciplined, formal, and consistent

> **UNCONVENTIONAL:** Free-spirited, open to change, negligent, creative, inconsistent, imaginative, whimsical, forgetful, reckless, aimless, frivolous, rebellious, irreverent, nonconforming, spontaneous, intemperate, anarchistic, undisciplined, impulsive, unfocused, disorganized, and quirky

Two UNCONVENTIONAL descriptors that need a little explanation are spontaneity and impulsivity, as they have been described as both positives and negatives by psychologists. In the *KPS*, spontaneity is doing something on the spot with some thought or rationale; impulsivity is doing something without thought.

When the Earth Shifted Profiles

Today, the ability to read the CONVENTIONAL–UNCONVENTIONAL wire is critical because of an unprecedented global behavioral change.

Up until the early 1900s, the world was about 90% agrarian. If you profiled our planet, it was CONVENTIONAL. Life was predictably rhythmical: prepare the soil, plant seed, and nurture and harvest the crops. My estimate is that approximately 10% of our population was UNCONVENTIONAL by 1900.[2]

Arthur Andersen

In 1918, an icon of the dominant CONVENTIONAL trait was Arthur Andersen, the founder of one of the largest accounting firms, which bore his name. His motto-directive was: *Think straight, talk straight.* And people did.

Then, almost overnight, with the injection of technology, people moved off farms and the profile of the Earth started to shift from CONVENTIONAL to UNCONVENTIONAL. Since the 1960s, the blistering rate of change has moved at warp speed, bewildering many.

If you stepped into a typical school classroom just 30 years ago, 75% or more of the students had the CONVENTIONAL trait and 25% the UNCONVENTIONAL trait.

Today it's reversed: 75% are now UNCONVENTIONAL, like Luke's class, and the only world they've known is one in which innovative approaches and variety are the norm.

Someone asked me, "What happens when everyone is UNCONVENTIONAL? Does that mean that everyone is CONVENTIONAL?" The answer is no. Just look at the actions. If you see the UNCONVENTIONAL actions—imaginative, free-spirited, and so on—it still means the group is UNCONVENTIONAL.

This shift is significant because previous ways of educating, nurturing, and mentoring youth, and leading people in the workforce often don't work. When Miss Higgins asked her class to perform CONVENTIONAL, tedious, nonstimulating tasks, she experienced a severe disconnect and performance meltdown.

The shift to the UNCONVENTIONAL trait has given parents, teachers, team leaders, and corporate boards fits—attributing difficulties to all sorts of pop theories. The reality is that it is predominantly a shift in traits.[3]

How our traits are formed. Traits are shaped from genetics, how we are brought up as children, and how we respond to life's circumstances. We can't control our genetics, which leaves childhood and adult experiences to shape our traits. Since the 1960s, phrases like "do your own thing" have been the steady drumbeat directed at youth and the rest of us. In effect: be more UNCONVENTIONAL. Take advantage of your new tools and innovate the next new thing—whatever that is.

My son, Luke, for example, learned how to edit a documentary on a computer in 2000. I learned the same skill seventeen years earlier when I produced my first documentary, but I paid $300 per hour just to step into a video-editing suite—and that didn't include instruction. With an inexpensive digital video camera, computer, and software, Luke informally earned his degree in production. The transition from $300 an hour to pennies was almost overnight and inspired books like *The World is Flat* by Thomas Friedman, which pointed out how even the weakest players can compete when armed with technology.

Exploration and innovation have been synonymous with the American consciousness beginning with the Declaration of Independence, which declared a daring new way to govern. Momentous adventures encouraged us to "Go West, Young Man" and even the moon. While many of the thought leaders and their visions for the future were UNCONVENTIONAL, the majority of the population was CONVENTIONAL. Then, in the 20th century, overnight the majority shifted to UNCONVENTIONAL and we were encouraged as individuals to be imaginative, spontaneous, and open to change.

Bill Gates, the UNCONVENTIONAL founder of Microsoft and technology leader.

If you told someone in the 1960s that you had a gizmo in your pocket that was a computer, phone, camera, and audio recorder, that it was smaller than a hip-pocket wallet, *and* could perform thousands of other tasks, access the world's database of knowledge, *and enable you to argue with people you never met*...well, they'd be generous to think you were only reading too many Dick Tracy cartoons. (Tracy sported a wrist watch that doubled as a two-way radio.) Innovation and new technologies have

Futuristic innovation in the 1930s–a time that was CONVENTIONAL.

appeared in previous generations, but nothing like the last few decades.

This shift even affects the simplest tasks, like making appointments, as one young professional discovered.

CONVENTIONAL relic from the past. This is the thirty- and forty-year diamond-studded lapel pin my wife's grandfather received for his service at Standard Oil. Notice the CONVENTIONAL name of the company "Standard"—at the time one of the largest American companies. Rarely, if ever, do people today work for the same company more than a few years because of rapid changes in technology and "flat earth" competition. Notice the finely machined fastener for the pins which is screwed onto the back of the pin to fix it to one's lapel.

A Winning Modification

Reducing cancellations. It's a game changer for anyone who has to keep appointments, like sales people. If you can make more presentations, and all other factors are even, you'll probably beat your competition because you'll have more opportunities to close deals. Here's how one insurance agent put the CONVENTIONAL–UNCONVENTIONAL trait to work with award-winning results.

It was Jeremy's first year in the business. While in college, he interned for one of the big-three insurance powerhouses. He came to me to see if he could get an edge using rapid-fire profiling. I asked him to detail every nook and cranny of his process: how he generated leads, established contact, set appointments, followed up, closed sales, followed-up after the sale, and cultivated relationships. In short: everything.

Jeremy's company had a reputation for the best new-recruit training in the industry—and it showed. Together, we hunted for where he could use rapid-fire reads to quantifiably generate more sales, shorten the sales cycle, generate more leads, and so on. Jeremy said his greatest frustration was cancellations; they were high—typical for new recruits.

For the next three weeks, I had Jeremy keep a spreadsheet of all appointments, both completed and canceled. I also had him make one snapshot read and identify if the potential clients were CONVENTIONAL (in-the-box, like accountants) or UNCONVENTIONAL (out-of-the-box, like research and development). A week later, the pattern I suspected emerged.

Clients who canceled with the greatest frequency were UNCONVENTIONAL. Potential positives of being UNCONVENTIONAL are open to change, spontaneous, innovative, and so on. Downside potentials are forgetful, undisciplined, and aimless. In sales, the negatives can drive cancellations. To reduce cancellations, Jeremy made one modification in his process.

Each time Jeremy set an appointment with a prospect with the UNCONVENTIONAL trait, he asked them how they usually logged appointments—hard-copy appointment planner, app on their cell phone, notes on the fridge, etc. Based upon their response, he added a couple of short follow-up reminders to complement their chosen method, or lack of method.

The result: Jeremy's cancellations dropped 13% in three weeks, and he became the number two first-year-out-of-college performer. The key factor that separated him from his competition: Jeremy delivered more presentations than his competitors because of a simple read and adjustment.

Dentists reduce cancellations. I first identified this cancellation connection when a group of dentists asked me about reducing patient cancellations. A short study revealed that most patients who didn't keep an appointment had the UNCONVENTIONAL trait. And, like Jeremy, when simple reminder modifications were applied, cancellations dropped. The only downside with the approach was that additional reminders might be provided for a patient who was CONVENTIONAL and didn't need it, but this was acceptable as no harm was done.

Surgeons providing aftercare. Surgeons in Switzerland found a similar application for aftercare with patients. They reasoned that if a patient had the UNCONVENTIONAL trait, it might be wise to provide more structured aftercare with more checkpoints than they did with CONVENTIONAL patients. Their reasoning was that those who were CONVENTIONAL would more likely follow instructions, while those who were UNCONVENTIONAL were less likely to. (They were of course considering groups of people and not specific individuals, which would be stereotyping.)[4]

They also pointed out that the worst outcome was providing more structure and guidance for someone who didn't need it. The benefits, though, included quicker recovery, fewer lapses, and lower cost to patients and the system.

Losing Key Personnel

The negative side of Jeremy's story is that he left his insurance agency within two years because its leaders didn't profile Jeremy. While known for their stellar training, they had a poor track record for retaining new associates that were UNCONVENTIONAL, which was Jeremy's trait.

He wasn't resistant to tackling something new. His management team was just the opposite. They were competent, but stiff and unchanging. They had a jewel in Jeremy but they never provided creative challenges or leadership. Jeremy quickly lost interest.

In a media interview, Jeremy's managing partner said that he was looking for people who were "smart, entrepreneurial, independent, and competitive." Today, most people who are entrepreneurs have the UNCONVENTIONAL trait. If you don't stimulate them with innovative ideas, there's a predictable outcome: You'll lose them. The manager told the reporter that his attrition rate for new recruits was two thirds. Although about 50% of his recruits were UNCONVENTIONAL, he didn't know why his attrition rate was so high. But it was because he didn't profile new associates like Jeremy and lead them based upon their traits.

More Offers at a Higher Dollar

Jeremy learned the hard way that it's not only the responsibility of employers to profile candidates, but also for candidates to profile employers. He realized that if he had profiled the partner, he wouldn't have taken the job. Jeremy passed this hindsight insight on to Phillip, who was graduating from a top law school and was looking for a position in a law firm.

Phillip learned the *KPS* and put it to work. He profiled each firm and partner where he wanted to apply. Phillip wrote target-specific letters of introduction, profiled the partners during the interview (to confirm snapshot reads he made from the observations of others), and conducted the interviews based upon the partner's profile. The result: He received more offers at a higher dollar than most in his graduating class.

What follows is an example where an employer made an accurate read and snagged the right candidate.

Leading Teams and Developing Capacity for Flexibility

While the trend is to the UNCONVENTIONAL trait, a new coach at a Division I school made two snapshot reads and realized he had a women's soccer team where the team leader was UNCONVENTIONAL but the majority of the team was CONVENTIONAL. Without a game plan to accommodate these opposites, there could be a real disconnect. He had to figure out a way for two completely different traits to unite and compete. Here's one of the techniques he used:

The team liked predictability during practice, but the UNCONVENTIONAL team leader, Sarah, liked it wild and crazy. To accommodate both, he told them, "Every day you will know what to expect, except one day. On that day you will never know what to expect and that day will be led by Sarah."

By doing this, he accomplished two things.

First, he developed the team's capacity to accept change, variability, and flexibility. This created the capacity for the team to follow Sarah.

Second, it kept Sarah engaged and honored her leadership.

The result: Overall performance increased, players decreased their 20-meter sprint times, vertical leaps increased, and it was their first season in years without a major injury.

The big lesson these examples highlight is that if you want people to elevate, we must honor who they are, leverage their natural assets, and create in both team members and leaders the capacity for working with others.

Avoid Stereotyping Career Paths

People who are UNCONVENTIONAL often change career paths, to which others will comment, "Oh, you're reinventing yourself." That may be true for some, but many need to be challenged with new ideas. My life is one example.

In 1981, I made a career shift to investigative journalism. If asked what I did before that time, many people speculate that I was a psychologist because of my interest in behavioral profiling. It was actually a very different field.

Beginning at 9 years old, I was a professional magician—I charged neighborhood kids a dime each for my first show. I was fascinated with solving riddles and puzzles and creating things that looked impossible. I learned and later invented my own sleight-of-hand effects (a magician's term for a trick), which I sold to other magicians while I was in high school. I never performed big illusions, but rather effects that required skill with the hands. My audiences ranged from 100 to 3,000.

When I was 15, I performed on television for the first time, and by the time I was 25, I had read over 10,000 books, magazines, journals, and other types of publications on the art of legerdemain and deception. Through my late twenties, I also authored and published books (written by noted experts) for magicians that are still read today.

From my studies, though, I became more fascinated with using what I learned to educate people on how *not* to be deceived, especially by those who claimed to have powers, such as cult leaders and fraudulent psychics and faith healers—all which were growing trends in the 1970s. Notable cases, like Charles Manson and Jim Jones, used sleight-of-hand deceptions to snare their followers. This led me to doing lecture/presentations for companies and college audiences on this and other subjects related to deception—like when it is and isn't acceptable to use deception. For example: a trick play in a ballgame versus telling the truth under oath. I even created a new word, *vrick* (a verbal trick), to specify a positive verbal deception—like tricking someone into coming to a surprise birthday party. This way, the word "lie" would only be used to denote a harmful deception.[5]

Because of my background, law enforcement agencies regularly contacted me for assistance when people who claimed to have powers were committing crimes. It was in that context, in 1981, that a family contacted me because their son had fallen into a dangerous cult-like group in its embryonic stage. That's when I formed a production company, and my professional career turned to investigative journalism, as explained in Chapter 2.

Today, with all the innovative tools available, we can't stereotype that there is one obvious path toward a specific endeavor or career. Many people, like Bill Gates, Steve Jobs, and the late Peter Jennnings have bypassed the traditional path of college to create and explore without presuppositions of how it's supposed to be done.

Reminders for Using the CONVENTIONAL–UNCONVENTIONAL Wire

When it comes to restraining a trait:

UNCONVENTIONAL: easier to restrain and be more CONVENTIONAL

CONVENTIONAL: harder to be more UNCONVENTIONAL

If you are UNCONVENTIONAL:

1. Practice restraining your trait. Deliberately insert yourself into situations that require a little more restraint and adherence to rules, regulations, and so on. It's a myth that to be creative you have to break all the rules. The ability to exercise some restraint when required will actually make you more creative and productive.
2. When presenting UNCONVENTIONAL options to people who are CONVENTIONAL, focus on the bottom line results that will be produced. Remember, not everyone is interested in new ideas and innovation, and that is okay.

If you are CONVENTIONAL:

1. Practice expanding toward the UNCONVENTIONAL side of your range. If you are 3 CONVENTIONAL, deliberately insert yourself into situations that require you to be just a little more tolerant of UNCONVENTIONAL so you can operate at, say, 1 CONVENTIONAL.
2. Resist stereotyping people who are UNCONVENTIONAL as self-centered, egotistical, etc. Remember, sharing ideas, innovations, and being different is part of who they are.

Snapshot reminder. Reread the three questions at the end of Chapter 1 to stimulate how you can use the CONVENTIONAL–UNCONVENTIONAL wire.

Because of the impact that the shift to the UNCONVENTIONAL has on us, regardless of our profile, in the next few chapters we'll look at important examples of how the CONVENTIONAL–UNCONVENTIONAL wire has and will affect our lives, and ways to navigate what's up ahead.

We'll begin with a cautionary tale of how the failure to make and heed just one CONVENTIONAL–UNCONVENTIONAL read led to one of the greatest collapses in American history and the story of a nation that did heed its read of its people and helped many rise from despair.

CHAPTER NINE

Collapse of a Giant

Protective Discipline for the Future

[When it's really important, you need more than a gut read.]

"Something is going to happen, and it's going to bring them down." I wasn't an industry expert. I didn't see any deception. I just made a snapshot read in the summer of 1998.

"It sounds crazy doesn't it?" I asked my colleague. He shook his head in disbelief because Andersen was an $8-billion industry giant and cash flush, supplying audit services to almost 20% of Fortune 500 companies. Over the next few months, I discreetly put the same question to others who were industry experts. All had the same reaction. Some talked about the usual *internal* disagreements (they had more than 28,000 domestic employees and 85,000 worldwide by 2002), but none saw or talked of a collapse. But, there it was: A simple read that said this can't work for long.

Have you ever noticed something about someone or a group, you knew it was accurate, but everyone else thought your observation was off? That's what happened to me. The collapse didn't commence until 2002, four years after a read anyone could have made. For me, it was also personal—friends of mine lost their jobs.

What I observed profoundly affects our personal and private lives.

Here's what happened.

Beginning in 1993, we trained hundreds of Arthur Andersen auditors. Andersen was one of the "big five" accounting firms, and its bread and butter was accounting, audit, and its growing consulting services. Arthur Andersen, the Midwestern no-nonsense founder, had a simple motto: "Think straight, talk straight." Not hard to profile him. He was CONVENTIONAL. Adherence to ethics and moral character were his standard.

As a group, the people we trained had the CONVENTIONAL trait and usually displayed the positive actions of the trait: organized, reliable, dependable, precise, persistent, logical, industrious, orderly, and self-disciplined. They used rapid-fire profiling to improve data collection during interviews and improve their ability to make presentations to boards that had to take action on their findings.

In 1998, I was asked to give a speech on profiling to Andersen partners. I expected them to have the CONVENTIONAL trait like their founder and staffs, so I prepared a speech that emphasized CONVENTIONAL themes, like consistency and bottom-line performance.

As I do before every speech, I check my reads of my audience, in this case the partners during our meet and greet at the resort. What I saw startled me. The group tilted significantly toward Einstein–UNCONVENTIONAL, and many who were CONVENTIONAL, were low CONVENTIONAL, about 3 or less on a 1–5 scale. I thought this was odd. It didn't fit. How can a band of UNCONVENTIONAL partner/leaders guide a CONVENTIONAL company whose core business relies upon being organized, reliable, dependable, precise, persistent, logical, industrious, orderly, and self-disciplined?

One reason for the increase of UNCONVENTIONAL leaders was a core conflict at Andersen. It began in response to auditors and others seeing the need for change—that surfaced in audits—in companies they were auditing, and companies wanting to facilitate that change.

In the process, the consultant practice at Andersen grew in order to implement innovative solutions. It should have been spun off as a separate company, led by a mix of UNCONVENTIONAL and CONVENTIONAL leaders, while leaving the tax and audit side of the house continued with a majority of CONVENTIONAL leaders, and just a handful of UNCONVENTIONAL leaders, who could help navigate needs for innovation and change. But that didn't happen. Instead, consulting started steering the CONVENTIONAL ship directed by UNCONVENTIONAL leaders.

Logically, when partners are running and gunning, promoting *new* products, ideas and ventures, the heart of the business—controls and discipline—are more likely to take a back seat. This increases risk and makes it easier for UNCONVENTIONAL bad guy(s) to slip into the fold who have the negative UNCONVENTIONAL actions: negligent, inconsistent, forgetful, reckless, aimless, frivolous, rebellious, irreverent, intemperate, anarchistic, and undisciplined.

At the meeting, I met several individuals who were reckless and undisciplined. I'm not saying all UNCONVENTIONAL people have destructive negative actions. That would be stereotyping. But those I talked to did. And for Andersen, this pointed to disaster.

It only takes one or two of these leaders to create an environment for collapse when the business is about compliance and controls. In Andersen's business, if you're convicted of a felony, you're prohibited from auditing public companies as per the rules of the Securities and Exchange Commission. When Andersen was convicted of criminal charges related to audits it conducted for one of its clients, it closed its doors, as did its client, Enron, the Houston-based energy giant.

The lack of positive CONVENTIONAL discipline at Andersen contributed to an even greater collapse at Enron,[1] which, in 2000, had 20,000 employees and revenues of more than $100 billion. It declared bankruptcy in 2001, and officers went to prison. Between the two companies, more than 100,000 people were sent packing; that's the population of a city like Green Bay, Wisconsin.

So there it was. Although not an expert on Andersen's business, I saw collapse coming with just one snapshot read. Some had "gut-check" reads, but few took to heart the potency of that one UNCONVENTIONAL read and the trait disconnect with Andersen's CONVENTIONAL business.

Hunting for Cowboys or Making Rapid-fire Reads

Jack Welch, the former chairman and CEO at General Electric saw Andersen's disconnect and said that there was "a real cowboy mentality" at Andersen and other consulting companies.[2] He was correct, but his observation is too subjective to hand off to someone else to check out. How do you define *cowboy*?

Imagine if you sent Brandon, one of your colleagues, into a room of Andersen leaders with the command: *Tell me how many cowboys are in the room.* You want him to report to you how the leaders *perform.* Brandon's accuracy, though, would hinge on his native intuitive skill. Without rapid-fire profiling, he could easily misread someone who was extremely EXPRESS and a bit boisterous as a *cowboy*—confusing a *talk* trait for a *walk* trait—and you don't get the read you need.

You also have to rely upon how Brandon defines *cowboy*, which can imply reckless and wild behavior. What if the leaders aren't reckless, but are just undisciplined, a negative UNCONVENTIONAL action which, in Andersen's business, could be just as devastating? If Brandon is looking for reckless and wild, he'd miss the key read because you didn't give him the CONVENTIONAL–UNCONVENTIONAL wire. This could lead to a disagreement about what is meant by *cowboy* instead of making a clean Queen Elizabeth–Einstein read.

Then, if you asked Brandon to relay his intuitively gathered perspective to others, the confusion multiplies.

That's why it's quicker, more efficient, and more accurate to use the CONVENTIONAL–UNCONVENTIONAL wire. This allows Brandon to base his reads on actions and motivations.

Do they tilt more towards Einstein or Queen Elizabeth?

And, if more toward Einstein, *Do they show the negative actions of that trait?* That could be disastrous for Andersen leadership.

If Brandon finds a significant number of leaders who are UNCONVENTIONAL, then he can drill down and find out who displays the negative UNCONVENTIONAL actions like *reckless, undisciplined, rebellious,* and *negligent* that could undermine the company. If significant negative actions are found in key leaders, then action can be taken to protect the company, followed by inspecting processes and systems to be sure they are in compliance.

I must emphasize that during the hour or so before my speech, I didn't observe any Andersen partners about whom I thought: *This guy's a crook.* I only observed an intolerable trait disconnect: too many UNCONVENTIONAL partners (and several who seemed reckless and undisciplined) leading a CONVENTIONAL organization. It was tragic, but only *after* the collapse did industry experts I talked to get it.

If Arthur Andersen were alive today, he'd probably amend his famous directive and add *act straight.*

Think straight.
Talk straight.
Act straight.

Major reason for misreads: talk misread for walk. Remember, *talk* is not *walk*. Thinking and talking isn't the same as talking and *acting*. It's a simple protective concept, but this confusion is one of the top causes for misreads. When Andersen dictated his directive, the world was CONVENTIONAL. It was assumed you'd perform with an emphasis on positive CONVENTIONAL actions like discipline, compliance, precision, and consistency.

Today, the world is UNCONVENTIONAL. The pressure is on to innovate—and do it fast. This means change is a constant and the new norm.

A journalist once quipped, "When the going gets weird, the weird turn pro."[3]

A less radical way to express this is: *When the day turns UNCONVENTIONAL, the UNCONVENTIONAL are the ones comfortable navigating the future.*

Our UNCONVENTIONAL world-in-constant-change equation, though, is unprecedented and tricky.

Today, many organizations have a CONVENTIONAL mission but must constantly inject change just to keep up, which means more UNCONVENTIONAL leaders on the team.

To promote stability, a core value must support positive UNCONVENTIONAL actions, like innovation, creativity, and imagination. Negative UNCONVENTIONAL negative actions, especially when they are extreme, are unacceptable—even more so in leadership.

And what about the rest of us, who aren't leaders? What do we do when we know change is coming, but we also want safety, security, and stability?

And what about companies that are UNCONVENTIONAL, like technology-driven companies, led by UNCONVENTIONAL leaders? How do you marshal restraint?

How we face these grave questions will dictate the stability of our collective and personal futures.

While the answers may be complex, there is a central theme that everyone can immediately grasp, apply, and use to steer the ship in the right direction. If you're raising or are responsible for a young person, it's one of the most important life values you can impart to them for their future.

Central Protective Theme for the Future: Innovate with Discipline Between the Lines

In another era, when we were a CONVENTIONAL planet, we had to guard against being stiff, autocratic, unbending, and insensitive—the negative CONVENTIONAL actions.

Today, we are UNCONVENTIONAL—a trend that isn't going to be reversed. Technology has insured that. This means the emphasis on specific protective themes must also change.

To navigate the UNCONVENTIONAL waters ahead with stability means we must cherish, teach, and activate a central lifeline value: *Innovate with discipline between the lines.*

Innovation is a blessing, but only when it occurs with discipline and between the lines and boundaries of ethics, rules, laws, and concern for the welfare of others. Here is a simple picture that illustrates this core value:

All tracks, courts, and fields where athletes compete have boundaries or sidelines, and rules of the game. Athletes can be as innovative as they want, as long as they stay within the lines. There is no limit on their creativity. But, operate outside the boundaries and you're penalized, disqualified, or ejected.

Tip for a Young Adult or Teen. If you're an UNCONVENTIONAL young adult or teen, make this principle active in your life. It will separate you from your peers, and more opportunities will open up for you. If you're being interviewed for a job and you emphasize how you've *innovated between the lines* in the past, with actual examples, you'll get hired before those who are more talented, because of your dependability.

The following is a story of how CONVENTIONAL and UNCONVENTIONAL teams learned to work together to leverage this concept.

Innovating with Discipline During a Transition

Two Fortune 500 companies, with very different cultures and profiles, were merging, and I was tasked to train a strategic team from each company in how to profile. The goal for the 60-plus professionals was to quickly reach consensus on how to navigate and integrate the two very different companies.

After a day of training, the teams attained 80% profiling accuracy. They were then instructed to profile both companies and identify the potential positives and negatives of each company's profile. Within 20 minutes they reached an almost unanimous consensus (which rarely happens with diverse cultures). They identified that Company A was high CONVENTIONAL (about 4), and might be resistant to change, while Company B was moderately UNCONVENTIONAL (about 3) and would be more likely to embrace change.

They then developed strategies so that the positives of each company were activated and leveraged, while negatives would be avoided, not activated, and workarounds developed.

A central strategy adopted was for UNCONVENTIONAL Company B to implement change and for CONVENTIONAL Company A to sustain the change until all units were successfully merged and integrated.

Both teams acknowledged the need for sustained innovation to remain competitive. They also agreed, however, that the concept of innovating with discipline between the lines was critical for stability and would be conveyed through leadership, integrated in relevant training, and so on.

At no point did they get stuck on intuitive, gut-check observations—because their reads were based on the wires. They quickly laid the foundation for future big-picture decisions and embraced specific values and interactive themes.

For our future, this starts with teaching core value to our kids in the classroom and the neighborhood, as in the next chapter.

CHAPTER TEN

Resurgence of a Nation:
It Usually Starts with our Kids

[And sometimes with our faith.]

"If you made a snapshot read, how would you profile your organization?" I asked a client, the VP of HR for a Fortune 500 company.

"Oh, that's pretty easy. We're conventional," he responded.

"Why is that?" I asked.

"Well, compliance, stability, and a sound public image are critical to our business. We're less about innovation and more about durable, stable service," he said.

"Would you say the majority of your employees are conventional?"

"Yes, that's probably right. They're pretty traditional."

"Well, how are you going to deal with the fact that about 75% of the high school and college graduates you'll interview are unconventional? How is that going to fit?" I added.

"You know, I've never thought about it that way. I don't know."

Significance of the Classroom Shift from CONVENTIONAL to UNCONVENTIONAL

Most people never grasp the overnight change to the UNCONVENTIONAL trait in school classrooms and what it means for our future in our personal and professional lives. They may have been frustrated by some of the negative effects they've experienced, but they haven't thought through the fundamental change itself.

It's human nature to focus on the negative effects first, like someone chronically showing up late for work, individuals creating mayhem because they buy into the pop philosophy that you have to break *all* the rules to be creative, or mega-cases like the collapse of CONVENTIONAL Andersen. But the impact of the shift, both positive and negative, starts when kids are in school where they spend years of their lives.

Education, as it exists today in most schools, is a CONVENTIONAL institution trying to teach UNCONVENTIONAL students. As a result, it's failing in its mission because it doesn't recognize and respond to the shift to the UNCONVENTIONAL trait. In short, there is a *huge* behavioral disconnect.

I've asked tens of thousands of educators to profile themselves, and they always identify their institution as CONVENTIONAL. (When educators profile themselves, about 60–65% identify their trait as CONVENTIONAL.) When asked to profile their students as a group, they always respond UNCONVENTIONAL—as already noted, about 75% of every class.

I then ask them, "So if CONVENTIONAL professionals are teaching UNCONVENTIONAL students, what can you predict will be the outcome?" That's when they get it and realize why their best efforts often fail to connect and produce results. It's like asking CONVENTIONAL auditors to train UNCONVENTIONAL research and development staff. How successful do you think that would be?

When Luke's CONVENTIONAL teacher used an extremely CONVENTIONAL approach to her class, her students failed to perform. What she innocently experienced is a daily occurrence globally.

Added to this are CONVENTIONAL government directives to produce better results. So what does this produce? We give UNCONVENTIONAL kids high CONVENTIONAL *standardized* tests for advancement. And, these tests don't even measure the competencies we want our kids to have and organizations need, such as: creativity, adaptability, ability to communicate, innovate, work as a team, etc.

The stiff, autocratic, unbending CONVENTIONAL pressure is so great from government, that teachers often spend 50% or more of their time teaching UNCONVENTIONAL kids how to take a CONVENTIONAL standardized test. In fact, the stressors are so high when we force UNCONVENTIONAL kids to mindlessly take these check-in-the-box tests that school *suicide ideation and attempts and random bombing and shooting threats dramatically increase.* The first school rampage that set the global trend occurred during high CONVENTIONAL standardized test week.[1] (Chapter 22 reviews intervention themes to bridge this gap.)

Here's an example of a young professional who was never taught and nurtured to have the capacity to *innovate with discipline between the lines:*

Common Example of Someone Who Doesn't Get It

Ironically, the day I started writing this chapter, a new IT contractor was scheduled to work on one of our systems. A 30-plus tech-savvy college-educated professional, he was UNCONVENTIONAL, exceptionally bright, articulate, and pleasant.

The appointment was set up for 9:00 a.m.; he arrived at 9:30. He forgot to bring a book with previous notes, failed to bring a checklist, and said the job wouldn't take more than an hour. Five hours later, the job still wasn't completed. On a previous visit, he had skipped doing an audit of our systems to determine if the solution he was integrating would work. Instead, he tried to wing it. Several times while talking to me he interrupted our conversation to take a call or read a text without even an "excuse me." Discipline and reliability were absent.

Failing to complete the system integration, we didn't take one step forward. When he left my office, he forgot to take the notes he generated. Inconsistency dominated. His actions were less about being forgetful and more about not being disciplined.

He was a hard worker and honest. I didn't take his poor performance personally, but he didn't realize that he was conveying with his *actions* that we couldn't trust him with critical future jobs, and his contract was terminated.

Does this sound like someone you know? Maybe you?

Usually, if someone is undisciplined at work, they're the same at home, and those we love deserve better.

We all have negative actions, and there's no stereotypical way to conquer every nuance of these actions. But, we can focus on one negative action at a time, like undisciplined, and work on it. If this sounds like you, find someone who is UNCONVENTIONAL who *doesn't* have that negative action and let that person guide you. Ask how *they* did it. This isn't difficult, but it does require commitment.

If you have people working for you, use this approach to save those who can be saved from dismissal, and simultaneously improve their lives. Today, we advise any client who is hiring staff to closely look at an UNCONVENTIONAL person's negative actions, if any, and do an assessment of whether that action could undermine the company or position for which they are being hired. (It's obviously advisable to do the same with those who are CONVENTIONAL, but the UNCONVENTIONAL factor isn't on most professionals' radar.)

If you are UNCONVENTIONAL but can innovate with discipline between the lines, you'll separate yourself from the masses who don't. You'll also make life a lot more pleasant and less stressful for yourself and everyone else around you—at work and at home.

When I speak to parents and they recognize the significance of the UNCONVENTIONAL shift, they all ask the same question: *So what do we do?* Here's another approach that brings this closer to home, and sometimes our faith.

Raising Our Children...and Ourselves

I stumbled across a remarkable article by *New York Times* writer John Tierney analyzing decades of studies confirming what many of us accept as common sense. His provocative 2008 New Year's Eve article was entitled, "For Good Self-Control, Try Getting Religious About It," (which he expanded in his book *Willpower*, coauthored with Roy F. Baumeister).

Churning through over eighty years of studies about people of faith, two psychologists at the University of Miami, found that "religious people tend to do better in school, live longer, have more satisfying marriages and be generally happier." This prompted them to ask if these folks were likely to have more self-control—a desirable character quality for *innovating between the lines.*

> As early as the 1920s, researchers found that students who spent more time in Sunday school did better at laboratory tests measuring their self-discipline. Subsequent studies showed that religiously devout children were rated relatively low in impulsiveness by both parents and teachers, and that religiosity repeatedly correlated with higher self-control among adults. Devout people were found to be more likely than others to wear seat belts, go to the dentist, and take vitamins. [For more from another scholar, see the Source Note.][2]

The psychologists, who described themselves as not particularly "religious," emphasized that just sitting in a church pew for "extrinsic" reasons like pleasing someone or making an impression wasn't sufficient. They had to be a "true believer,"[3] with a genuine belief in God, like the man in the next story.

A Neighborhood and a Nation Transformed

Most people have never heard of Robert Raikes. He was a CONVENTIONAL guy who did something extremely UNCONVENTIONAL. His story reminds us that we don't have to be UNCONVENTIONAL to do something UNCONVENTIONAL that changes out-of-control lives.

Raikes was a newspaper man and ran the *Gloucester Journal.* Gloucester, about two hours east of London, was an industrial town noted for manufacturing fine pins and bell foundries as well as textiles. One simple action by this working stiff to teach young people self-imposed restraint changed the direction of his country...and the lives of millions of others.

In 1780, Gloucester experienced a terrible blight of juvenile crime, as did the rest of the nation. At that time, kids were forced to work 10 hours a day, six days a week. Their only day off was Sunday. Parents were tired, and kids ran wild. Up to 100 cases of juvenile crime were brought each year to the magistrate. Unrestrained, these kids, like those incarcerated today, often have the dark side of the UNCONVENTIONAL trait—reckless, anarchistic, undisciplined—living unrestrained and out-of-control in alleys and byways. Raikes, in a 1784 letter to Colonel Townley, a "gentleman of Lancashire," told how he stumbled across his need to act.

> The beginning of this scheme was entirely owing to accident. Some business leading me one morning into the suburbs of the city, where the lowest of people (who are principally employed in the pin manufactory) chiefly reside, I was struck with concern at seeing a group of children, wretchedly ragged, at play in the streets. I asked an inhabitant whether those children belonged to that part of town, and lamented their misery and idleness.[4]

Convinced something had to be done, Raikes hired four women and a minister. He paid them to teach about 100 6- to 14-year-olds how to read and write. The Bible was the text used to affect the "reformation of manners," as it was termed by Lord William Wilberforce, an engaged politician. They also learned the catechism and many were baptized into the Christian faith. Raikes used his newspaper to report personal stories of the transformation in these young lives.

By 1792, Gloucester juvenile crime had ceased, and as word spread across England in newspapers, so was the birth of "Sunday School" and England's education system.[4] The *Gentlemen's Magazine*, which published Raikes's letter to Colonel Townley explaining the phenomenon, noted that over 1,800 children "were engaged" in the town of Leeds, which had followed the Gloucester example.[5]

Newsman Raikes's modest effort contributed to another profound change in England and the world—a change that has been lost to dusty history books.

Wilberforce, after he experienced his religious conversion to Christianity, decided in 1785 that he would work in Parliament until two goals were completed. The first was the freedom of the slaves and the end of that evil institution. The second was the "reformation of the manners," which referred to the severe moral decay prevalent throughout England, which Raikes observed firsthand, and which Sunday School began to address in the lives of youngsters.

When the juvenile crime rate plummeted as the new and innovative Sunday Schools spread across England, the English demonstrated through UNCONVENTIONAL actions that failing taking care of their weakest was no longer an option. If the English wouldn't take care of their own children, why would they care about enslaved Africans and abolishing slavery? As the heart of the nation changed in local neighborhoods, pricking the souls and conscience of the British, the English passed a law in 1807 to abolish slavery 27 years after Raikes started the Gloucester "Sunday School."[6] Slavery didn't end then, but with consistent local pressure, Parliament eventually passed its final legislation in 1833 abolishing it. Wilberforce, who championed the movement, died three days after the law passed.

If you ever wondered how Sunday Schools started, now you know. A CONVENTIONAL man took UNCONVENTIONAL action because the times demanded it, which fueled another UNCONVENTIONAL act for the times: the abolition of slavery.

Present day, and on a much smaller scale, I witnessed how genuine faith and an UNCONVENTIONAL approach changed the lives of over four hundred inner-city youth whom I worked with from 1986–1992 through an outreach at the church we attended. Although one-third of the students had seen someone shot, stabbed, or murdered, not one youth joined a gang, not one teenage girl became pregnant, and a large number began making all A's and B's, prompting calls from local teachers inquiring as to what we were doing.[7] (See Source Notes for more.)

What Raikes and the Gloucester community did was UNCONVENTIONAL for the times, but it brought severely needed discipline *and* love into the lives of children and families as they were educated. (As one educator said, rules without compassion breeds anarchy.) This is where the notion for *innovation between the lines* must begin—in our homes, schools, and places of worship...and then where we work.

The shift to the UNCONVENTIONAL doesn't have to be a curse so long as our morals, values, and the essence of character remain consistent. Telling the truth and not lying, for example, is a constant for the ages.

We already have our inspiration points which provide us with direction. We just need to do it.

Next, let's look at a powerful principle when making snapshot reads that allows us to see people and situations with even greater clarity.

CHAPTER ELEVEN

Situational and Behavioral Reads

Keeping them Separate

[Is it the person or the situation?]

"My entrepreneurial clock is ticking. I'm starting another restaurant," Terrence explained. He'd been in the restaurant business for years.

"I want to create a concept for the locals to ease some of the pain of seasonality. There's a lot to consider. Do you think profiling could help?" he asked me.

Terrence's restaurants, which have seasonal swings, are located in a waterfront resort area off Lake Michigan. He's thinking about another restaurant to attract locals in order to keep a steady cash flow and his staffing consistent. His challenge was expanding and contracting staff and finding strategies to keep his best employees. He had learned the *KPS* and wanted to know if rapid-fire reads could help.

Terrence is typical of many entrepreneurial clients: They have lots of factors to consider and they need clarity quickly. The failure to separate *behavioral* reads from *situational* reads is one of the most common reasons for confusion, and a common reason for errant snapshot reads.

Behavioral reads are those we make using the four wires and how they may impact a situation. *Situational* reads are all the other factors—the who, what, why, where, when factors and how they impact a *situation*.

Ever had a situation where you had a lot to consider and you just wished you could see things with greater clarity? If so, the principle Terrence used will help. To get an idea of how to separate and use behavioral and situational reads, let's watch how Terrence broke down his observations, beginning with an email he sent me.

> How do I go about profiling a community? I have lived here most of my life, but I can't seem to pinpoint the overall demographic. We have over 65% second-home owners and tourists, which seem to be my current customers. I have thought about my regular customers and they seem to be all over the board. At my seafood and Italian restaurants they tend to be conventional. A lot could be situational though and this is where I lose it.
>
> I have a gut feeling that the people I am targeting with the new restaurant fall into the conventional trait. I think that because of the people I see eating at my competition. The food they serve there is very basic, service is very predictable and cost is low. Do you think profiling a community could help me build a business and improve my current businesses?

Using his email, let's breakdown a couple of his *situational* reads:

Location and season dependent: The resort area is a seasonal business so most of his sales were during peak seasons. Sales didn't drop during off-peak times because of the quality of Terrence's food or service, but rather a shortage of patrons.

Type of Food: The clientele like his seafood restaurant because it's near water and it's fresh. They like his Italian restaurant because of the excellent quality, and because most people like Italian.

Both of these situational reads are important, but by themselves aren't behavioral reads like CONVENTIONAL or UNCONVENTIONAL.

Here are some of Terrence's behavioral reads:

Appeal to the UNCONVENTIONAL: He has dishes with a twist on each menu for those who like to experiment and try something new.

Staff is UNCONVENTIONAL: Terrence identified their profile as a group. He made this read as we discussed their compatibility with the proposed restaurant, which would feature CONVENTIONAL fare.

Competitor and target clientele is CONVENTIONAL: His competitor serves the year-round locals standard fare that appeals to people who are CONVENTIONAL.

Terrence's main objective was to stabilize his cash flow and employee base during the off-season. He made a situational read that his competitor offers a conservative menu. He profiled the customers as CONVENTIONAL, and Terrence's conclusion was to create a restaurant that appeals to this crowd. There is a problem, though.

As a team, he profiled his staff as pretty high UNCONVENTIONAL—about 4. Some of the staff will form the hub for the new restaurant. This is significant as they may not be enthused about working in a CONVENTIONAL restaurant—they might find it boring, which could lead to less than enthusiastic customer service. One option we discussed was moving those who were low UNCONVENTIONAL (1 or 2 on the 1–5 scale) to the restaurant, provided their knowledge, skill, ability, and experience (the situational reads) are up to the task.

A key situational read was that everyone wanted steady work and a consistent paycheck during the off-peak season. This meant that with reminders from the team leader they could probably sustain their customer service edge over the other competitors. Another option was to rotate staff to work at the new restaurant for a month and then return to the seafood or Italian restaurants. This would behaviorally inject change/variety, deliver a consistent paycheck (situational read), and keep them happy.

When Terrence started his evaluation process, he didn't have an assumption of what type of read was more important. To provide clarity, he made behavioral and situational reads, weighted each separately, and then examined how each read impacted the other.

If Terrence didn't profile his potential customers and his staff, he'd be stuck with a "gut" decision. But, by keeping his situational and behavioral reads separate, he was able to lay out his plans for others to grasp quickly—from investors to staff. As he received their input, he added it to his behavioral and situational list of reads, making connections clearer for everyone. This minimized emotional decision-making as part of the equation. It directed discussions away from *I feel* to *we can see.*

TERRENCE'S BEHAVIORAL AND SITUATIONAL READS

Behavioral Reads

- Staff: UNCONVENTIONAL, must keep engaged
- Customers: CONVENTIONAL
- Type of food locals like: CONVENTIONAL
- Terrence's peak-season menus: UNCONVENTIONAL

Situational Reads

- Most customers are seasonal
- Goal: attract locals in off season
- Location: resort

Summing up the principle. Keep behavioral and situational reads separate to provide clarity. It's time efficient and can be used over a period of time in situations where there are multiple factors and observations. It can also be applied in any situation where people are involved, such as acquisitions and mergers, considering a career change, entering into or terminating a personal or professional relationship, designating responsibilities in a marriage, and mentoring and disciplining kids.

The simplest way to record your observations is to draw a line down the middle of a piece of paper and list your behavioral reads on one side and the situational reads on the other. In addition to giving you clarity, you can use it when explaining the factors, options, and your decision to others.

Keeping behavioral and situational reads separate is also useful in spontaneous situations, like in the following story which is an amazing example of someone who used the principle to instruct others and put people at ease.

Good to See You...

"You said you want a full house, queens over twos?" asked Richard, renowned as the world's greatest card mechanic.

Sylvia nodded.

"How many players?" he asked.

"Five," she responded.

"Who gets the winning hand?"

"The second player," she said, pointing with the deck she had just shuffled at an imaginary spot on the table.

"Are you satisfied the deck is thoroughly shuffled?"

She nods.

"And it's impossible to know where the queens and twos are?" Richard continued.

"Yes." Sylvia then handed the deck to Richard.

Name any card and Richard Turner can deal it from a deck you shuffle and make it look like it came from the top. His second, bottom, and center deals are considered the most fluid and undetectable the world has ever seen. Legend has it that a mobster offered him $1 million to play in a high-stakes game in the Middle East. Richard refused the request and needed law enforcement to protect him—*because he's that good.*

The 40 of us watching Richard were all sleight-of-hand card buffs. Assembled in the back room of a suburban Dallas Chinese restaurant in 2006, we were more than astonished; we were stunned by his expertise. Ever since I was a teen, going to lectures presented by the greats was an event, and watching Richard took me back in time to those early days.

I was seated so I could see underneath the card table where Richard was seated. Oddly, his feet were in an aggressive athletic stance, shoulder width apart, left foot forward and his right foot poised on its ball. Unusual for someone seated at a table demonstrating card techniques. I assumed that it was a technique he adopted as a black belt in karate. Or, maybe it was from his days as an extreme rock climber.

Immediately after Sylvia handed Richard the deck she had just shuffled, he shuffled it some more with effortless concert pianist precision. I also noticed that he never looked down at the deck, only at us. Then he dealt the five poker hands, sailing five cards each to five imaginary players at the table. At any time, Sylvia could take the cards from Richard as he was dealing and shuffle them, and she did—twice.

When he finished, he said, "Turn over player number two's hand."

Sylvia did and blurted out, "Oh my gosh!" as she turned over a full house, queens over twos. (Remember, she shuffled the cards at anytime while he was dealing. Crazy!)

Anytime, anywhere, that's the result when Richard is at the table. His moniker is "The Cheat," and he quips how odd it is that he's made a small fortune with 52 pieces of paper.

Oh, and one more detail about Richard the premiere card mechanic, sixth degree black belt in karate, and extreme rock climber . . .

Richard is *blind*. That's right, legally blind since he was 9, and by early adulthood, he could see only peripheral shadows. Today, even that is gone.

Imagine manipulating and controlling a hand of cards called for *when you can't even see the faces of the cards*. Astounding. Then, when he shows you *how* he does it, it gets worse. Even the best card experts in the world struggle to replicate his knuckle-busting techniques.

Added to this, he qualified as a black belt in karate by going 10 rounds with 10 different black belts, an accomplishment featured on the front page of the sports section of the *Los Angeles Times*. The video can be viewed online.

Richard lost his sight because of deteriorating macula in each eye. He told me that to overcome his fear of what he couldn't control, he became an extreme rock climber in his twenties. To say he is gifted trivializes his abilities, but what happened next in that restaurant elevated him to almost mythical status, and emphasizes that sometimes you have to *hear it* to see it.

"Is there a teenager here?" Richard asked. He wasn't feigning, he really didn't know.

"Yeah, Chris is a teenager," said one of the guys.

"Chris, would you come up and sit next to me?" Richard asked, gesturing at an empty seat to his right.

"Thanks, but I'm a bit shy," Chris replied timidly. Chris was sitting on the windowsill. "Please don't be offended," he added, now standing with his back against the windowsill.

"Please, I'd really appreciate it," Richard gently urged.

"No, I'd rather stay back here," Chris resisted.

"Chris, you're about six-foot-four inches and you used to play football, am I right?" Richard asked, restraining the assertiveness in his voice to coax him forward.

It was extraordinary. Richard rapid-fire profiled Chris as NONASSERTIVE and a CAUTIOUS decision maker from the tone of his voice. In response, Richard restrained his ASSERTIVE trait by lowering his voice and leaning back a bit in his chair. Richard also made a lightning *situational* read.

When Chris replied to Richard, he stood up. Richard is so spacially attuned to where people are around him, that he gauged Chris's height from the change of location of his voice when Chris stood. He made these reads in seconds and responded appropriately, putting Chris at ease by applying the philosophy: *I know who you are. Good for me, better for you. It's the art of treating a person right the first time.*

This was the second time in 24 hours that I watched Richard, rapid-fire profile. He didn't use a profiling system, just his intuition. The night before, he rapid-fire profiled two people simultaneously, again making both behavioral and situational reads.

Providing Instruction Based Upon Reads

I met Richard for the first time the evening before at the home of a friend, an IT professional who was also a serious amateur magician. It was a private coaching session. I arrived late and quietly sat at the dining table as Richard coached two fellows through his technique for dealing from the bottom of a deck. I unconsciously profiled each magician and Richard. As I watched, I was stunned.

Richard made a situational read of their level of expertise as each held a deck of cards in their hands. As he instructed them, Richard cupped their hands in his and bent his head so it was right next to their hands, heightening his ability to hear each card dealt. If improperly executed, the card makes an almost imperceptible clicking sound as it clears the bottom. If the deal was properly executed, no "click"—just the expected sound of a card gliding off the deck.

What was extraordinary, though, was that Richard changed his *style* of instruction for each fellow *matching their behavioral profile.* It was evident that his change of instruction was deliberate. One fellow was ASSERTIVE and CONTROL and the other was NONASSERTIVE and EXPRESS.

Richard used his ASSERTIVE trait and restrained his EXPRESS trait when working with the first fellow, who was ASSERTIVE/CONTROL. Then he restrained his ASSERTIVE trait and used his EXPRESS trait when coaching the NONASSERTIVE/EXPRESS second magician. He was the first person without sight I had met who could rapid-fire profile.

It's one thing to be able to dazzle with a deck of cards, which he can hold and feel. It's another to be able to thoughtfully modify his instruction with people he couldn't see.

The clue to how Richard intuitively learned to make rapid-fire reads is found in his greeting when he meets you: "Good to see you!"

Richard teaching us his second deal at the lecture.
(Dan Korem, December 2006)

I met a blind pianist 30 years ago who did the same. It was a lighthearted way to put those of us with sight at ease. But for Richard, it was more. He really does create a picture of you in his mind.

Because he is blind, Richard has no choice but to make situational and behavioral reads. For Richard, the performer, this is integral to his interactions with an audience, which often doesn't know he is blind until many minutes into his presentations.

In 2013, at the famed Magic Castle in Hollywood, before anyone realized that Richard lacked sight, one young woman, flummoxed by Richard's skill, blurted out, "Yeah, but can you do it blindfolded?"

"I don't know," Richard coyly responded. "Why don't you cover my eyes." She did, and the audience roared with laughter when she realized his true condition!

The reality is that Richard can *see* what others can't, and because he chooses to see what's important, he can treat people in a way they uniquely deserve to be treated. It's what endears him to others. He even helped direct a scene in the movie *The Tree of Life*. That's right, a blind performer advised a sighted director on how to visually shoot a scene.

You might say, "Well, because he's blind, his other senses are heightened."

That may be true, but *do you have to go blind before you can make reads that a blind man can see?*

If a blind man can immediately read and treat others uniquely to entertain, teach, and mentor, why can't we do the same? And we have an advantage. We can see and read non-verbal actions and reactions like hand gestures, body posture, and facial expressions, which Richard *can't* see.

At home, Richard doing a one-hand riffle shuffle while taking a phone call. (Dan Korem, December 2013)

As you might suspect there is more to Richard's story, and although loaded with talent, he'll be the first to admit that he still has rough edges to be chiseled away. (In 2015, *Dealt*, a fascinating feature-length documentary on Richard's life, will be released. Through an unusual turn of events, my son, Luke, is producing and directing the project.[1])

Kids See the Darndest Things

Before we leave Richard, what do you think is his favorite type of furniture?

Answer: Antiques, especially those with unique carvings.

When one of my granddaughters was 7 years old, I told her about Richard and his love of antiques, and I asked her, "What is his favorite thing to do in the house?"

Quick as a button, she said, "Dust the furniture! He likes to feel the furniture because he's blind!" she beamed.

Kids can often make situational reads faster than adults because they're uninhibited and can see themselves in another person's shoes.

When kids watch sleight of hand, they often blurt out the secret before adults. This is because they don't see limitations and don't consider how a solution *isn't* possible, while adults assume *well he couldn't have done it this way*. The direct-path approach kids take is one reason why they learn to rapid-fire profile so quickly, and the wires let them see the shortest path with clarity.

So if kids, a restaurateur, and a blind chap deemed "The Cheat" can make situational and behavioral reads, what excuse is left for the rest of us?! (Yes, an exclamation after a question mark is a bit UNCONVENTIONAL!)

Finally, here is an everyday situational/behavioral read by comic Jerry Seinfeld:

> So they're showing me on television the detergent getting out bloodstains. I mean, come on, you got a T-shirt with bloodstains all over it. Maybe laundry isn't your biggest problem!

Richard attended a speech I gave to San Antonio business leaders in 2013 on profiling and snapshot reads. They viewed and profiled video clips using interactive keypads. Before I showed them how to increase accuracy, they only scored 35%—the typical result globally. Richard, however, profiled every clip correctly, even though he only made reads based on what he could hear. Notice the intensity of his "gaze" directed at the audio speakers. It was the same intensity I observed when he modified his instruction based upon the profiles of students he was teaching when we first met in 2006.

My son, Luke, left, and his crew filming *Dealt*, a feature length documentary on Richard's life. Here Richard is wowing magicians at the joint 2014 International Brotherhood of Magicians/ Society of American Magicians convention in St. Louis.
(Dan Korem, July 2014)

For years, Richard and I knew of each other but never met. We both even performed at the famed Magic Castle in Hollywood in the early 1980s.

When we finally met in December 2006, we became close pals. After a late-night card session at my house that week, I gave Richard a prized possession: the deck used by legendary card magician Ed Marlo, when I shot him in 1982 for one of the first professionally recorded instructional videos for magicians. At that time, the best video of Marlo was on 8mm film.

When Marlo, who called himself a "cardician," demonstrated his bottom deal for the cameras, he was holding a cigar in his right hand—the same hand that dealt the cards. He explained that years earlier, whenever he dealt from the bottom, the lit tip of the cigar hit the table and the ashes flew. It was a sure tip-off that he dealt from the bottom. This led Marlo to modify his technique so that his right wrist didn't turn and the ashes didn't fly! At the end of the session, Marlo took the cigar band and tied it into a knot and said, "I always do this. So if you find this at a crime scene, you'll know I'm the one who did it!" I also gave Richard Marlo's knotted band. It meant a lot to him.

About Richard, Marlo said, "Technicians, as a rule, are not usually good actors or entertainers. Richard Turner is all three."

Notice in the photograph Richard's eye contact with the camera. He explained to me that while it is common for the eyes of some people who are blind to drift upwards, he physically works to direct his eyes towards the sound of a person's voice.

CHAPTER TWELVE

Solve A Mystery: ADHD

[Didn't see the solution
because we didn't pay attention?]

The teachers were upset.

"We think that most of our students who have been diagnosed as having ADHD don't have it and shouldn't be given drugs. What do you think?" they asked me.

It was 1999 and ADHD was a new trend.

Today, millions of people complain about millions of others who are bright but seem scattered, can't stay focused or finish assignments on time. The complaints are directed at people with the disease/disorder called Attention Deficit Hyperactivity Disorder (ADHD). In 2011, the Centers for Disease Control (CDC) said it affected over 5.4 million kids and 4.4 million adults (18–48).

By 2013, the CDC stated *20% of all high school-aged boys* and 11% of all school-age kids have been "diagnosed" with ADHD—the number one youth disorder. That's 6.4 million kids out of 54 million in school. A jump of one million in just two years. *Can this really be true?*

People complain because of inconvenience and an estimated "cost" of $36–52.4 billion (as posted on the CDC website) for everything from medications, therapies, special education, discipline costs, and more.

People also complain because they can't make one simple read which would enable them to connect the dots and provide a simple thematic remedy for the majority of "cases."

This is the story of how hundreds of teachers who could make snapshot reads solved the three big ADHD riddles:

- What is ADHD *really* (in most cases)?
- Why did ADHD seem to suddenly appear?
- How to immediately help almost any student or adult perform successfully in the classroom or on the job.

This is also a story of what happened when reading the human factor was neglected; millions were needlessly medicated; and for many people, creativity was deliberately flatlined.

Today, if you see a doctor who uses the current and fifth edition of the *Diagnostic and Statistical Manual of Mental Disorders (DSM-V)*, the diagnostic guide for mental-health professionals, and you show just *five* of the symptoms shown on the book jacket to the right, you will be diagnosed as having a mental disorder—ADHD. Common sense says that millions might have these behaviors, but does that

YOU ONLY NEED **FIVE** OF THESE TRAITS TO QUALIFY FOR AN ADHD DIAGNOSIS. . . .

- [x] Fails to pay close attention to details
- [ ] Has difficulty sustaining attention in tasks
- [ ] Does not seem to listen when spoken to directly
- [ ] Does not follow through on instructions
- [x] Has difficulty organizing tasks/activities
- [ ] Avoids or dislikes tasks requiring sustained mental effort
- [ ] Loses things necessary for specific tasks
- [x] Easily distracted by external stimuli
- [x] Forgetful in daily activities
- [ ] Fidgets with hands/feet
- [ ] Leaves seat in situations where remaining seated is expected
- [ ] Runs about when inappropriate to do so
- [ ] Has difficulty engaging in leisure activities quietly
- [ ] Often on the go or acts as if driven by a motor
- [x] Talks excessively
- [ ] Blurts out answers
- [ ] Has difficulty awaiting turns
- [ ] Interrupts or intrudes on others

BUT WHAT IF THE DIAGNOSIS IS WRONG?

2014 book, "ADHD Does Not Exist" by Richard Saul, M.D., member of the American Academy of Pediatrics, the American Academy of Neurology, and the Society for Behavior and Development.

mean they *all* they have a *behavioral disorder*?

Because of the impact on our lives, now and long into the future, we will take a more in-depth look at the snapshot and situational reads people made to solve this mystery. Let's begin with teachers who told me they made a snapshot read and saw something others didn't.

Teachers Frustrated by Student Lack of Attention

We were training thousands of teachers in scores of school systems across North America in how to prevent school rampages like the 1999 Columbine massacre in Littleton, Colo. During workshop breaks, many told me they spotted another pattern using their new profiling skills. The collective observation/complaint I heard hundreds of times was: *Most of our students who have been diagnosed as having ADHD don't have it and shouldn't be given drugs.* And there was more.

"We profiled our students who are labeled ADHD and most are *high* UNCONVENTIONAL. The problem is we've been taught to use CONVENTIONAL teaching techniques, and these kids just don't relate. We think they need more innovative assignments, change of routine, and a quicker pace in the class. There is enormous pressure on us to go along with the medication route, and we don't think they have a disorder. What do you think?"

ADHD wasn't on my radar because my kids didn't have it, but I investigated their concerns. (At the time, doctors were saying that if a student struggled paying attention it was ADD, and if they were also extremely hyperactive it was ADHD. Most now just refer to it as ADHD.)

In 2004, about 5% of the workforce were told they had ADHD, and doctors were saying millions more had it but didn't know it. A 2004 feature article in the *New York Times* listed these ADHD actions of adult professionals:

- Forgetfulness
- Disorganized
- Restless
- Creative
- Whimsical
- Hard to stay focused

- "There's an amusement park going on in my head"
- Becomes antsy and bored
- Tends to unravel as the work devolves from interesting to routine
- Has lost jobs that had neither the structure nor the flexibility he needed[1]

Profile the list of actions listed in the article using your CONVENTIONAL–UNCONVENTIONAL wire. As a group, do the actions tilt toward Einstein–UNCONVENTIONAL or Queen Elizabeth II–CONVENTIONAL? If you profiled the actions as UNCONVENTIONAL, you're correct. They are very similar to the UNCONVENTIONAL actions listed in Chapter 8. This is the same read the teachers made regarding their students diagnosed as ADHD.

Teachers Solve the Riddle

Here was the logic the teachers used to solve the riddle and the progression of their reads:

First, they agreed that up to 75% of their students in a typical classroom were now UNCONVENTIONAL, a severe shift from 25% or less just 20–30 years earlier (noted in Chapter 8).

Second, they said that as the number of students with the UNCONVENTIONAL trait increased, the number of kids with the *high* UNCONVENTIONAL also increased (4 or higher on a scale of 0–5).

Third, they profiled the students who were diagnosed as ADHD as high UNCONVENTIONAL and these students displayed UNCONVENTIONAL actions such as inconsistent, spontaneous, imaginative, impulsive, undisciplined, etc.

Fourth, they said there was a severe behavioral disconnect between the teachers and these students. They profiled the *institution* of education as CONVENTIONAL, and they profiled their administrators and the leaders who steer the ship as *high* CONVENTIONAL.

Probing their reads. Each time teachers approached me about the ADHD high UNCONVENTIONAL connection, I had them describe their students' actions and bring me student papers and assignments to test the accuracy of their reads. Often, I met their students, which was possible because workshops were usually held on school campuses.

Then I probed deeper.

My first question was: *In which classes do these kids have the most and least difficulty focusing and performing?*

The answer confirmed my suspicions: math, science, language arts (like grammar and composition), and history were the lead culprits—the CONVENTIONAL disciplines. The UNCONVENTIONAL classes, like art or shop, weren't even on the radar—no complaints there.

My second question was: *What is the profile of the teachers who teach math, science, language arts, and history who didn't complain about kids not focusing?*

For over 14 years, virtually every one of the teachers they identified was UNCONVENTIONAL—or they were CONVENTIONAL teachers who learned UNCONVENTIONAL techniques for instruction. In other words, teachers using UNCONVENTIONAL techniques weren't complaining about ADHD students. Their students performed. The UNCONVENTIONAL themes they applied in the classroom were change, variability, and flexibility (CVF). Simultaneously, they encouraged innovation with discipline between the lines, as explained in Chapter 9.

If you're an instructor/teacher/team leader for these "ADHD" students and adults, which would you try first? Would you modify your instruction and leadership with CVF themes and UNCONVENTIONAL assignments? Or, would your first move be to give them medication to make them more compliant and flatten out their thought process so they could focus? The obvious answer is to modify instruction and leadership. Meds should only be a part of the remedy for extreme cases (perhaps 2–5% from the millions labeled ADHD)—if verified by a doctor who is looking at the big picture and not quick-on-the-draw to dispense meds.

The *New York Times* reporter, those she interviewed, nor the CDC could rapid-fire profile, and none broached the possibility that a trait disconnection might be the culprit. The teachers we trained who could profile, however, solved the riddle for most of their students.

Years later, doctors and professors in the medical disciplines finally caught up with the teachers, like Richard A. Friedman, a professor of clinical psychology and director of the psychopharmacology clinic at the Weill Cornell Medical College, who, in late 2014, wrote in the *New York Times* about a man who changed his environment, and voila, lost his ADHD disease.

> In short, people with ADHD may not have a disease, so much as a set of behavioral traits that don't match the expectations of our contemporary culture...he would multitask, listening to music and texting, while "working" to prevent activities from becoming routine. He is much happier and—little surprise—lost his symptoms of ADHD. My patient "treated" his ADHD simply by changing the conditions of his work environment from one that was highly routine to one that was varied and unpredictable.[2]

Who Complains the Most About ADHD?

Who do you think complains the most about others having ADHD? Those who are CONVENTIONAL or UNCONVENTIONAL? If your answer is CONVENTIONAL, you're right again. So to refine Friedman's observation, it isn't our "contemporary culture," but rather CONVENTIONAL people and systems that collide with those who are high UNCONVENTIONAL.

When the CDC released its 2013 data, I was stunned, but not surprised, by their demographic map. It showed that states that were the *most* CONVENTIONAL, such as Alabama and Iowa, had the greatest number of students labeled ADHD, while the highest UNCONVENTIONAL state, California, had the *lowest* number per capita. Nevada, Colorado, and New Mexico, which are also high UNCONVENTIONAL, ranked near the bottom.

Just like you can predict in which classes high UNCONVENTIONAL kids will struggle, you can also predict geographic regions where UNCONVENTIONAL kids will be labeled ADHD. (There are a couple of mysteries, though, as with all human behavior—like why are there so many cases in Rhode Island, but a lot fewer in similarly small states like Delaware and Connecticut? Or, why isn't Washington state, which is high UNCONVENTIONAL, ranked as low as California? More puzzles for researchers to chase down, but the big pattern is clear.)

It is evident that CONVENTIONAL states complain the most about kids with "ADHD" like CONVENTIONAL teachers of the most CONVENTIONAL classes—math, science, history, and English (the language arts).

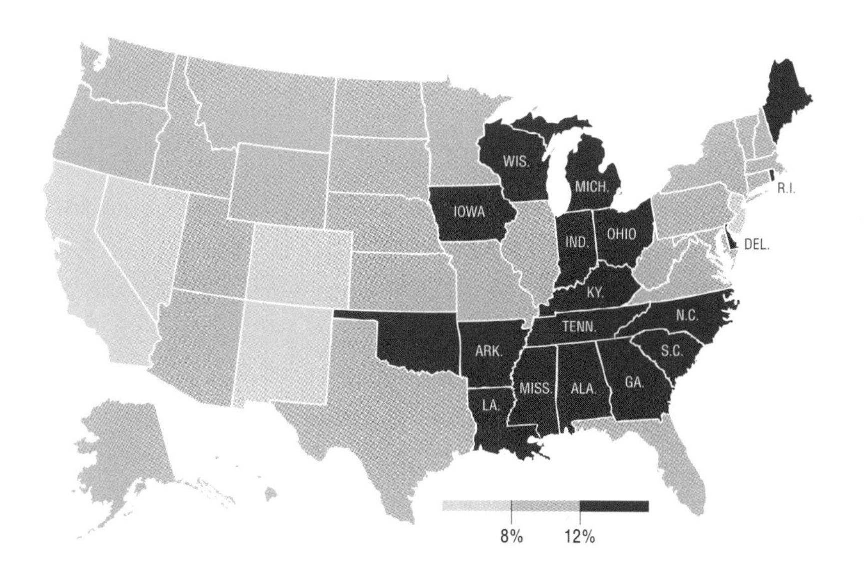

Patterns between countries? There may also be a correlation between countries like the U.S. (which tilts toward UNCONVENTIONAL as a nation) and Britain, which tends to tilt toward CONVENTIONAL (think of Britain's love of their Queen), although its youth population is steadily becoming more UNCONVENTIONAL like the rest of the world.

In 2003, a science editor noted that 8% of American kids at the time were given a diagnosis of ADHD but only 2% in Britain. But, like the U.S., the British rate is now as high as 5%, according to the British Health Service.[3] Perhaps this is because youth globally are becoming more UNCONVENTIONAL?

And then there is UNCONVENTIONAL France, where only 0.5% of their kids are "diagnosed" as ADHD. *That's 20 times less than the U.S. rate.* Why? Similar to the teachers who approached me in 1999, French doctors "prefer to look for the underlying issue that is causing the child stress—not in the child's brain, but in the child's social context."[4]

Theme for a Solution

Teachers who have been trained to profile and inject more CVF in their instruction see students perform better because the majority need more stimulation, a quicker pace, more change, and so on. And the teachers who don't, are losing their kids.

We remember stories from history, like UNCONVENTIONAL Einstein who couldn't stay focused in the classroom. A century ago, UNCONVENTIONAL students didn't overwhelm the education system because their numbers were small. Today, the significant numbers confound teachers stuck in CONVENTIONAL approaches that don't connect. The same is true in the workplace, like the equation we already reviewed: *Do you want CONVENTIONAL people with CONVENTIONAL techniques leading and educating those who are UNCONVENTIONAL?* Of course not; it's like asking audit to train research and development.

Immediate classroom improvement. In early 2001, I donated training to a Dallas inner-city school. One of the teachers at the school, who went on to obtain her Ph.D., helped me develop the first instructional module that provided strategies for educating UNCONVENTIONAL students *simultaneously* with those who are CONVENTIONAL. The results were predictable.

Academic performance increased, complaints about ADHD students dropped precipitously, and behavioral referrals decreased. More than 13,000 teachers received this instruction with similar results. The obvious question is why more schools aren't deploying these strategies. The reasons include a lack of exposure, a lack of interest by education researchers, and the difficulty of obtaining funding for research.[5]

Demanding that UNCONVENTIONAL kids take standardized tests: Really? On the broadest platform, high CONVENTIONAL K–12 *standardized* check-in-the-box tests are used to measure annual performance, but they don't deliver. First, they don't identify creativity, ability to communicate, work on a team, and other core competencies that are sought in the workforce. Second, most K–12 teachers and administrators will express severe frustration about how the demand to perform on these tests shifts the classroom from a learning environment to one that narrowly instructs kids to robotically check boxes. *In addition, standardized tests are behaviorally discriminatory and biased against UNCONVENTIONAL students, who perform better when given change, variability, and flexibility in a learning environment.* In fact, the explosion of ADHD complaints/cases paralleled changes in the law that incentivized getting kids to pass these tests.

> Stephen Hinshaw, a professor of psychology at the University of California, Berkeley, found that when a state passed laws punishing or rewarding schools for their standardized test scores, ADHD diagnoses in that state would increase not long afterward. Nationwide, the rates of ADHD diagnosis increased by 22% in the first four years after the 2001 "No Child Left Behind" act was passed [the first federal effort to link school financing to standardized test performance].[6]

Adam Rafalovich, a sociologist at Pacific University, adds that the beginning of ADHD "epidemic" trend paralleled governmental policy changes that incentivized diagnosing kids and adults with ADHD: For the first time, the diagnosis came with an upside—access to tutors and time allowances on standardized tests.

By the late 1990s, as more parents and teachers became aware that ADHD existed, and that there were drugs to treat it, the diagnosis became increasingly normalized, until it was viewed by many as just another part of the experience of childhood.[7]

Faced with the inability to solve the riddle and raise the instructional bar, public schools, which are CONVENTIONAL government agencies, turned to exotic classroom "management" techniques (that didn't work), and eventually meds for help.

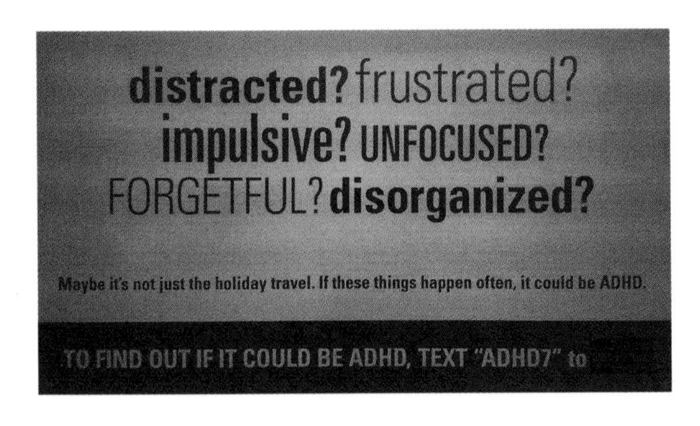

2011 poster at Philadelphia Airport with descriptors that lead to stereotyping UNCONVENTIONAL adults and kids as ADHD.

The Rush to Take Meds Followed by Behavior Therapy

In 2011, the Centers for Disease Control posted specific "treatment" recommendations on its website for kids diagnosed with ADHD. Note the absence of *any* suggestion that there might be a behavioral classroom disconnect or suggestions for applying UNCONVENTIONAL teaching strategies. Instead, what is recommended is a rush to medicate and apply therapy, and ADHD drug sales increased from $4 billion in 2007 to $9 billion in 2012.[8]

The CDC recommendations are:

- Primary care clinicians should establish a treatment program that recognizes ADHD as a chronic condition.

- The treating clinician, parents, and child, in collaboration with school personnel, should specify appropriate target outcomes to guide management.
- The clinician should recommend stimulant medication and/or behavior therapy as appropriate to improve target outcomes in children with ADHD.
- When the selected management for a child with ADHD has not met target outcomes, clinicians should evaluate the original diagnosis, use of all appropriate treatments, adherence to the treatment plan, and presence of coexisting conditions.
- The clinician should periodically provide a systematic follow-up for the child with ADHD. Monitoring should be directed to target outcomes and adverse effects, with information gathered from parents, teachers, and the child.

No doubt drug companies apply pressure to the equation, but the more compelling factor is the absence of recommendations to look at a student's core behavioral trait first. It's not a part of the CDC equation.

Adults and Kids Figure It Out

In 2008, the *New York Times* ran another ADHD article entitled "Patient Voices: ADHD," that featured audio interviews on its website. (Although the *Times* never connected the dots, they became a persistent player in providing the "dots" that helped solve the ADHD riddle.) Just like the list of descriptors in the 2004 *Times* article profiled as UNCONVENTIONAL, the kids and adults interviewed in 2008 were also UNCONVENTIONAL, like Robert Cimera, a special-education professor at Kent State University.

Cimera detailed his UNCONVENTIONAL approach to move forward despite his diagnosis—meds were never a part of the equation. He said he stumbled across the connection while working on his master's degree. He was leading a discussion group about ADHD with adults and students—some whom were diagnosed with ADHD and others who weren't.

He said someone stood up and said that their mind was like a "wall of television sets and I don't have control over the remote." That's when he realized that he was the same—with several different thoughts going full bore at the same time. He thought everyone was like him "but could just handle it better." He now realized that he "wasn't the screw-up that his teachers and siblings" portrayed.

"People describe ADHD as a contextual condition. If you ask me to do something for a long period of time, I can't do that," he said.

In class, he uses his need for change to his advantage and says his students really appreciate it "because I'm always keeping things moving, doing things that are funny or creative, or odd."

He says that he gets his class preparation tasks done by doing more than one task at the same time. His brain wants more stimulation from multiple directions, and that's what he gives it.

"If I try to sit myself down to read or force myself to write, I can't concentrate. And it becomes like throwing gasoline on the fire. So what I do is try to do a bunch of things at the same time. For example, I have two computers at my desk. Sometimes I'm writing a paper and then I'll work on something else. I multitask. So every two or three minutes I do something different. I'm actually more productive breaking tasks down into small increments."

While Robert can multitask, it's stereotyping to suggest that this applies to every UNCONVENTIONAL person. Some can, some prefer not to, but all do like and immediately respond to UNCONVENTIONAL approaches.

The successful themes for interaction and instruction, though, are operative for Robert: change, variability, flexibility—the same themes thousands of teachers have used with no complaints from students, parents, or caregivers. Like K–12 students, Robert learned to thrive in a CONVENTIONAL institutional environment.

He also found that exercise helps him focus, removes the "fog" in his mind, and works better than medication. He is emphatic, though, that what works for him may not work for everyone.

As I've emphasized, and Cimera discovered, while we can identify someone's core trait and identify themes for interaction, there is an infinite variety of ways to employ those themes. The good news is that teachers or organizational team leaders don't have to be UNCONVENTIONAL to apply them—they just need some direction. This not only includes instruction and curriculum modifications, but even classroom setups. Some schools have rearranged seating so everyone faces the center, engaging everyone.

Keith Bryant, the former president of the Mid-Size School Association of Texas and the former superintendent of the Bullard Independent School District, an upscale small-town community in Texas, created an UNCONVENTIONAL classroom at his high school.

As seen in this photo, the furniture and layout are extremely UNCONVENTIONAL, replacing the standard-fare desks and chairs (to augment their updated instruction, which includes CVF), just like you find in some advertising think tanks.[9]

In the absence of innovation, though, things can turn dark.

Meds shut down creativity. The 2008 *Times* article also described the destructive impact some drugs can have—the negatives that the teachers who came to me observed.

Kendrick Royal, an exceptionally articulate 12-year-old student from New Orleans, explains why we should be concerned.

"Well, the advice that I give is don't try too hard to be creative when you're on medicine. You won't be as creative as you would be off medicine. I like [the medicine] when I'm doing school work, but I don't like it when I'm in my art classes because it kind of shuts down my creative mind. It's easier to be focused but it seems like my creative mind is off."

Screen grab from *NYT* online article.

It's terrible that Kendrick couldn't create while on drugs, which inhibited his UNCONVENTIONAL trait. While he is able to focus on CONVENTIONAL tasks, why should he be forced to be the person the *institution* wants? If teachers who have used our education strategies taught Kendrick using the CVF themes, he would have probably have been okay.

I personally watched many friends follow well-intentioned medical advice and give their kids drugs to control their thinking. In virtually every case, the kids were high UNCONVENTIONAL and struggled in the CONVENTIONAL classes with CONVENTIONAL instruction. Not one psychologist or doctor recommended looking at modifying instruction to be trait specific to the child's UNCONVENTIONAL trait.

No doubt, there may be a small percentage of kids and adults who have some kind of mechanical brain disorder and need medical and/or behavioral help. But to reemphasize: *Most "ADHD" kids do well without meds in UNCONVENTIONAL classes or CONVENTIONAL classes that utilize UNCONVENTIONAL instructional techniques.*

My friend Richard, whom you met in the last chapter, said that if ADHD was around when he was in school in the 1960s and, 70s, he would have been labeled and given meds. Richard's brain craves stimulation and he's always in motion—mentally and physically. Can you imagine how his life might have unfolded if he was given drugs—which he didn't need—to flatten out his creativity? Diminishing his creative genius, he would never have inspired so many lives.

Finland example: Like other countries, Finland has experienced an increase of kids labeled ADHD, but meds haven't been the chosen method of addressing kids' need for stimulation.[10] While I was in Finland in 2009, lecturing to Finnish behavioral specialists, a psychologist there whose son was diagnosed with ADHD and Asperger traits told me that her school applied the CVF themes and many of his dysfunctional issues were mitigated. She said that what she learned from the American cases in my lectures confirmed her conviction. In a letter to me, she wrote:

> The school is the remedy because it is very safe: you have the same teacher from 1st grade all the way to 8th grade. Everyone is valued as an individual. The school is very structured so the children always know what is coming next, but it also offers variety, because they study intensively one subject for 4-5 weeks and then leave that subject and take up another. For example, you can have only history for one period, let's say the Romans. You hear the stories, you make the sculptures out of clay, you draw the pictures (they use no school books, the children make their own books).

Notice the balance of structure (an extension of innovating between the lines, which is also a protective factor that diminishes fear) and how, like their American counterparts we've trained, Finnish teachers applied the CVF themes in a way that worked for their students.

Here is one more extreme example of a first-grade student and a first-year teacher, whom we'll call Lisa, who had left the business world to make a difference. The comments are from an older teacher who watched Lisa's process of applying CVF themes.

> The class had 19 students and most were from very low income homes and few had two-parent households. The teacher who began the year didn't last but after about 4 weeks left one day saying she was going to be out sick, but decided she just couldn't some back to this class. She literally left all her personal stuff and walked out. They were unable to find a teacher and a sub wouldn't return to the class after being in there

once or twice. Then Lisa took the job. It was her first class and it had 3 or 4 students with major discipline problems. One little boy would become mad very quickly and begin throwing things, scream, and sometimes run. Nothing the administration had suggested would work, so Lisa began trying different things to see what might work with him [we'll call him Ben].

She would have other students come up to give her hugs during the day, so she began watching his reaction. Ben seemed to look like he wanted to hug her, but just didn't know how. She had talked to the parents and caregivers regarding "hugging" and all of them were happy she was willing to care for her children that way.

Lisa decided to create a separate "cool-down" desk for Ben in the class and she covered the desktop with colorful paper, because he liked to draw. The other students would always ask why he was so mad and mean. She talked with them one day when Ben was absent and explained what she was doing to help him, so they wouldn't think he was getting something special.

She invited Ben to eat lunch in the classroom with her one day and explained that she had made that desk for him and it would be his "cool down" desk when he knew he was getting mad. He asked her if he could call it his "chill" desk and she agreed that was a better name for it. She told him she would leave a couple of colored pencils in the desk and that instead of throwing things, hitting, or yelling when he was mad, he should just go to his desk and draw on the paper. Lisa told Ben that when he felt better that he could come up and tell her that he was "ready to hug it out" if he wanted to.

The 1st week Lisa would have to ask him to go to the desk when he began acting out, but then after that he would take himself there and sit for usually no more than 15 minutes, drawing on the desk. He still wasn't at the "hug it out" stage, but he would approach her then change his mind. The 2nd week he started going to the chair on his own when he began melting down. When she could tell he was calming down, she decided to approach him and ask, "Are you ready to hug it out with me?" He looked at her and smiled, hugged her, and then after that he asked on his own. She figured that he would at least still be part of the class if she could get it to work and that's what she wanted. I know this won't work for all children, but it made a big change in her classroom!

As already noted, many in the behavioral sciences lament that psychologists and other mental-health practitioners aren't taught how to rapid-fire profile and identify healthy traits. When you can't, you miss so much—sometimes what is extremely obvious, like the need for CVF. There is a movement in the profession, though, to introduce a broader range of skill sets that extend beyond identifying and treating disorders. Until then, they rely upon a controversial diagnostic manual for "disorders."

The encyclopedia of mental disorders known as the *Diagnostic and Statistical Manual* is built on a principle that many therapists find simplistic: that people's symptoms are the most reliable way to classify their mental troubles.[11]

The frustration is that most parents and teachers aren't aware that teachers, who could profile, solved this riddle more than 10 years ago. And, that many children have been needlessly prescribed medication their minds didn't need.

An Asset in the Workplace

As more people with the high UNCONVENTIONAL trait enter the workforce, more are labeled ADHD. Yet, professionals and leaders find their high UNCONVENTIONAL trait an asset, even as it's mislabeled a "disorder."

[Many] are grateful for the disorder, who consider it the best part of themselves. David Neeleman, for instance, the founder of JetBlue Airways, has said that he will not take medication for his ADHD, fearing

> that it would make him just like everybody else... .
>
> "It's the source of my creativity and my drive," echoed Thomas Apple, who was given a diagnosis about seven years ago, when he was in his early 40's, and went on to create the world's largest video display for stock market quotations. "You can think outside the box because you're not in a box."...
>
> "ADHD is the greatest thing that happened to me," said Sam Grossman, who became a partner in the Albert Corporation, a real estate company based in Brookline, Mass., two years ago, when he was 22. "I wish I could hire four or five people like me with ADHD," he said. "The impulsivity that comes with this means I can walk into a building, see things an ordinary person wouldn't see and act on my gut right away."[12]

Some of my high UNCONVENTIONAL executive clients tend to move faster because they need more stimulation. An unintended by-product is shorter meetings, fewer unnecessary and unproductive meetings, and they keep staff on their toes.

For balance, I often recommend that they are paired with an assistant or executive who is low CONVENTIONAL with a tolerance for change, variability, and flexibility.

I've recommended that people who struggle to focus in meetings where there are windows to position themselves so they're facing a wall and not a window (where they can be distracted by what is happening in the office or plant). This reduces potential lapses of attention, which can be interpreted as rude or uninterested by others in a meeting.

For those who struggle with self-discipline, but are motivated, consider the lawyer who was always chronically late to pick up his son from school. He noticed a paralegal who always left promptly at 5 p.m., and he instructed her that "she wasn't allowed to walk out the door without me," even if she had to "physically yank me from my chair."[14]

Quick summary. Change, variability, flexibility (CVF)—coupled with innovating with discipline between the lines—works for most kids and adults who are high UNCONVENTIONAL.

Why ADHD Seems to Decrease as People Get Older

Predictably, as kids exit puberty and pass young adulthood, ADHD drops off severely. The part(s) of their young brains that regulate impulse control changes and their actions become more controlled. Society has always intuitively recognized this. To the extreme, it's one reason why kids aren't given the death penalty for murder, like the three high UNCONVENTIONAL teenagers who assassinated Arch Duke Ferdinand in 1914—the assassination that ignited WWI.

A Perfect Storm: Other Factors That Inflame the Inability to Focus

In addition to the shift to the UNCONVENTIONAL trait, there are other factors that are creating a perfect storm for inattentiveness and inability to focus in kids.

- Too much media stimulation
- Possibly pesticides and additives in processed foods
- At-risk kids who are severely stressed
- Not enough delta sleep

Too much media stimulation. Do we need to say that again? The American Academy of Pediatrics for years has issued dire warnings about not letting toddlers under 2 watch TV. A 2004 study published in *Pediatrics* concluded that every hour a preschooler watches TV each day increases their chances by 10% of having ADHD problems—even "rewiring" the brain.[13] So 2 hours a day theoretically increases risk by 20%.

My kids watched the older-generation—grainy by today's standards—televisions which initially caused pediatricians to speak up. Then along came high-definition television on giant screens with more stimulation on steroids—overpowering young developing brains. Since then, the pediatrics association has expanded its dire warnings to include too much stimulation from Internet interaction, video games, and electronic devices like tablets and cell phones. Parents take note: the danger exists *even* when the programming has positive messages. (More on this in Chapter 24.)

In light of all the anecdotal and scientific evidence, I recommend reducing all visual and audio media—not just for toddlers, but for all kids and adults. This includes reading from a computer screen. (None of the top copy editors I've hired over the last 10 years, like Paula LaRocque, who has written two of the leading books on writing style, will edit and read copy from a computer screen, except in small doses. They only use hard-paper copies as they notice a significant deterioration in the quality of their work and the work of others.)

If I were raising my kids today, they wouldn't watch more than a few minutes a day, if at all, until they were at least 2 years old. I've also seen excessive stimulation affect adults.

In the early 1980s, when I was producing documentaries, I noticed something that happened to my video editors: After an hour or two of watching thousands of images fly by on their monitors, their ability to make cognitive decisions diminished. They could make *emotional* decisions regarding whether a clip *felt* right, but cognitive decision-making disintegrated. So I made them take a break every hour and a quarter.

I also observed this in leading newsrooms. A friend ran the news edit bays for the ABC television affiliate in New York. In 1982, we had dinner at an Italian haunt, near his office. My pal was glib, easily conversant, and spot-on when talking about facts. After dinner, we walked across the street to the station. As we entered a hall with over a dozen editing suites, all fired up with editors whizzing through thousands of images, my friend's eyes glazed over. It was like a catatonic state that I had seen in cult members. It was bizarre. Tough, critical thinking wasn't present like it was at dinner, and I saw this in other newsrooms.

Historically, one of the principal agents of change for the movement toward fast-changing images in large doses was MTV. Thirty years ago, MTV came on the scene pitching potential advertisers with ads in major newspapers boasting that it knew how to sell to kids. MTV reached kids on an emotional level with massive doses of fast-changing images never before seen in history. MTV is where watching images changed forever and helped foster a hyper need for stimulation. Television news directors complained that it directly reduced the length of news interview bites from substantive lengths of 20 to 30 seconds down to just three to five—and with it, cognitive information became trivialized.

Through the 1980s and 1990s, during the rise of MTV, I researched and wrote extensively about youth culture and subculture trends, and interviewed hundreds of students. I also spoke to tens of thousands of youths in live presentations, and I watched their attention spans plummet almost overnight. It wasn't because my presentations were boring. I usually used powerful sleight-of-hand demonstrations to illustrate points. Still, I found that as their attention span shortened, I had to quicken the tempo of whatever I did and constantly come at them from unexpected angles, just like forward-thinking teachers are now doing in classrooms. This all happened in the span of just a few years.

It is my opinion that for young developing brains, excessive media in all visual forms (except for print that isn't on a computer screen) develops an aberrant need for stimulation. If the brain doesn't get this stimulation, the diagnosis is ADHD for some kids who are actually high UNCONVENTIONAL. In fact, large volumes of media with all its boundary-pushing messages also push kids toward the UNCONVENTIONAL trait.

Our brains crave stimulation—but not destructive over stimulation, especially for toddlers through young adults. The hope is that our brains are resilient enough to rebound and reverse a generation of punishing over stimulation, but we won't know that for years to come. It is a certainty, though, with the constant bombardment of attention-distracting intrusions—from cell phones, to texting, to movies available on devices that fit in our pockets—kids and adults will have more difficulty paying attention.

At-risk kids who are severely stressed. From 1986 through 1992, I worked as a lay volunteer at a church with more than 400 severely at-risk kids, grades K–12, from an inner-city type of community. One-third had seen someone shot, stabbed, or murdered. Many were nonaffect, nonemotive—just staring ahead. Others were constantly jittery, couldn't sit still and would be diagnosed today as having an ADHD disorder. It was during this time that I also did my research for the book *Suburban Gangs—The Affluent Rebels*, and when I uncovered the Missing Protector Strategy (*MPS*). When this intervention was applied with the students, their visual discomfort and inability to focus disappeared within weeks. It was so startling that I videotaped the transformation, as I had never encountered it before. Their public school teachers called us and asked what we were doing because most of the kids had significant improvement behaviorally and academically (many started making all A's and B's). The *MPS* worked as follows:

An at-risk youth was matched with an adult "Protector" near the neighborhood where they lived. The Protector called the youth once a week to check in on the youth and met with the youth face-to-face every other week. Protectors were, of course, carefully screened. Then, if youths faced any type of crisis, they called their Protector—who had a short list of professionals they could call if needed. I have written about this extensively and here are the typical outcomes when the *MPS* was deployed:[15]

- One of the most significant deterrents to suicide
- Gang recruitment and assaults stopped
- Truancy plummeted
- Teen pregnancy severely dropped
- Academic performance significantly improved

Results in real numbers. Approximately 70% of the kids involved were African-American, 20% Hispanic (half couldn't speak English), and the balance were Asian and Caucasian. Not one youth joined a gang or was arrested for an assault, and not one girl became pregnant. None of the students, to my knowledge, received any behavioral-therapy meds. Similar outcomes occurred in almost every school system that used the *MPS*, including Plano, the upscale Dallas suburb. For years, Plano had the highest suicide rate in the nation but it went off the radar the year the *MPS* was deployed in 1998.

Plano's issues point out that the number of severely troubled youth who *aren't* from economically disadvantaged communities has skyrocketed—also triggered by severe family deterioration. Like their inner-city counterparts, these kids struggle to focus because they are afraid and insecure.

Chemical factors in the environment. The *Journal of Pediatrics* published a 2010 study that seems to indicate that a common pesticide increased the risk of a child being diagnosed as ADHD.[16] Similarly, a British study found that food additives in some processed foods are also a contributive factor.[17] At present, these studies are limited, and while not yet definitive, should be watched carefully.

Not enough delta sleep. Here's another surprising factor that may be artificially boosting ADHD diagnoses: lack of sleep, specifically delta sleep—the deep, rejuvenating, slow-wave kind kids need for proper growth and development. You'd think that if you didn't get enough sleep, you would be the opposite of hyperactive. But that's not what happens for some kids and adults.

Vatsal G. Thakkar, a clinical assistant professor of psychiatry at the New York University School of Medicine, says:

> Youngsters sleep more than an hour less than they did a hundred years ago. And for all ages, contemporary daytime activities—marked by nonstop 14-hour schedules and inescapable melatonin-inhibiting iDe-

> vices—often impair sleep. The result is that some people have the same symptoms as those who have ADHD: procrastination, forgetfulness, a propensity to lose things, and, of course, the inability to pay attention consistently.[18]

He says that a number of studies have shown that a huge proportion of children with an ADHD diagnosis also have sleep-disordered breathing such as apnea or snoring, restless leg syndrome, or nonrestorative sleep, in which delta sleep is frequently interrupted. He points out that when the root cause of the lack of delta sleep is addressed, ADHD symptoms often dissipate or completely disappear.

If you or someone you know could benefit from more insight into this factor, read the Source Note for this article for more data. It's compelling. Thakkar even points out that "moves about excessively during sleep" was once listed as a symptom of ADHD in 1980—the first time ADHD appeared in the *Diagnostic and Statistical Manual of Mental Disorders.*

Online newspapers. This last one is a *distractor enhancer.* Many times when I log on to a newspaper website, a pop-up sales pitch ad blocks my reading or an ad in the right hand column has an annoying moving image (although the *New York Times* and the *Dallas Morning News*, my local "paper," have gotten better). I've resorted to putting Post-it Notes on my screen to block them out.

Even the best news outlets try to distract us from reading important information in order to sell us something. There is no *"Please can we tell you something?"*—just a rude interruption. My teachers in school said, *"Pay attention,"* but electronic media-delivery systems tell you, *"No you won't."* Maybe this attention distractor trend will diminish so I can get back to being educated about the facts of the day. (Ironically, the *Times* has been the leader on reporting on behavioral issues, like the articles I reference in this chapter, but they have gotten better online and are less intrusive.)

Brief summary. Most people diagnosed today as ADHD are actually UNCONVENTIONAL and need more change, variability, and flexibility (CVF) coupled with innovating between the lines (Chapter 12). Beginning in 1999, teachers demonstrated that most of their kids didn't need meds, but rather their slow-to-move CONVENTIONAL institutions of education needed to change—but rarely did. (I recommend reading Richard Friedman's article referenced in the Source Notes for more on the science behind all this.)

Are there people who truly do have ADHD and might require medication? Sure. But not 20% of all American teenage boys and 11% of kids. Are there other factors that are probably adding to this mix and creating a perfect storm? Probably.

This chapter isn't intended to be the final word on ADHD. But if you or someone you know has been diagnosed with ADHD (or whatever it will be called in the future), first take a look at the patterns and themes for remedies that thousands of teachers have used before resorting to a medication. Rarely do you find a team in education or the workplace that can't find ways to apply the commonsense themes provided in this chapter—especially with all the tools we have available to help us innovate.

CHAPTER THIRTEEN

Solve A Mystery: The Yips Caper

[A story of what happens when systems collide with CONVENTIONAL people... and sometimes with those who aren't.]

Imagine there was something that you could do all of your life, and all of a sudden you couldn't. And, what if that something was your livelihood or your favorite pasttime? That's what this chapter is all about. It's called the "yips" and it bedevils millions. You're going to solve the mystery of this nemesis with one snapshot read using your CONVENTIONAL–UNCONVENTIONAL wire, just like the teachers who solved the ADHD riddle. And with what you learn, you'll be able to bring relief to yourself or someone you know.

You'll be equipped with background data, clues, and reads to solve a riddle that has confounded experts for years and has afflicted a wide range of people, from the world's best golfers to concert pianists to attorneys writing technical briefs to news anchors unable to report the news. Trapped, they often hide their secret from everyone around them. Even the famous Mayo Clinic attempted to solve this bedeviling problem and failed.

But you have an edge. You can make snapshot reads using your CONVENTIONAL–UNCONVENTIONAL gauge. As you do, you'll also get a feel for what it's like to profile people you don't know but whose traits you can identify.

This mystery is a potent parable of what can happen when we create systems to replicate human performance without considering the mental price on our minds, especially for people who are CONVENTIONAL—but also those who are UNCONVENTIONAL. You may even stumble across a nuance that leads to an amazing new approach that can be used in other applications.

Just be sure to make your snapshot reads within 10 seconds of taking in new data as you read the chapter. You may change your mind as you make additional reads. That's okay. *Anything worth reading once is worth reading twice because we will make mistakes.*

Suddenly Without Warning

Heralded by his peers as one of golf's premier instructors, Hank Haney had a secret: He hadn't played a round of golf for years because he developed an invisible tick in his swing—what golfers call the *yips.* "It was so frustrating, because my swing looked great—except for the moment of impact," he writes. "Doing it over and over again just makes that problem worse. So I started trying to make my swing 'perfect.'"[1]

For six years he coached the top golfer in the world, Tiger Woods, but when he swung his own driver—look out! Hank's ball would dangerously launch in random directions.

And he isn't alone. There are adept professionals in many fields who suddenly can't perform a simple task they could do all their life, such as:

- Concert pianists who suddenly can't play even the simplest of pieces
- Lawyers who can no longer make handwritten notes—they can only type their thoughts
- Baseball pitchers who can't make a simple toss to first base
- Baseball catchers who can't toss a baseball to the pitcher
- Basketball players who can't make the easiest shot—a simple free throw
- Radio newscasters who can't read the news to their audience

Major League Baseball players call it the *thang*, Steve Sax Syndrome (if you can't make a simple throw to first base), and Steve Blass Disease (if you suddenly lose control as a pitcher, wildly throwing the ball in the dirt or ten feet over the catcher). Pianists and lawyers just cower and don't call it anything. A 25-year news broadcaster heard about my research and asked, "My mind just can't comprehend what's happening to it. How do I overcome major yips when doing the news? I've always been an ad-libber... and now I stumble when the words just suddenly become jumbles."

For our purposes, we'll call it all the yips, and they aren't caused by physical infirmities, neurological disorders, or choking under pressure.

Serendipitously, I solved the yips riddle back in 2004, when I made just one snapshot read that solved why people get them, how to permanently eliminate them, and how people who are at highest risk for getting the yips can build capacity and inoculate themselves against ever getting them.

We'll first focus on how the yips affect golfers, where the term originated. Then we'll look at how this affects other disciplines.

Using your CONVENTIONAL–UNCONVENTIONAL wire, you're going to solve this riddle by profiling various observations I make of:

- Hank
- People who typically *do* and *don't* get the yips
- The specific golf shots when people *do* and *don't* yip

As you profile my observations, which represent the highlights of my research (the balance of which could fill another book)[2], we'll connect the dots to this mystery, solve the riddle, and perhaps bring relief to someone you know. Don't worry if you don't know anything about golf. You'll still be able to make the necessary reads.

About the Yips

Hank didn't have the yips because of physical infirmities, he wasn't paralyzed by fear, and he didn't lack control of his nerves because of inexperience. There was nothing wrong with his mechanics or his driver. Disaster struck only at the moment the clubface contacted the ball—at which point he had some kind of sudden jerking/freezing that he calls "one of golf's dirty little secrets."[3] Like most yippers, it *never* affected his backswing, only his *downswing*—at the moment results have to be delivered. In his book, *Fix the Yips Forever*, in which he presented his theory on how to cure the yips, Hank writes:

> The yip itself is an uncontrolled movement of the hand or wrist during the stroke.[3] We don't have a clear idea of why or how the yips start in one player instead of another, or why a specific kind of drill or treatment works with one player's yips but not another's.[4]

I first heard of the yips during the Masters in April of 2004. The eccentric term was coined by pro golfer Tommy Armour in the 1960s to describe the "tremors in his hands that made it impossible for him to putt."[5] The commentators talked about how it had ruined or hampered the careers of many pros, including Johnny Miller, Mark O'Meara, Seve Ballesteros, and Chris DiMarco.

A month later, I went to Hank's driving range near my home (he lives in the Dallas area). I heard that Hank had the yips with his driver (for nongolfers, it's the first club you use on most holes to hit off the tee, and with which you hit the ball the farthest).

At the time, I was in the middle of writing *Rage of the Random Actor—Disarming Catastrophic Acts and Restoring Lives*, and my thoughts 24/7 for three years were focused on stopping catastrophic acts like homicide-suicide terrorist attacks in Iraq. I was averaging a couple nights of sound sleep a week, and Sandy pushed me out the door every week to play golf as a mental break.

As a lighthearted distraction, Sandy challenged me to solve the riddle, so over the next couple of weeks I wrote a paper, "Conquering the Yips," in which I laid out a two-part solution based on snapshot reads I'd made of Hank and others over the previous five years, as well as predicting who I believed *wouldn't* get the yips and *why.*

As you read each of my observations, profile them and ask yourself: *Does this sound like the* CONVENTIONAL *or* UNCONVENTIONAL *trait at work here?*

As a behavioral pattern emerges, our goal is to strategize a theme for an antidote which must not only *control* the yips, but prevent the yips from returning, and build capacity in a person so they never get the yips.

Profile Hank

Observation #1: Hank the teacher and technician, fall of 1999. I bought Hank's new book, *The Only Golf Lesson You Will Ever Need*, to help me resurrect my game. As my two sons were ready to graduate high school, I planned to shift my time from playing basketball and baseball with them, to golf. From Hank's own words from his book, profile his CONVENTIONAL–UNCONVENTIONAL trait:

> Hi, I'm Hank Haney. Thanks for coming to me for a golf lesson.... When I start an analysis of your game, I first look at the flight of your ball. Then I work back. The flight of the ball basically tells you what happened at impact. Changing what your shots are doing means first changing what happens between club and ball at impact. Your main goal is to change how the ball flies, so you have to change impact. That will lead us to the swing plane. Changing that, changes impact. But in order to change your swing plane you must change something your hands and arms and/or your body are doing. So you go (a) ball-flight, (b) impact, (c) swing plane.[6]

Quickly, in 10 seconds, based upon Hank's approach to instruction, does he tilt more toward Einstein–UNCONVENTIONAL or Queen Elizabeth–CONVENTIONAL?

It's pretty easy to profile him as high CONVENTIONAL, from his precise, logical, orderly, and easy-to-follow instructions and the cover photo on his book. If he weren't a golf instructor/coach, you could picture him in engineering or a profession where parts must predictably work together.

I purchased Hank's book because he demystified the game by presenting a logical plan, which gave me confidence. There wasn't a hint in his book that he struggled with the yips.

Observation #2: Hank, first impressions, spring of 2000. As I read Hank's book, I realized that he lived in Dallas and had a beautiful driving range north of the city. After I finished hitting a bucket of balls on my first visit, I noticed a tall, lean fellow meticulously adjusting one of the signs near the rustic pro shop. He seemed a little more focused than the average guy—a little *too* focused. He'd adjust it, step back, and readjust it—*and he did this several times.* So what's your read? UNCONVENTIONAL or CONVENTIONAL?

When I watched him, I thought, "This is a ranch. Leave it alone. It doesn't have to be *that* precise. He's got to be high CONVENTIONAL, with little tolerance for ambiguity." This is a common characteristic of many clubhouse pros—no chit-chat, just keep it orderly, gents and ladies. Then I recognized it was Hank from the photos in his book.

In addition to my observations, other people who knew Hank confirmed he was CONVENTIONAL.

Profile Golfers Who Typically Do and Don't Get the Yips

Observation #1: Golfers most affected by the yips and the profile of most golf instruction. Oddly, the golfers with the best scores—who practice the *most*—are most likely to get the yips. This is particularly true if they practice with the themes on the cover of *Golf Digest* shown here: *consistency* and *repetition.* Which side of the wire does this type of practice tilt toward?

This is pretty easy to profile as CONVENTIONAL, especially with the cover line that emphasizes "Repeat." If you profile how golf is typically taught, it's usually CONVENTIONAL, with the message: *don't deviate, be consistent, just repeat.*

So what is the connection between CONVENTIONAL people (like Hank), CONVENTIONAL instruction, and the yips? (Hint: There is a certain *type* of *repetition* during practice that can lead to yips, and a different type of repetition that will inoculate someone from getting the yips.)

Observation #2: Age of golfers most affected by the yips. According to Hank, golfers over 45 are most likely to get the yips. I've observed this to be especially true for CEOs and senior executives in large companies. As a group, do you think they are probably UNCONVENTIONAL or CONVENTIONAL?

The Answer: CONVENTIONAL, and often high CONVENTIONAL. (The susceptibility of this age group may decrease in the future as more people who are UNCONVENTIONAL reach this age.)

Observation #3: Golfers least affected by the yips. Those who like to regularly experiment and practice hitting out of difficult and even bizarrely rare conditions almost never get the yips.

Do these golfers sound more UNCONVENTIONAL or CONVENTIONAL?

The answer is, of course, UNCONVENTIONAL.

Do you see the pattern emerging? People who are CONVENTIONAL and practice the most with CONVENTIONAL regimens and instruction are most likely to get the yips.

Now let's look at the types of shots that cause golfers to yip. Be prepared for some surprises.

Profile Golf Shots Most and Least Susceptible to the Yips

Observation #1: Most affected shots—least creativity required. The most common shots affected by the yips are uncomplicated ones that don't require strength, flexibility, or creativity. And, the number one shot affected is putting, the simplest stroke on the golf course. In fact, the simpler the putt, the more likely a golfer will yip. In other words, golfers are most likely to get the yips for shots that require the simplest *point-to-point* action and a simple *repetitive* motion—the CONVENTIONAL shot.

Observation #2: Most affected shots—shortest shots that are under 100 yards. The most common shots affected by the yips are the shortest shots—those under 100 yards that don't require strength or flexibility. Example: When a golfer hits a short shot up onto the green—called a chip. Chipping is also a simple *repetitive* motion. So, profile the shot.

Answer: CONVENTIONAL. (This applies to most chip shots although there are exceptions where extreme creativity is required. *Golfers rarely yip when creativity is required.*)

Observation #3: Most affected shots—hitting driver. Another commonly affected shot is the extremely *repetitive* shot with the driver, when the ball goes the furthest. This is when Hank was affected. Does this shot tip toward UNCONVENTIONAL or CONVENTIONAL?

Answer: CONVENTIONAL. This applies to most tee shots.

Observation #4: Least affected shots—those over 100 yards that require creativity. The shots least affected by yips are those over 100 yards with irons where there are numerous complications that have to be navigated. For example, you rarely see competent golfers yip when they have to hit an exotic, complex shot around a tree on an uphill lie in the face of a howling wind while standing on slippery pine straw. They may not execute the shot, but it won't be because of yips. They've accepted that they may not get exactly what they want, but if it's close, that's okay.

To summarize, golfers don't yip when executing complicated shots with lots of factors that require some creative thought. So, does this shot tip toward UNCONVENTIONAL or CONVENTIONAL shot?

Answer: UNCONVENTIONAL.

Observation #5: No yips during practice strokes. According to Hank, virtually no one yips during practice strokes—only when it counts and they feel they must produce a *predictable, no surprises result.*[7] They don't yip during a practice stroke because there is tolerance for some *variability* and *ambiguity.*

This is a little tougher observation to read, but practice range strikes tilt more toward UNCONVENTIONAL, as there isn't the expectation that every swing will produce exactly the same result. On the practice range, there *is* the tolerance for *some* variability.

Observation #6: When Hank didn't yip. In his 2006 book, *Fix the Yips*, Hank describes his first successful attempt not to yip, and how it worked. Profile the shot he describes: UNCONVENTIONAL or CONVENTIONAL?

> I almost completely stopped doing clinics that required me to hit drivers in front of people. The only way I could do it if I absolutely had to was to look back at the crowd while I hit shots. I'm sure that seemed like some kind of neat trick shot to those audiences, but it was literally the only way I could hit those shots.[8]

Answer: Hank used an UNCONVENTIONAL shot, and his yips disappeared.

The Pattern Becomes Clear: Don't Abuse the Brain with Unrelenting Requests to Perform CONVENTIONAL Tasks

You probably see what's going on. When CONVENTIONAL people are asked to perform golf's CONVENTIONAL point-to-point uncomplicated shots, like putting and chipping, and they're expected to repeat *exactly* the same result in exactly the same way, they can get the yips.

If, however, a golfer has to execute a complicated shot where they have to make all kinds of modifications—in essence an UNCONVENTIONAL shot—they don't yip. Also, golfers who are UNCONVENTIONAL rarely get the yips. And CONVENTIONAL golfers who follow an UNCONVENTIONAL training regimen won't get the yips.

The bottom line is this: Our brains, packed with over 200 billion cells, crave stimulation and were never meant to perform like a machine with assembly-line execution. If you abuse the brain by demanding thousands of repetitions without giving it change, variety, and flexibility, it may rebel. Consider these observations by Dr. Paul Brand, the late world-renowned surgeon and leprosy specialist:

> During each second of life [our brain] performs about five trillion chemical operations...and is bombarded with a hundred million messages...It appears the brain needs this ceaseless turmoil. When a person reduces the number of sense impressions, for example by lying in a dark tank of warm water cut off from most sensations, before long the brain begins to hallucinate and fill the void with sensory content of its own devising. And during sleep billions of cells spark through the night, their level of activity barely diminishing from daytime levels.[9]

We aren't machines. The message here is: *Don't abuse your brain with machinelike expectations.*

During the afflicted swing or putt, the dialogue from the golfer's brain says: Stop abusing me. I am perfectly capable of thinking on my own, on the spot, as needed. I don't like what you are doing to me. Can't you lighten up just a little bit? I want a bigger range in which to perform tasks and tell the muscles, tendons, eyes, hands, arms, and all the rest what to do. I want a little more time on the UNCONVENTIONAL side of your natural range.

Can you see how CVF—change, variability, flexibility, combined with tolerance for some ambiguity—can become a power antidote to retard the yips? Teachers in the last chapter used CVF to educate high UNCONVENTIONAL students labeled ADHD so they could learn, but here it can prevent yips in people who are CONVENTIONAL so they can continue to perform as they always have in the past. It's powerful, isn't it, what one simple snapshot read and treating people right the first time can produce?

The same pattern in other professions. In sports, the yips appear in the simplest, point-to-point CONVENTIONAL actions. There are basketball players who yip when shooting a simple free throw, but never during an acrobatic driving shot to the net. Baseball and softball pitchers can carve the plate with an 85-mile-per-hour fastball, but can't make a simple toss to first base. And the pitch in baseball most affected by the yips is the four-seam fastball, which is the most straightforward pitch and has the least amount of movement—similar to golf's most direct shot, the putt. There are also catchers who can make quick-as-a-cat throws to second base to catch base runners trying to steal, but they can't toss the ball back to the pitcher.

Outside of sports, concert pianists who don't have stage fright freeze up on well-known passages that everyone expects to be played to perfection. Jazz pianists, by definition UNCONVENTIONAL musicians, rarely—if ever—get the yips. I've also seen yips in people who write technical documents, like attorneys. They can't take handwritten notes as they self-demand that every letter look *exactly* the same without variability, forcing them to type everything.

I even had a friend, a leading radio news talk show host, tell me how one day he couldn't perform the simplest, most repetitive part of his job: read news on the air.

"I literally had to focus on reading it word by word. I dreaded it," he said. "And I never knew why that happened."

Can People Who Are UNCONVENTIONAL Get the Yips?

Anecdotally, I estimate that UNCONVENTIONAL golfers make up about 5–15% of all yippers, and many I've observed have been exposed to oppressive, CONVENTIONAL instructional regimens. So, at least related to golf, they lose their tolerance for slight variances and ambiguity. We'll briefly look at two cases later in the chapter, including a case where another trait also came into play.

Who Doesn't Get the Yips and *Why*?

To test my theory, I asked: *Which professionals must execute repetitive, fine-tuned, and precise tasks with their hands but don't experience the yips?*

It didn't take long and to come up with a hit. My first profession: accomplished sleight-of-hand magicians. As a group, they never get the yips, and what they must do with their hands is even more fine-tuned than golf.

When profiled, most magicians—both professionals and amateurs—are UNCONVENTIONAL and have a natural tolerance for CVF. Some performers might get momentary stage fright, but not the yips. None of the dozens of magicians who I ran the idea by could think of a single performer who perfected an effect (what magicians call a trick), incorporated it into a routine, and then suddenly couldn't perform it again. This is significant because there are moves with cards or coins that take years to perfect. This means thousands of repetitions in practice followed by many performances in front of audiences. So what's the difference between these technicians and those who yip, like Hank?

Magicians know that all sleights (or moves) will eventually fail during a specific performance, so they always create outs—another direction or method to employ if something breaks down. There's always a backup which takes the heat off of: "I must do it *exactly* the same way *every* time."

One exception I found, however, was UNCONVENTIONAL performers who felt chained to an act—especially a short act. For example, my friend and magician, the late Tommy Martin. He was one of the top acts in vaudeville, making $1,000 a week, and bookers refused to let him change his short act. They didn't want to tinker with success. Tommy said he performed it so many times that often he felt himself separated from his body, like he was watching his own act. In despair, he said the mind-numbing tedium drove him to drink to dull the pain and he became an alcoholic, something I'd seen happen to other magicians (and one reason I stopped drinking with friends, for fear I'd innocently cause someone to fall off the wagon). In other words, even though he and his act were UNCONVENTIONAL, he became chained to something that became unrelentingly CONVENTIONAL, just like golfers who become changed by unrelenting repetitions without CVF.

Tommy and I met years after he retired from show business when he was a successful real estate appraiser in Houston and sober for years. He explained that he was afraid to step out and do something new because the act paid so well. Our discussions confirmed to me a decision I had intuitively made as a teen:

I determined *never* to perform the same routine twice in a row, so my performance would never become robotic, as I had seen happen to others. Repetitive and boring were out. I continually changed the order of my effects, adding and subtracting new ones. The possibility that an exceedingly difficult technique might go south because of a

I'm often asked if I still keep up my sleight-of-hand magic. The answer is yes. I still find it invigorating to invent a few effects every year. It keeps the brain sharp, creative. And, I use them when making points in speeches and presentations. In fact, I've found that golf is a lot like learning a new trick. I enjoy practicing a new shot and then executing it more than shooting a low score. It's the challenge of doing what looks impossible or improbable that keeps us engaged!

change actually kept me sharp, alert, flexible, willing to adapt, and more engaged.

At the time, I never realized that what I did was protective from getting the yips or descending into despair like some of my friends who needed more stimulation. Only after I talked with the teachers who solved the ADHD riddle did I fully understand the wisdom of my choice and the protective barrier I had put around myself.

Why Solving the Yips Riddle Matters

There is a much bigger issue here than just golf. With technology, we have become masters at systematically breaking down activities, like a golf swing or any other isolated movement, and then creating systems to replicate them. This is good to a point, but if we don't respect that our brains need variety and stimulation, then yips can appear in almost any discipline—and even in people who are UNCONVENTIONAL.

The Two-Part Solution

CONVENTIONAL people using CONVENTIONAL training, executing the simplest point-to-point CONVENTIONAL shots, is the most common pattern when yips appear. Logically, the remedy is to insert a little more of the UNCONVENTIONAL, combined with CVF and tolerance for ambiguity—during practice *and* while playing the game. In effect, you're expanding a person's trait *range*, described in Chapter 4.

Here are the two components to prevent the yips so they cease and don't return, or never occur in the first place:

Part 1: Develop tolerance for CVF and some ambiguity. Golfers may or may not have to change their swing or putting stroke, but their mindset on the course and during practice must accept that there can be more than one way to execute a shot or manage a situation.

Part 2: Tolerance for CVF and some ambiguity should become a natural part of how one thinks both on *and* off the course. If you only perform something like a new technique over and over, or change the style of putter, eventually the new will become old and routine—CONVENTIONAL—and the yips can come back, which often happens for elite golfers.

Solution: Part One
Develop Tolerance for CVF (Change, Variability, Flexibility) and Some Ambiguity

As you've learned, our traits can have upsides and downsides. Hank's CONVENTIONAL trait enabled him to write his instructional book with clear, easy-to-follow logic. He also developed a terrific system for instruction. That's the upside.

The downside is that he developed an unhealthy need to always reproduce the same swing with his driver. It's the *intolerance for flexibility and variability* that caused the misfire in his hands. It's the same thing I saw when he was adjusting the sign a bit too much. This isn't the same as being a perfectionist, which can affect any profile when high standards are demanded. It's different. It's *an intolerance for even a small amount of change, variability, flexibility, and ambiguity.*

High CONVENTIONAL surgeons, but no yips. The former chief of staff of a major Dallas hospital, Dr. Kathryn Waldrep, says she's never known of a surgeon who had the yips—probably because surgeons accept the fact that they may need to adapt and modify due to the unknown in any operation. Dr. Waldrep says she has worked with surgeons who are just as CONVENTIONAL as Hank, but they have accepted the need to be flexible.

Hank solves Part 1. Hank came up with dozens of new swing techniques that yippers could try (I've highlighted key words).

> I've always taught a pretty **traditional** grip...so the one I came up with for myself was a big departure. It is **unconventional in the extreme**—natural golf and then some. Instead of holding the club in my fingers, I moved it down into my palms. I virtually removed hand action from my swing.[10]

Although the Mayo Clinic never solved the yips riddle, it found the best putters access *both* the left and right sides of the brain—the CONVENTIONAL *and* UNCONVENTIONAL sides of our thought process—the concrete *and* the more ambiguous subjective lobes. Repetition in practice isn't detrimental as long as variation is inserted and a player isn't mentally chained to one method or technique.

In fact, it's common for coaches in all sports to inject new variables—something *different*—during training regimens as the body will adapt to new stimulus to a point, and then will no longer respond, even if you intensify the same stimulus and increase the volume of work. In lay terms, it's like the body becomes insensitive, and that's when appropriate change must be injected.[11]

Shawn Humphries (Chapter 7) does this regularly to inoculate his kids, doing things like what he calls yoga golf, where students are given just six balls and have to take 20 minutes to hit them in slow motion. It not only perfects their technique, it also is a fun way to inject some CVF.

UNCONVENTIONAL people and their yips. As already noted, people who are UNCONVENTIONAL inherently like and embrace change and variety, and handle ambiguity better than those who are CONVENTIONAL—and they are less likely to yip. However, if they demand of themselves that they produce *exactly* the same result in *exactly* the same way, they can get the yips—especially with shots that require the *least* creativity, which is what derailed the career of the late Seve Ballesteros, one of the most creative golfers to ever play the game.[12]

Related to Hank's solution, just doing something different won't work long-term for many people. It only treats the symptom—the brain's need for stimulation/variety. As soon as the new stroke becomes old and *routine*, the yips can come back—and they often do—which leads us to the second part of the solution.

Solution: Part Two
Solving the Root Problem

Hank's mission was to *control* his yips, and in his book, *Fix the Yips*, he shows you how to adopt different strategies, techniques, and grips to *minimize* or *neutralize* the spasm or jerk. It won't, however, solve the root problem for one simple reason:

The brain doesn't want to be abused.

When a pro or amateur adopts a *new* putting technique, they practice it with exceeding repetition over and over. Then, for most, the yips come back because the new becomes old and *routine*. They then try another yip-controlling technique, and the cycle starts all over again. New technique, repetitive practice, yips return. That's why just making a modification by itself doesn't work for most amateur and pro golfers. Many quit in frustration, or rely upon other parts of their game to continue to compete. For professionals, it costs them their livelihood. For amateurs, they lose their love of the game and a wonderful pastime.

But there is an answer. You don't *control* the yips, you...

Develop capacity for flexibility and tolerance for ambiguity in one's personal AND professional life. Golfers "groove" a swing through thousands of repetitions. The golf swing itself is an unnatural movement. It feels awkward until you're used to it. So there's nothing wrong with repetitive practice to develop coordination, muscle memory, etc. Concert pianists face a similar challenge. However, if you build capacity for flexibility and variability in your personal life, *as well as* in your game or occupation, it then becomes part of who you are. When you do this, it's almost impossible to get the yips for most golfers. So what can people do to develop that capacity in their personal lives?

For Hank, it might be to deliberately leave the sign slightly cocked two or three days a week. A decorator we'll call Mary might deliberately tilt a picture on the wall a bit differently each day, or use a work technique that is more UNCONVENTIONAL just for a day. Alex might work with UNCONVENTIONAL Jay for a week and implement one UNCONVENTIONAL idea that he wouldn't have considered (providing it's a good one). The specifics depend on the person and what he or she does during the natural rhythm of their day.

Remember, the themes described here can be applied by anyone in any discipline who has the yips—like those described earlier in the chapter. It's just that I stumbled across the antidote when observing Hank.

Record-setting pitcher can't lob ball to first base—gets fixed off the diamond. One remarkable turnaround for an athlete took place *off* the field to correct a very embarrassing problem.

A pal, Don "Slugo" Slaught, a hitting coach for the Detroit Tigers, called and asked, "Dan, have you ever heard of what we call 'the thang?' It's when a pitcher can't make a simple lob to first base. I've got a college coach who has a pitcher who has the *thang* and I think you can fix this."[13]

Don said he thought the *thang* contributed to the Tigers losing the 2006 World Series, when multiple pitchers couldn't make easy *routine* throws to first base.

Working with an assistant coach, we injected the themes in this chapter into the pitcher's *personal* life and within weeks, the record-setting pitcher's yips were gone, confounding sports announcers. One snapshot read, a couple of modifications, and it was fixed within weeks *off the field*.

Here's what was significant: No changes were made at all to the pitcher's on-field performance or how the player practiced. (We also helped the pitcher learn to make CONFIDENT decisions *separate* from native athletic ability, a concept explained in Chapter 18, enabling an athlete to perform in any unfamiliar situation, but also applicable in any part of life.)

Instruction tip with a CONVENTIONAL person. Never assume that a person with the CONVENTIONAL trait is a CAUTIOUS/FEARFUL *decision maker* as these are two completely different traits.

For example, when helping a CONVENTIONAL person accept or make a change, *never* say, "John, what are you afraid of? Why not try a new grip? Why not try something new?"

This is one of the most offensive things you can tell this person, especially if he is a CONFIDENT decision maker (a trait we'll cover in Chapter 15). He's not afraid, he just likes things to be the same, and there is nothing wrong with that. It's like asking John, "Why don't you try another restaurant? Why do you always eat at Lawry's? What are you afraid of? Don't you want to live a little?" He's *not* afraid, he just likes the same thing.

A better approach is: "John, we're going to exercise your capacity to incorporate something new—a little at a time." This puts the focus on the activity that has the yips and not the person.

Wrap-Up

That we can use technology to create systems to replicate performance is a positive, but it comes with a warning label. Our brains and bodies weren't created to replicate *anything* with perfection over and over. We leave that to machines. For us, it's okay if it doesn't always work out. It's okay if we do something a bit differently. Our brains want all of the lobes engaged. If we don't respect this reasonable requirement, we can create huge unforeseen dysfunctions—even in those who are UNCONVENTIONAL.

The yips is like the flip-side of what happened at Andersen where there was a need for *greater* discipline (Chapter 9).

And, in a weird twist, the yips and ADHD are somewhat related. The yips predominantly affects CONVENTIONAL people who need more CVF, while ADHD affects UNCONVENTIONAL people who also need more

CVF. The big message here is that our brains require varied stimulation, regardless of our profile.

If you or someone you know is high CONVENTIONAL and these strategies aren't applied, professional careers and leisurely pastimes could be put at risk. Like golfers, there's nothing wrong with practice and repeating shots, but as history shows, it can lead to disaster if we don't develop tolerance for CVF and some ambiguity. While this small chapter isn't the last word on the yips, the basic principles can bring relief to many who are afflicted by this subtle nemesis.

As a convenience for golfers, a condensed, easy-to-read shortlist of who is and isn't likely to get the yips is provided in the Source Notes.[14]

And, on a lighter note, for my golfing buddies out there: *The reason you and I go out and play a round of golf or head out to our practice ranges is so that we can unburden ourselves of our stress, and go home and be better spouses, parents, employees, and employers to those in our charge. So hit 'em long, straight, and stress-free!*

CHAPTER FOURTEEN

Don't Leave CONVENTIONAL Behind

And snapshot reads for selecting a doctor

The doctor was frazzled. His patient needed to take blood-pressure medicine. Diet, exercise, and other options didn't reduce Fred's blood pressure. An 80-year-old patient and retired minister, Fred was pleasant and kind, but seemed a bit stiff when it came to taking meds. The doc thought it was because Fred was high CONVENTIONAL and a bit old-fashioned.

The doc misread Fred. Yes, Fred was CONVENTIONAL, but that wasn't the problem. Fred asked me what I thought. I told him, "What could it hurt to try it? You can always say no later."

So he agreed to try the medication, which ended up being a good option for him. The doc could have convinced Fred the first time, but he stereotyped Fred as someone who was just resistant to change.

Fred's case is an example of why we shouldn't stereotype people who are CONVENTIONAL, and why we must make behavioral reads *separate* from situational reads. As the number of people who are CONVENTIONAL continues to shrink, we can't leave CONVENTIONAL people behind. They not only add variety to life, but they're often the glue that keeps families and organizations together and functioning.

What's Driving Fred?
His Situation or His Trait?

What the doctor didn't realize was that Fred's father had died years ago because of care provided by a doctor. Fred's dad was diagnosed with polyglycemia—a condition where one has too many red blood cells—and was given an injection of radioactive phosphorus to correct the condition. According to Fred, he was given too much, which killed the bone marrow and gave him "man-inflicted leukemia." The doctor meant well, but Fred thought the treatment killed his father.

Then Fred's best friend, Dirk, had a similar experience. Dirk's father had a spider bite, and was told by his doctor to soak his leg in hot water with Epsom salts, which Dirk believed caused the infection to spread and kill his father.

Taken together, it's easy to understand why Fred was a bit skeptical of jumping into medical treatments without thinking them through first.

The doctor correctly profiled Fred's CONVENTIONAL trait, but mistakenly thought Fred's hesitancy was trait driven. Fred was actually willing to try UNCONVENTIONAL alternative healthcare options and investigated those that didn't require medicine. Fred didn't have an aversion to new medications, but was hesitant because of his previous experiences.

The doc's misread could have easily been corrected if he had asked Fred a couple of simple questions when new care was suggested: *Have you or someone close to you ever seen a doctor and had a positive outcome? Have you or someone close to you ever seen a doctor in a situation that didn't have a positive outcome?*

Fred might have shared the two stories, allowing the doctor to factor in Fred's experiences. Instead, he stereotyped Fred's hesitancy. A short conversation with Fred could have helped the doctor differentiate between being hard-headed and resistant. Hard-headed is when someone refuses to accept the truth in the presence of evidence. Resistant is when someone won't follow a prescribed solution an expert because that doctor doesn't understand his or her past experiences.

After following this case and several others, I talked to the chiefs of staff of a number of major hospitals and they agreed that rapid-fire profiling could measurably improve hospital care and significantly reduce costs, especially during new-patient intake or when new options are presented.

Rapid-Fire Reads When Selecting a Doctor

"Doc, I have a little problem with my shoulder. Do you know a shoulder guy who's unconventional and likes to solve riddles?" I asked.

My dermatologist, Dr. Cook, is UNCONVENTIONAL and a real delight. He always passes along helpful health tips beyond skincare that relate to me uniquely. He does it with everyone. He makes a quick read of a patient, uses common sense, and he's always on the mark. So when I asked him my question, he furrowed his brow a bit, as he knew there was more behind the question.

"Unconventional, huh?"

"Yeah. I don't want a brass-tacks carpenter type of guy. I've already seen one orthopedic doctor who is good, but he's not the creative type. He doesn't look beyond the obvious or try to figure out why I've got the problem. He only focuses on the symptom. I need someone who will think out of the box and help me solve the riddle about my shoulder," I explained.

"You know," I added, "not all doctors who work on the same part of the anatomy have the same profile."

"That's for sure." He nodded.

Knowing that I write about profiling, he said, "You should write a patient's profiling guide for selecting doctors."

So taking his cue, I've listed a few snapshot reads for using your wires. They work equally as well with male or female doctors. Like most other tips, these are typical patterns and may not apply to a specific physician.

(Oh yes, my shoulder got better. Dr. Cook said that sometimes if you just wait, certain injuries heal themselves, and that's what happened.)

How does the doctor communicate?

ASSERTIVE

- Does he listen? Poor listening doesn't mean lack of competency, but it does increase the risk that important details will not be taken into consideration.
- Does he try to just run you over with jargon? If so, it can mean he is impatient or arrogant.
- Does he get annoyed when you ask an appropriate question?

NONASSERTIVE

- Usually are better listeners.
- If he's quiet, you may have to carefully tease out all information. It's best if you have a list of questions and ask him to walk you through each one so you can be sure to follow all his instructions, understand all the factors, etc. (I would suggest doing this with any doctor so that you can remember to cover all important questions.)
- May be more likely to minimize importance of bad news.

EXPRESS

- If he shows emotions, this is often reflective of good bedside manner, but doesn't necessarily mean he is competent.

CONTROL

- If he doesn't show emotion, be certain he does display care and concern through his actions (like the case of the flight attendant in Chapter 5).

Questions to read CONVENTIONAL–UNCONVENTIONAL

- Ask what they like about their specialty.

- What does he like about his practice?
- Ask other patients about their experience. Remember, even a doctor who is difficult to deal with, but has good outcomes, will have patients who'll say he's terrific.
- Don't be fooled by CONVENTIONAL attire, office decor, website, or business card. They may or may not tell you anything about this trait.

CONVENTIONAL

- He may tend to treat the symptom and not dig for the cause of the problem. They're okay for nuts-and-bolts procedures that don't require a lot of creativity.
- Don't expect him to display much curiosity. For him, it's more about "What's the problem?" and "Here's the fix."
- Does he continue to do research beyond attending the obligatory medical convention?

UNCONVENTIONAL

- Does he carefully review all steps? Be sure to write down what the doctor tells you.
- Look at how the office is run. Most doctors are terrible business people. If you see it is well run and appointments run on time, this is a good sign, but not determinate, that the doctor is thorough.

Additional CONVENTIONAL–UNCONVENTIONAL reads

- How carefully do they record their notes? For important medical issues, ask a couple of questions that relate to answers you were given in your last visit to check the thoroughness of his note-taking. You can't stereotype that a CONVENTIONAL by-the-book doctor will be more diligent, because he or she could be lazy, distracted, etc. And, you can't assume that the UNCONVENTIONAL doctor won't be meticulous when recording notes. The great ones know that having all the data allows them to more effectively consider a different path for treatment.

Dr. Cook, my UNCONVENTIONAL skin doctor, and Dr. Miskovsky, my CONVENTIONAL orthopedic "hand doctor," are competent, patient-first, can-do-attitude doctors, and passed the snapshot test. (Dan Korem)

Different May Not Mean UNCONVENTIONAL... and Preserving the CONVENTIONAL Trait

Historically, if we said someone was really *different*, we meant that someone was UNCONVENTIONAL. Times have changed. Today, *different* may mean someone who is CONVENTIONAL, or someone who has a different trait from the majority.

We have spent more time looking at the shift to and the impact of the UNCONVENTIONAL trait, its increase in society, and unique reads and applications. I've spent less time on the CONVENTIONAL trait, as it is less mysterious to most people. We must, however, consider the decrease in the CONVENTIONAL trait and the preservation of the trait.

Imagine if the majority of the professionals in the following disciplines were predominantly UNCONVENTIONAL: accounting, quality assurance, audit, and systems. Long term, we might lose the trait firepower to sustain change with stability. It's easier for CONVENTIONAL people to work in these roles—not that those who are UNCONVENTIONAL can't work in these professions, but it's harder to find those who will, and enjoy it.

While it's inappropriate to artificially steer people toward one trait or the other, we *can* increase a person's range to be a little more or less of their actual trait. Or, people might be able to learn one action outside their trait for a specific situation.

One way to preserve the CONVENTIONAL trait is to specifically increase the range of people who are low UNCONVENTIONAL (2 or less), allowing them to operate at low CONVENTIONAL. This can be encouraged at home, school, and the workplace by giving them tasks and assignments that are CONVENTIONAL, while being mentored by those who are *low* CONVENTIONAL. You want to use people who are low CONVENTIONAL because it's usually easier for them to relate to someone who is low CONVENTIONAL than a person who is high CONVENTIONAL. As they work together, strategies and methods are developed to adapt and expand the range.

Remember, though, that just because people can expand their range doesn't mean that they will necessarily take on all the attributes of an UNCONVENTIONAL person, like creativity.

Resist Trait Prejudice

A subtle bit of "trait prejudice" often comes into play by people who are UNCONVENTIONAL thought leaders, like David Kelley, the genius entrepreneur, teacher, designer, and more, who created the first mouse for Apple. In a thought-provoking speech delivered at TED (March, 2012), he said:

> When we have clients in to work with us side by side, we eventually get to the part of the process that is fuzzy and unconventional. And these big-shot executives whip out their Blackberries, and they say they have to make really important phone calls, and they head for the exits. And, they're just so uncomfortable. When we track them down and ask them what's going on, they say something like, 'I'm just not the creative type.' Well, we know that's just not true. If they stick with the process, they end up doing amazing things.

While unintentional, there is a subtle message that says unless people are UNCONVENTIONAL and creative, they're deficient. But that just isn't the case.

It's much better to frame this kind of discussion by talking about thoughtfully expanding our range, *just a little*. People can grasp that, and it's attainable. Implying that most high CONVENTIONAL people can learn all or most of the positive UNCONVENTIONAL actions—such as, free-spirited, open to change, imaginative, spontaneous, and creative—just isn't true. You can, however, pick a couple, work on them a bit for specific situations, and expand your range. Kelley's company, IDEO, helps specifically with creativity, and that's good. But, for some people learning to be just a little more open to change or tolerant of the imaginative ideas of others can be just as powerful.

Similarly, we don't want to place the expectation on a high UNCONVENTIONAL person that they can take on all or most of the CONVENTIONAL actions, such as: organized, reliable, dependable, precise, persistent, logical, industrious, orderly, self-disciplined, and consistent. Can they learn a couple, like being a little more disciplined or reliable? Sure. But the whole inventory? Not likely.

Steven Spielberg Gets It

In 2011, while working on the set of the historical movie, *Lincoln*, director Steven Spielberg, who is UNCONVENTIONAL, did something CONVENTIONAL. For him, the situation required it. He wore a coat and tie on the set—every day.

"I'd never worn a suit before," he explained to *60 Minutes*.

"... we were recreating a piece of history. I didn't want to look like the shlubby, baseball-cap-wearing 21st-first century guy."

He got it. A slight move and expanding his range, doable. Complete makeover, forget it.

We've talked a lot about providing CVF—change, variability, and flexibility—for people who are UNCONVENTIONAL, but it's just as healthy to expand their range a little bit toward CONVENTIONAL for the benefit of others or the situation.

Steven Spielberg: A slight move to CONVENTIONAL attire when required (his tie is still comfortably open).

The 21st century guy. (Screen grab from *60 Minutes*)

CHAPTER FIFTEEN

CONFIDENT–CAUTIOUS/FEARFUL

Your Fourth Wire

[DECISIVE, decisive, decisive]

Making choices. Seth owned a jewelry story that specialized in high-quality silver sporting pieces. He wondered if showing more or fewer pieces to each customer would increase his sales. He found one rapid-fire read that increased his sales about 15%.

His first hunch was that he'd show *fewer* selections to customers who were CONVENTIONAL because they probably wouldn't be interested in variety. When he tried that, though, he found it didn't matter. Those who were CONVENTIONAL usually knew the style they liked and quickly eliminated everything else. It's like a CONVENTIONAL banker buying a suit; he'll usually go to the dark, conservative colors no matter how many suits are on the rack.

Seth's next theory was that he'd show *more* pieces of a different variety to customers who were UNCONVENTIONAL, as he surmised they'd like to consider the options. Here, he was correct. They liked the variety, but it also added time to the sales process, which was acceptable because it met his customers' needs.

The next read, though, had the greatest impact on closing sales in the shortest amount of time.

Seth used his CONFIDENT–CAUTIOUS/FEARFUL gauge, which identifies how people make everyday decisions.

To customers who made CONFIDENT decisions, he showed *more* pieces. It wasn't stressful or confusing for these customers because they could make decisive decisions, and it didn't take significantly more time.

To customers who were CAUTIOUS decision makers, he showed *fewer* pieces. This made the process less stressful and uncluttered and reduced the amount of time per sale.

Seth found that the more CONFIDENT a customer:

1. The more choices they can be offered.
2. The less time they need to make decisions.
3. The less likely they will second-guess decisions.

Conversely, he observed that the higher customers are on the CAUTIOUS/FEARFUL side of the wire:

1. The fewer choices they should typically be provided.
2. It's best to factor in additional time (and counseling) for processing and making a decision.
3. Anticipate and plan for second-guessing after a decision is made—and a thoughtful process for exchanges/returns.

By using his CONFIDENT-CAUTIOUS/FEARFUL gauge, Seth saw repeat sales increase across all profiles because his customers sensed *Seth and his staff understand us.* They liked Seth's jewelry *and* his process. What Seth learned can be applied in any situation where you have to help people make decisions.

Overview of the Wire

The CONFIDENT-CAUTIOUS/FEARFUL wire helps quickly identify:

- Who needs more or less time to process a decision.
- Who to give more or fewer choices.
- Who is decisive and who is most likely to second-guess decisions.
- Who needs more support, coaching, and training before making decisions.
- Who should lead and who should follow.

Anyone can use these themes: teachers, team leaders, parents, clergy—*anyone*. Other ways to use this wire are explained in later chapters, including:

1. How to help anyone increase their capacity to make CONFIDENT decisions (Chapter 18).
2. How to lead people with the CAUTIOUS INNOVATOR profile—the fastest growing profile, which is confounding team leaders, parents, and friends (Chapter 21).
3. Related to safety and security, how making just one read with this wire and responding appropriately has prevented numerous catastrophic attacks and massacres (Chapter 22).

More Complexity. This gauge has more complexity than the other three wires because it has *three* spots on the wire to identify someone's traits. They are: confident, cautious, and extreme fearful.

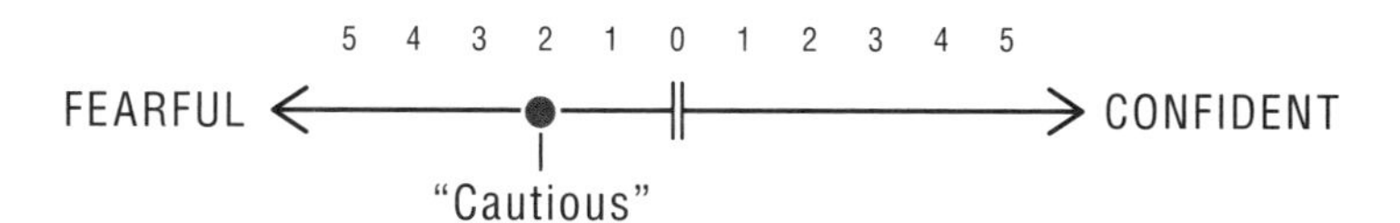

The reason it has three key points is so we can accurately read the degree of fear people have on the CAUTIOUS/FEARFUL side.

Those who are at 0–3 are CAUTIOUS, over 3 are FEARFUL, and 5 is full-blown fear or paranoia. The paranoia may be just extreme fear or a diagnosable condition, like paranoid schizophrenia. Also, a person who is about 4 FEARFUL might spike out to 5 due to a stressor.

Here are common positive and negative actions we see when people make decisions:

Confident: Assured, poised, self-reliant, candid, conceited, decisive, independent, bold, callous, durable/stable, arrogant, and action-oriented

Cautious/Fearful: Cautious*, guarded*, restrained*, careful*, measured*, insecure, anxious, indecisive, timid, unstable, envious, passive, self-pitying, defensive, cowardly, gullible, and paranoid (when extreme)

(The CAUTIOUS/FEARFUL actions that have an asterisk may be present in people who are 3 or less on the 0–5 scale.)

Five Clarifying Concepts Before Using the Wire

Before you use this gauge, there are five important concepts to clarify.

1. **What we're looking for is how people makes decisions *separate* from their giftedness/natural competency or what they've been trained to do.**

For example, people may be naturally gifted in the arts or well trained in engineering, and when they have to make a decision in their discipline, it will be a CONFIDENT one.

But we want to know how people make decisions *separate* from their giftedness/natural competency or area in which they've been trained. We want to know how people make everyday decisions, such as tackling a new project, buying a car, ordering off a menu, or choosing which class to take. We're looking for how they make decisions when they *can't* rely upon giftedness/natural competency/training. Reading how they make these kinds of decisions will be their core trait.

If his core trait *is* CONFIDENT, he'll make a CONFIDENT decision after he has gathered and reviewed all the facts. And, the higher his CONFIDENT trait, the quicker the decision.

If, however, his core trait is CAUTIOUS/FEARFUL, he will take *longer* to make a decision the *higher* he is on the 0–5 CAUTIOUS/FEARFUL side of the wire.

Reading the CONFIDENT-CAUTIOUS/FEARFUL trait *separate* from giftedness/natural competency/training gives us greater insight into *how to treat someone right the first time.* When these two reads are *not* made separately, the following misreads can happen:

Abigail, a team leader, assumes that Hailey is CONFIDENT when in reality Hailey is CAUTIOUS/FEARFUL. Abigail misreads Hailey because Hailey's past decisions relied upon her competency/training. Then, when Abigail gives Hailey a new task/project/challenge for which she *hasn't* been trained, or is outside her natural competency, Hailey hesitates and isn't as decisive. Now Abigail incorrectly assumes that Hailey isn't interested, won't follow her lead, is giving her push back, etc.

Later in the chapter we'll look at how to work with a person who is CAUTIOUS/FEARFUL but also gifted/competent/well trained. (For you personally, it's also beneficial to consider your trait and how you make your everyday decisions.)

2. The time versus second-guessing factor.

Whether or not a person takes time to analyze a decision may not necessarily be a factor, unless it is excessive because they are driven by fear. Anyone can analyze a decision. The more complex or unfamiliar someone is with the strategic factors, the more time may be needed to analyze data, options, consequences, and possible outcomes before making a decision. People who are on the CAUTIOUS/FEARFUL side, though, will typically take longer to make a decision regardless of the complexity, unless it's an area in which they have competency.

So, here's what you should look for:

After the facts have been analyzed and a decision has been made, does this person keep looking in the rearview mirror, wondering if their decision was the right one?

People who are CONFIDENT won't second-guess their decision, especially the higher CONFIDENT they are (3 or higher). Once a decision is made, they are decisive. (Remember, we're looking at everyday decisions, not life-changing or life-threatening decisions.)

People who are CAUTIOUS/FEARFUL are more likely to second-guess their decisions or make sudden reversals. This doesn't mean they will, but related to their trait, are more likely than a CONFIDENT person.

3. The moral and protective factor.

How people make moral decisions may or may not be reflective of how confident they will be when making daily task-oriented decisions.

Some people drink excessively to numb their emotional pain, which can be an indicator that they are FEARFUL decision makers. There are also CONFIDENT decision makers, however, who excessively party and abuse alcohol.

Moral decisions are a reflection of character. People on *either* side of the wire can, as an act of character, refuse to drink excessively, ingest cocaine, honestly report their taxes, and choose to tell the truth. So when making snapshot reads using your CONFIDENT-CAUTIOUS/FEARFUL wire, be sure to read daily task-oriented decisions *separate* from moral decisions.

And be careful that you don't make a read based upon a protective survival decision, like the fear of physical harm or losing one's family or job. Any profile can take protective action, make a quick decision, reverse a decision, or be paralyzed by fear.

4. Most common misread: confuse talk for walk.

This occurs when people are ASSERTIVE and *talk* confidently but make decisions *cautiously.* Remember, *talk* isn't *walk.* That's why we read each wire *separately.*

This was a key misread by the YPO executives who asked that I create a rapid-fire profiling system for negotiations. They insisted on being able to read how people communicate *separate* from how they make decisions because they had experienced costly situations where someone *talked* confidently but didn't *make decisions* confidently. Statistically, it's one of the most common misreads. Even experienced negotiators can struggle with this read if they can't profile.

Similarly, if someone is NONASSERTIVE and doesn't talk confidently, it doesn't mean that they can't make a decision confidently. Maybe they can, maybe they can't. You have to read their CONFIDENT-CAUTIOUS/FEARFUL trait *separately* to avoid the stereotypical trap that they can't make decisions confidently simply because they aren't ASSERTIVE.

5. Other common misreads.

- Someone is NONASSERTIVE. You're discussing a CONFIDENT decision you've made or are contemplating. Because they are attentive to what you are saying and your position/perspective, you assume they are also CONFIDENT.
- They are EXPRESS and emotionally connect with your decision and you misread that they are also CONFIDENT.
- They are CONTROL and outwardly don't seem rattled and you misread this as CONFIDENT.

6. 5 FEARFUL: no positive actions.

The only point on any of the four *KPS* wires where there aren't any positive actions is 5 fearful. These people are extremely FEARFUL and always struggle with making decisions outside their area of competency.

Personalize Your CONFIDENT–CAUTIOUS/FEARFUL Wire

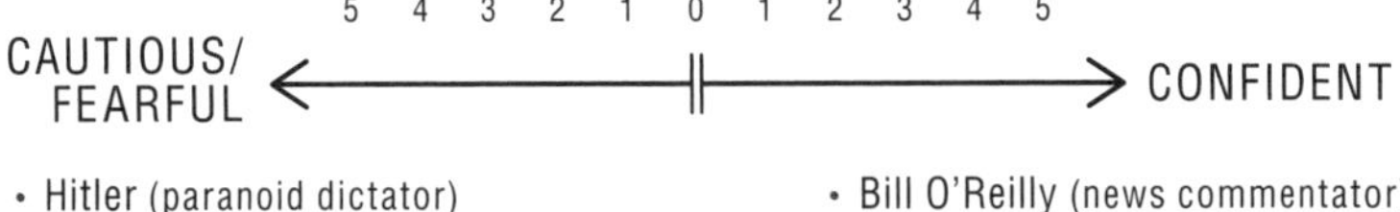

- Hitler (paranoid dictator)
- David Koresh (cult leader)
- Charles Manson (cult leader)
- Some people who have extreme phobias

- Bill O'Reilly (news commentator)
- Martin Luther King, Jr.
- Margaret Thatcher
- Russell Crowe (in *Gladiator*)

- Alan Greenspan (cautious Fed chair who set interest rates)
- Prince Charles (cautious and measured in all of his actions)
- Taylor Swift (when she was young)
- Some air traffic controllers

Consider the examples for each of the three points—extreme CONFIDENT, CAUTIOUS, extreme FEARFUL—and select who you will use to represent each of the three points. As you did before, select someone you can instantly recall and visualize. If you choose someone you know, they must be as extreme as the examples provided or your gauge will be off.

History is the best predictor of future decision-making. To help you make reads using this wire, you'll use a tried and tested principle: Past behavior is the best predictor of future behavior. This is true when reading any of the four wires, but is especially handy for reading the CONFIDENT–CAUTIOUS/FEARFUL wire. One way to make your read is to ask others about decisions someone has made in the past, and evaluate the decision(s) separate from his or her competency. Here are a couple of examples:

> **Example 1:** When Rachel was tasked with a new project, how did she handle it...especially when she had to deal with areas where she wasn't trained?
>
> **Example 2:** How does Toby typically make everyday decisions at school,

home, and when it involves friends? Does he ever second-guess himself? Please be specific.

When counseling someone, ask if they ever had to make a similar decision in the past. *What were the circumstances? What happened? In hindsight, would you make the same decision—and why?*

As you listen, make your read. Does this person seem more like Russell Crowe, Alan Greenspan, or Hitler? Don't overthink it. If it's a decision in their area of competency, you may have to make another read. Here's an example:

The perfect snapshot. Jacob and his son came up with a quick way to identify their customers' traits at their camera shop. If uncertain, they asked: "Do you bracket your shots?" Bracketing is when a specific picture is shot at several incremental exposures.

If they get an affirmative, they follow with, "Why? Do you do it as a safety, to be creative, or because of experience?"

The follow-up questions identify:

1. Is the customer a CAUTIOUS decision maker?
2. Do they just like to be creative (which is UNCONVENTIONAL)?
3. Is the decision a result of experience, like working for an art director who wants more selections from which to choose (a situational read, Chapter 11)?

Jacob's question is shrewd because it quickly drills down to cause and effect without being intrusive.

When making snapshot reads of how people make decisions,
the key is to observe what people do and listen
to the why behind their decision.

Here are other everyday examples of how you can use the wire:

Selecting a CONFIDENT babysitter: Ask how they've made quick decisions in the past when taking care of other children.
Selecting a future employer: Inquire how the team leader you might work for handled the last downturn or major change, such as the adoption of a new system.

You May Have to Use Two Strategies

Reading a person's CONFIDENT–CAUTIOUS/FEARFUL trait raises an obvious question: *What if my friend/child/colleague makes CONFIDENT decisions in his area of competency but everyday decisions are made cautiously? How do I know how to lead, counsel, coach, or work with him?*

The answer is that you may have to adopt *two* different strategies. First, in his area of competency, you can trust that he'll be CONFIDENT. Outside his area of competency, expect CAUTIOUS. This means you'll need to allocate more time for him to process or receive additional counsel/training. If time is a factor, someone else may have to make the decision.

Recognizing that you may have to use two different approaches when working with someone is especially valuable when *change* and *unfamiliar factors* are injected into a situation—when he doesn't know what to expect. While it's possible, don't expect him to operate confidently; expect caution.

Recognizing this twofold strategy is important because more people today operate on the CAUTIOUS/FEARFUL side of the wire than at any other time in North American history.

Tip for when someone asks you for help: Evaluate their trait so you can gauge the time required for counseling/mentoring. This will help you wisely select where and when to invest your time, which is valuable and limited.

Major Shift to the CAUTIOUS/FEARFUL Side of the Wire

In the 1950s, the majority of Americans were CONFIDENT decision makers. We fought two world wars and a depression, and won. Then something happened. Families began to disintegrate at a frightening rate to the point where now more than one out of every two first-time marriages ends up in divorce.[1] Now ask yourself this question: Did this trend, that affects over 32 million youth, increase or decrease CAUTIOUS/FEARFUL decision making for children from these homes? The obvious answer is *increased*, and most carried this trait into their adult lives. Added to this are millions of youths from dysfunctional or abusive homes or homes where parents have never married. The number of American youths from broken and high-risk homes far exceeds the entire population of Canada (36 million).[2]

I have researched and written extensively on how various violent youth trends emanate from this family deterioration factor. When kids are insecure and the world is shifting under their feet, their confidence in making decisions evaporates. Educators and law-enforcement professionals globally voice the same opinion because they see its effect daily.

The shift toward the CAUTIOUS/FEARFUL side and its impact on society is perhaps even more significant than the Earth's shift to the UNCONVENTIONAL trait. In a typical school 40 years ago, about 75% of the students were CONFIDENT decision makers. Today, it's down to about 50% or lower in middle- and upper-middle class neighborhoods—and much lower in the inner-city.

As these student enter the workforce, there is now a potentially crippling effect that is a part of the corporate landscape: the inability to make CONFIDENT decisions when decisions and changes are needed to compete and keep up with changes in markets and technology. Some of you are struggling with this right now and wondering what you can do.

There is an antidote. In Chapter 18 you'll learn a practical, can-do strategy that develops a *capacity* for increased CONFIDENT decision making separate from one's area of expertise, giftedness, or training. It's one of the most important concepts in the book. I originally taught it to thousands of teachers who used it with other strategies to successfully stop school-rampage massacre threats and attacks from 1997–2014 (Chapter 22). I then watched many apply it with any student who struggled to make CONFIDENT decisions, not just those threatening violence or self-harm, and the results were the same: within weeks most increased their capacity to make CONFIDENT decisions. And, more broadly this strategy can be applied with anyone—youth or adult. I now teach student leaders in high schools how to increase their CONFIDENT decision-making capacity and help others students do the same, and the results are always stunning (more in Chapter 19).

Interaction Suggestions When Simultaneously Reading the CONFIDENT–CAUTIOUS/FEARFUL and CONVENTIONAL–UNCONVENTIONAL Wires

When *change* and *unfamiliar* factors are injected into someone's life, it is best to make snapshot reads of both the CONFIDENT–CAUTIOUS/FEARFUL and CONVENTIONAL–UNCONVENTIONAL wires.

For example, someone who is CONVENTIONAL *and* CONFIDENT might resist change. This person shouldn't be confused for CAUTIOUS/FEARFUL just because they are resistant to something new, which is a common misread. Here is an easy-to-use short list of suggestions when working with people making decisions based upon your read of *both* the CONFIDENT–CAUTIOUS/FEARFUL and CONVENTIONAL–UNCONVENTIONAL wires.

UNCONVENTIONAL & CAUTIOUS/FEARFUL

They want to look at all the options, but will struggle making a decision and can consume significant time.

Focus: Show them variety in small doses, break their decision down into smaller bites, and watch your time.

CONVENTIONAL & CAUTIOUS/FEARFUL

They won't take as much time to identify what they want, but they may struggle to make a decision and commit, or second-guess their decision. **Focus:** Break their decision down into smaller bites as they focus on their selected option. This will help them make a series of small decisions out of confidence rather than one big one.

CONVENTIONAL & CONFIDENT

They can quickly weed out what they don't want and make a decision. **Focus:** Help them narrow down the specific option to be considered. Don't be fooled, however, if they are resistant to change and misread them as CAUTIOUS.

UNCONVENTIONAL & CONFIDENT

They may take more time to view more options but they'll be decisive. **Focus:** Because they are decisive, you can suggest purchasing/pursuing more than one option, but be prepared to spend more time to allow them time to consider all the options.

The list you just read hints at the increased insight you'd have if you did snapshot reads of all four traits simultaneously.

SNAPSHOT REMINDER #1
It is easier to restrain something you have than to create and do something you don't have.

SNAPSHOT REMINDER #2
Be sure to reread the three questions at the end of Chapter 1 to stimulate how you can use the CONFIDENT–CAUTIOUS/FEARFUL wire.

Before we look at other ways to use the CONFIDENT–CAUTIOUS/FEARFUL wire, let's take a short detour and look at TYPES and COMPREHENSIVE profiles, which are richer layers of information available when we combine two or more traits together.

CHAPTER SIXTEEN

Types, Profiles, and Two Safety Checks on Accuracy

[More insight when you need it]

"Would you please cut my hair again?" Jasmine, an administrative assistant, asked Pierre, a high-end hairstylist.

"Dan, I see her once a year and it's always the same story: She wants a new look, but when we're finished, she asks me to cut her hair again so it's almost like it was when she came in. What do I do?" he asked.

"I only get about two or three clients like this a year," he continued, "but it's frustrating, and they only pay for one cut when they get two."

He asked for my input, and I thought some snapshot reads might help him shape a solution. Here's how Pierre profiled Jasmine.

> **PERFORMANCE traits:** CONVENTIONAL (when performing tasks) and CAUTIOUS (when making decisions)
> **COMMUNICATION traits:** NONASSERTIVE and EXPRESS

Using me as a sounding board, he worked on a tactful solution that would also keep Jasmine happy.

"Why do you think she does it?" I asked.

"She probably wants to be different but it's really not her comfort zone," he correctly surmised. "Jasmine is CONVENTIONAL, she wants to be different (UNCONVENTIONAL), but when she sees the new style, she knows it's not 'her.' She's also afraid to stick with a decision. She comes to me because she knows I like to push the envelope tastefully, but she's cautious."

Pierre pinpointed that he needed to focus on a plan to tactfully work with Jasmine's PERFORMANCE traits. Here were his two solutions:

First, he said he could explain to her that he'll have to charge her twice for a second cut if she requests it.

The second option was to cut the back of her hair a bit more UNCONVENTIONAL and the front more like her usual CONVENTIONAL style. This way she can have her secret wish to be a bit different, but she'll see her regular style first and won't bail because of her CAUTIOUS trait.

"That sounds like it might work," I affirmed, not knowing a thing about women and hair styles. But, it seemed reasonable, and he gave me examples where he had combined two styles in the same cut and clients were pleased.

"How will you explain this to her?" I asked.

"Well, I'm also NONASSERTIVE and EXPRESS, so I can gently and politely suggest this as an option, with a bit of emotive expressiveness so she knows I care."

Snapshot reads had now moved into the delicate high-wire world of women's fashion! And it worked!

Both Pierre and Seth, the jewelry store owner in the last chapter, needed to read more than one trait to serve their clients. As explained in Chapter 2, this book is a short primer on how rapid-fire profiling works and how you can make and use snapshot reads today. The *KPS*, though, was designed so you can access as much or as little information as you need.

The simplest level is to make a snapshot read of a trait, like CONTROL–EXPRESS, and interact with someone based upon that trait.

The next level up is when you read two traits and identify a person's COMMUNICATION or PERFORMANCE TYPE, which identifies another layer of actions.

Next, when you read and combine all four traits, you can identify someone's COMPREHENSIVE PROFILE, revealing more than two pages of insight that includes:

- Strengths, shortcomings, and other tendencies
- Which traits drive which behaviors

The profile also provides tailored suggestions for interaction, including:

- General interaction tips
- How to sell/present ideas, products, etc.
- How to confront/disagree
- How to lead/motivate

Below is a graphic representation of the *KPS* engine and how TRAITS when combined together reveal TYPES, and when TYPES are combined

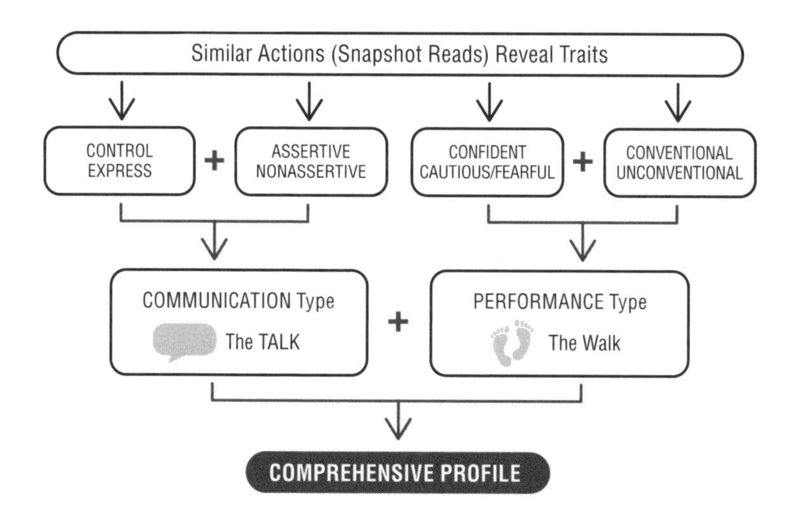

together they create COMPREHENSIVE PROFILES.

The *KPS*, as presented in *The Art of Profiling*, explains how to identify TYPES and COMPREHENSIVE PROFILES. In this chapter you'll be introduced to both to help you decide if you want to learn the rest of the *KPS*.

Finally, you'll learn how TYPES and COMPREHENSIVE PROFILES can be used as a powerful safety check on the accuracy of your snapshot reads. For many, this alone is worth investing the extra effort.

Now let's look at the three steps to identify a person's TYPES and COMPREHENSIVE PROFILE.

Step 1: Identify a Person's COMMUNICATION TYPE

After you have identified someone's COMMUNICATION traits using the ASSERTIVE–NONASSERTIVE and CONTROL–EXPRESS wires, you combine the two traits together to identify a person's COMMUNICATION TYPE. Jasmine, who Pierre profiled as NONASSERTIVE and EXPRESS, is an ARTIST TYPE as shown below.

The identifiers for each TYPE were carefully selected and tested for use with an international audience. SALESMAN, for example, was chosen

COMMUNICATION TYPES

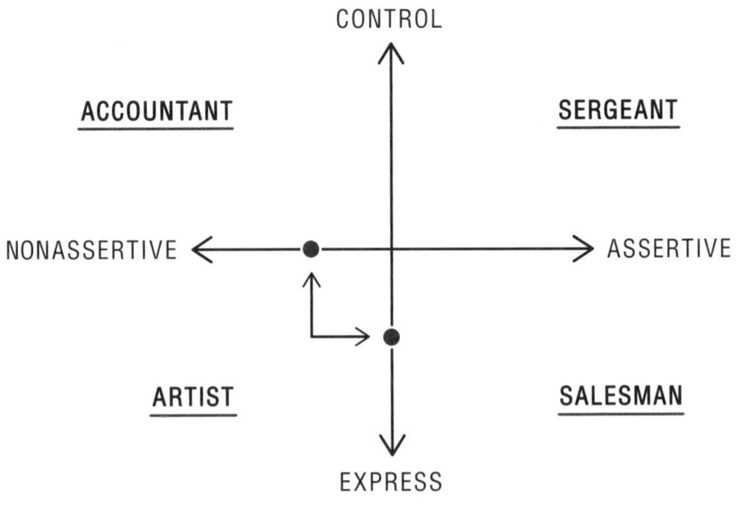

CONTROL

ACCOUNTANT

SERGEANT

NONASSERTIVE

ASSERTIVE

ARTIST

SALESMAN

EXPRESS

because some cultures don't have a male and a female identifier for those in sales. If you don't relate to a specific identifier, you can use another one that communicates the essence of the two traits like the following:

- **SERGEANT** or COMMANDER
- **SALESMAN** or COMMUNICATOR
- **ARTIST** or COUNSELOR
- **ACCOUNTANT** or DETAILER

You may have seen four quadrants used in other behavioral models. In this case, it's simply a graphic depiction of what happens when you combine traits together. A person who is EXPRESS and ASSERTIVE, for example, will communicate using different actions than a person who is EXPRESS and NONASSERTIVE.

When you identify someone's COMMUNICATION TYPE, you're able to identify positive and negative actions, as well as other tendencies. Access to these actions provides additional insight to the ASSERTIVE–NONASSERTIVE and CONTROL–EXPRESS actions. (Reminder: The difference between the *KPS* and other systems is that you can use the *KPS* on the spot without written tests, batteries of questions, etc.)

Shown below are possible actions for an ARTIST, like Jasmine, who had the positive actions of sympathetic, agreeable, loyal, thoughtful, and amiable.

Remember, COMMUNICATION actions only identify how a person *commu-*

ARTIST: EXPRESS / NONASSERTIVE

Positive Actions	Negative Actions	Other Tendencies
Thoughtful	Critical	Idiosyncratic
Sympathetic	Moody	Respectful
Agreeable	Appears weak	Tolerant
Curious/Inquisitive	"Spineless"	Passionate
Supportive	Emotionally rash	Sensitive
Compassionate	Weak	Focuses on feelings
Deep-feeling	Unsure	Naive
Self-sacrificing	Resists interaction	Dramatic
Loyal	Appears uninformed	Avoids conflict

Condensed list from *The Art of Profiling, Expanded 2nd ed.*

nicates and not how they perform tasks and make decisions. While Jasmine may communicate expressively with creativity and sensitivity, it doesn't mean that she will perform creatively. (The list of ARTIST actions provided here is a condensed list for illustrative purposes. The complete list for each TYPE is provided in *The Art of Profiling, Expanded 2nd ed.*)

Like the possible ASSERTIVE–NONASSERTIVE and CONTROL–EXPRESS actions in Chapters 4 and 5, not everyone who is an ARTIST will have every action or show their actions exactly the same way. To imply they do is stereotyping.

It is also possible that someone may have one or two communication actions from another TYPE. For example, an ARTIST, like Jasmine, might have an ACCOUNTANT action because ARTISTS and ACCOUNTANTS both have the NONASSERTIVE trait. However, most of her actions will come from the ARTIST TYPE list of actions (there are exceptions, as noted in *The Art of Profiling*).[1]

The TYPE action list is extremely useful for quick interactions or where you must focus on a specific action, as in the case of Jasmine, who had the specific CAUTIOUS action of indecisive that Pierre had to navigate.

TYPES as a Powerful Safety Check on Accuracy

TYPE actions not only provide more information about someone, but they also allow you to instantly check the accuracy of your reads. It removes the guesswork of your accuracy when making snapshot reads. And, when you do make a misread—and we all do—you can immediately correct it and modify your interaction.

For example, imagine that you profiled Jasmine as an ARTIST (EXPRESS and NONASSERTIVE). But, when you look at the list of ARTIST actions you find that as a *group* the actions don't fit her. This means you misread either Jasmine's CONTROL–EXPRESS or ASSERTIVE–NONASSERTIVE TRAIT—or perhaps both traits.

To correct your misread, you would first look at the lists of ACCOUNTANT and SALESMAN actions. You start with these two TYPE lists because each shares a trait with the ARTIST. ARTISTS and ACCOUNTANTS (shown below) both have the NONASSERTIVE trait. ARTISTS and SALESMEN both have the EXPRESS trait.

Typically, when we misread someone's TYPE, we usually miss just one trait and not both.

If you find that the ACCOUNTANT actions are a better match for Jasmine,

ACCOUNTANT: CONTROL / NONASSERTIVE

Positive Actions	Negative Actions	Other Tendencies
Easy-going/Agreeable	Uninvolved	Introspective
Thoughtful	Weak	Indifferent/Aloof
Analytical	Suspicious	Picky
Detailed	Pessimistic	Stubborn
Poised	Unexcitable	Introverted
Calm and cool	Slow	Tranquil
Dependable	Resists interaction	Proper
Curious	Critical	Debater
Efficient	Compulsive	Perfectionist

Condensed list from *The Art of Profiling, Expanded 2nd ed.*

this means you thought she was EXPRESS when she was actually CONTROL. Changing your snapshot read on the fly from EXPRESS to CONTROL allows you to immediately modify how you interact with her.

For example, if you are presenting Jasmine with a proposal, instead of using expressive language, you might be more restrained and just focus on the facts (which people who are CONTROL typically prefer—as we learned in Chapter 5). Knowing now that Jasmine is CONTROL is a reminder that she may not show much emotion as you share your thoughts so you don't to jump to the conclusion that she isn't interested.

Step 2: Identify a Person's PERFORMANCE TYPE

PERFORMANCE TYPES reveal actions of how someone prefers to perform tasks and make decisions. To identify someone's PERFORMANCE TYPE—the *walk*—you use the same process just described, but you combine snapshot reads of CONFIDENT–CAUTIOUS/FEARFUL and CONVENTIONAL–UNCONVENTIONAL.

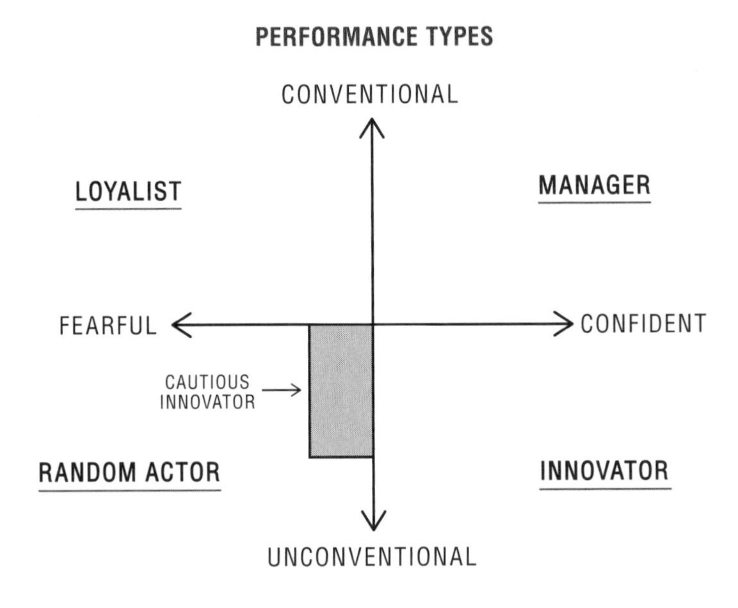

LOYALIST: CAUTIOUS-FEARFUL / CONVENTIONAL

Positive Actions	Negative Actions	Other Tendencies
Loyal	Unquestioning	Obedient
Manageable	Subservient	Compliant
Precise	Uninteresting	Analytical
Reliable	Uncreative	Guarded
Cautious	Indecisive	Rule oriented
Supportive	Mindless	Follower
Dutiful	Insecure	Compulsive
Organized	Fear of failure	Avoids risk
Orderly	Gullible	Unbending

Condensed list from *The Art of Profiling, Expanded 2nd ed.*

In the case of Jasmine, she is a LOYALIST TYPE (CONVENTIONAL and CAUTIOUS), and her possible inventory of actions is also shown below the PERFORMANCE TYPES graph on the previous page. We use this additional insight to refine interactions with her.

You'll also notice there are *five* PERFORMANCE TYPES. The fifth, the CAUTIOUS INNOVATOR, was added in recent years and is discussed in more detail in Chapter 21. These are people who are 0–3 on the CAUTIOUS/FEARFUL wire and are UNCONVENTIONAL.

As you've learned, the TYPE actions are also used as a safety check on Jasmine's PERFORMANCE traits: CONVENTIONAL and CAUTIOUS.

Once you've identified a person's COMMUNICATION and PERFORMANCE TYPE everything is in place so you can identify their COMPREHENSIVE PROFILE.

Step 3: Identify the COMPREHENSIVE PROFILE

To identify a person's COMPREHENSIVE PROFILE, you just combine the COMMUNICATION and PERFORMANCE TYPES together, and then read the profile. The *KPS* provides 20 COMPREHENSIVE PROFILES. Each one is almost three pages of information and guidance how to interact. Below is a graphic reminder of how the pieces fit together.

Jasmine's COMPREHENSIVE PROFILE

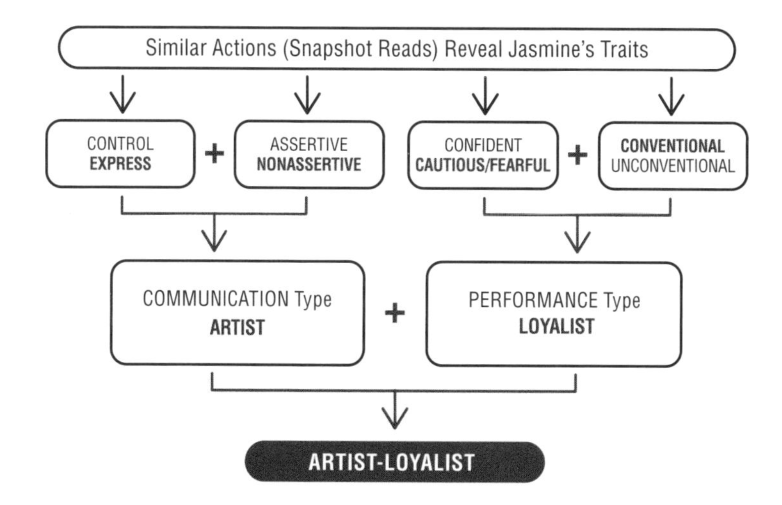

COMPREHENSIVE PROFILES as another safety check. You can also use the COMPREHENSIVE PROFILE as a second safety check on the accuracy of your snapshot reads. If you read the profile and it doesn't seem to fit, you can correct your read by rechecking the TYPE actions.

Using TYPES and COMPREHENSIVE PROFILES as safety checks is a key reason people use the *KPS* with confidence, as it provides greater control over accuracy. This ability to make on-the-spot corrections is one of the most powerful aspects of the *KPS* because we can all make mistakes.

Example of a COMPREHENSIVE PROFILE. What follows is Jasmine's COMPREHENSIVE PROFILE, the ARTIST–LOYALIST. Like the list of TYPE actions, not every action or suggestion for interaction will apply to everyone with this profile, which would be stereotyping. What you have, though, are high-percentage insights into how a person will operate as well as *how to treat someone right the first time.*

Take a minute and review the ARTIST–LOYALIST, and as you do, ask yourself if this additional level of information can be useful for you. If it can, then you might consider learning the entire *KPS*, which provides all twenty profiles.

ARTIST–LOYALIST (From *The Art of Profiling, Expanded 2nd ed.*)
The ARTIST–LOYALIST has the following combination of traits:

- EXPRESS–NONASSERTIVE
- CONVENTIONAL–CAUTIOUS/FEARFUL

People with this profile have the COMMUNICATION type of an ARTIST—open, expressive, and sensitive. What is seemingly contradictory is that they aren't UNCONVENTIONAL. They are open in relationships, but prefer more conventional tasks. Because this profile's PERFORMANCE type is characteristically compliant and obedient (CAUTIOUS/FEARFUL and CONVENTIONAL), these people don't translate their emotional sensitivity into new, creative, or unique performance. This seeming contradiction between their COMMUNICATION and PERFORMANCE TYPES can result in tension for some, which can create neurotic actions the stronger their CAUTIOUS/FEARFUL and EXPRESS traits; they're sensitive and want to step forward, but they are stymied by their fear. This uncommon profile demonstrates the need to avoid preconceived stereotyping. While we tend to expect ARTISTS to take some risks in personal relationships because of their willingness to express emotion, we find that for these ARTISTS their "talk" doesn't match their "walk." In this case, ARTIST–LOYALISTS reduce their potential because they require predictability in their performance and a safe, risk-free environment for managing their lack of confidence. This is very different from ARTIST–INNOVATORS, for example, who are willing to accept risk and try new ventures, taking advantage of their creative capacity.

Typical Strengths

- Open COMMUNICATION TYPE coupled with willingness to loyally follow; a very yielding COMMUNICATION TYPE.
- Has potential for combining a precise work ethic with a creative bent.
- Not likely to overreact like other ARTIST TYPES because they are restrained by their LOYALIST TYPE.

Typical Shortcomings

- Won't try new ideas and adventures, despite open COMMUNICATION TYPE.
- Avoids risks that might endanger relationships with others, even in the face of opportunity.
- Under emotional stress, inclined to be impulsive when they communicate and then "take back" what they have said or done.
- While they appear open and easy to understand, they make decisions in ways that appear mundane or boring, earning the label

of "underachiever."

Other Tendencies

- Can be hard to read because of contradictions in COMMUNICATION and PERFORMANCE TYPES.
- Can serve as good "eyes and ears" for SERGEANT TYPES who want to be more "in touch" with others; may be seduced into informant role.
- Avoids conflict.

Trait Indicators

- High NONASSERTIVE makes this profile the most useful "eyes and ears."
- High EXPRESS may produce implosive reactions.
- High FEARFUL will cause profile to appear untrustworthy to peers and to those not in control.

Interaction Tips

- Don't force into quick decisions or reaction situations.
- Like ACCOUNTANT–LOYALIST, don't ask them to give others negative or critical feedback.
- After an agreement is reached, allow time for it to "settle in" before assuming it is a "done deal."
- Like all LOYALIST profiles, encourage to recognize their natural tendency toward loyalty and to carefully consider the integrity of those whom they serve—without paranoia—so that their trusting nature isn't abused.

Sell/Present

Like other LOYALIST profiles, resist approaching them with important decisions the higher their CAUTIOUS/FEARFUL trait. ARTIST–LOYALISTS require a lot of time to process requests, and the strategic use of a person with a low or moderate ASSERTIVE trait may be helpful to get them to "move." (However, the longer the process, the greater the likelihood that their CAUTIOUS/FEARFUL trait will kick in as they mull over the options. Additionally, ASSERTIVE presenters will typically be ineffective in reaching them over a long, sustained period of time.) Avoid too much EXPRESS, which may trigger more irrationality in their CAUTIOUS/FEARFUL decision-making process. Best advice: Find backup support, like one of their colleagues, to bolster their lack of decision-making initiative.

Confront/Disagree

You are confronting people who have both fear and sensitivity and will retreat into themselves. For this reason, these people usually aren't dangerous or highly volatile. Use an ARTIST or an ACCOUNTANT (who is low CONTROL) to establish dialogue and trust, and a low ASSERTIVE person to encourage a decision or bring closure, but only if a NONASSERTIVE person (an ARTIST or an ACCOUNTANT) isn't successful. Finally, in most cases, ARTIST–LOYALISTS won't attempt crippling or life-threatening retaliation.

Lead/Motivate

Can be led by those who are more ASSERTIVE and CONFIDENT. This includes someone who is lower NONASSERTIVE and is CAUTIOUS—but lower CAUTIOUS. Lead and motivate them in their area of expertise and competency. Do not present with critical decisions or significant change and provide tangible rewards. The higher the CONVENTIONAL trait the more likely they will resist change, so emphasize loyalty to the organization and provide time to absorb opportunity. Emphasize team effort and safety nets along the way. Remember, even though you may connect with their EXPRESS trait, this doesn't mean they are on board. Mentor how to make small bite-sized CONFIDENT decisions separate from area of competency to expand capacity for increased CONFIDENT decision making.

Time Required to Develop Competency Using the *KPS*

It takes about 6–8 weeks of following the lessons in *The Art of Profiling Expanded 2nd ed.* to develop competency, achieve 65–75% profiling accuracy, and be able to access all the information provided. With sustained application, accuracy will increase. In a workshop environment, the time required to achieve 75% accuracy or higher is reduced to 1–2 days. With sustained application, 80–90% accuracy is common.

Pocket PeopleReader®

For years, many have asked me for an app and/or computer software that allows immediate access to all the TYPES and COMPREHENSIVE PROFILES. After several years of development the Pocket PeopleReader® was created. One version is available for cell phones and another is in development for integration into contact databases.

With the app, you make snapshot reads by tapping the screen with people you've selected to represent the extremes of each trait. Next, up pops a short summary of what you should be seeing. You can then view the actions for each TYPE (which is also a check on the accuracy of a snapshot read). You also can access the COMPREHENSIVE PROFILE and suggestions for how you would effectively interact with someone based upon your needs (everything from hiring interviews, purchasing, closing sales, even hiring a babysitter). For more information, see the Korem & Associates website.

Summary of What You Can Access with the KPS

TYPES

1. Make two snapshot reads using COMMUNICATION or PERFORMANCE wires and you can identify someone's TYPE actions.
2. TYPE actions provide more insight into a person's specific actions.
3. TYPE actions are also a safety check to confirm the accuracy of your reads.

COMPREHENSIVE PROFILES

1. Make four snapshot reads using all four wires.
2. Combine the traits to identify the COMMUNICATION and PERFORMANCE TYPES.
3. Combine the TYPES to identify the COMPREHENSIVE profile.
4. Use the COMPREHENSIVE profile as a final safety check on the accuracy of your reads.
5. Review the profile actions and suggestions and apply as needed.

You now have a big-picture view of all the information available and safety checks to review your accuracy. Before we return to ways to use the CONFIDENT–CAUTIOUS/FEARFUL gauge, we'll pause for a very interesting visual in the next chapter.

Pocket PeopleReader® App Screenshots

HORSE LISTENER SNAPSHOTS

Monty Roberts is known as the legendary "horse whisperer" who would rather be known as *The Man Who Listens to Horses*, the title of the book he wrote at the urging of Queen Elizabeth II after Monty trained her staff on his legendary Join-Up ® system for leading and training horses.

Monty is a master of making snapshot reads of horses and enabling others to become "trauma-free" trainers. He explains that the horse is a "prey" animal and his inherent defense is to flee. Horses are flight animals. Once you recognize that, you can make accurate snapshot reads and *treat horses right the first time*. Monty says, "I did not create my training concepts. I only discovered what nature already had in place."

Monty was raised in an abusive home as a child. He and his wife, Pat, have three children and they also helped raise 47 foster children. He loves people and horses and has a gift for helping those who have faced tragedy—abused children, wounded vets, and many others. And, he brings them together with horses to help them heal, which has been featured in documentaries.

When I read another of Monty's books, *From My Hands to Yours*, I was astounded to discover that many of the explanations and diagrams for how to interact with a horse are just like what you have learned in this book.

Below are illustrations of the proper open-body position and other recommendations that allows a horse to feel at ease. The horse interprets our actions in light of how they view any animal. When our body and eyes are squared to a horse, they interpret us as an animal of prey. Remember, how Urs in Chapter 6 opened his body and thoughtfully restrained any ASSERTIVE motions with his hands so people would feel relaxed during an interview? It's the same idea with a horse.

If you want to expand your ability to make snapshot reads of people and animals, and gain greater insight into how to treat each more effectively, read Monty's books and learn more about him at MontyRoberts.com.

Eyes on eyes, shoulders square.

I am getting ready to be "predatorial."

Shoulders at 45°, arms down and folded across midline, eyes off eyes.

I am inviting you to feel safe around me.

CHAPTER SEVENTEEN

Profile the Artist-Creator

Infinite Variety
Same Construct

There is a pattern in nature in which the simplest elements are combined together with infinite variety and majesty. Billowing clouds, hidden caves, sunsets and sunrises, forests, ever-changing dunes, and more. That each of us has four behavioral traits that reveal themselves uniquely is another example. Snowflakes are another.

Kenneth Libbrecht is a physics professor at the California Institute of Technology who photographs snowflakes right after they fall, using a special microscope he developed. His coffee-table books, including *The Art of the Snowflake*, are masterpieces.

Above is a snowflake he photographed. It's what we typically think a snowflake will look like.

Yet, this is also a snowflake. Stunning, isn't it?

So let's profile the artist-creator of these crystalline wonders.

First, we find that no two fully formed snowflakes that have ever fallen since the beginning of the world are identical. They are all unique. Every one of them.[1]

The fact that snowflakes are created with limitless variety and creativity points to an artist-creator who is extremely UNCONVENTIONAL. That's an easy read.

There is a problem, though.

Although each is different—often dramatically different—the trillions upon trillions of other snowflakes that fall each year have a common characteristic. They all have six points. (Actually a million billion descend to the Earth every year.)[2]

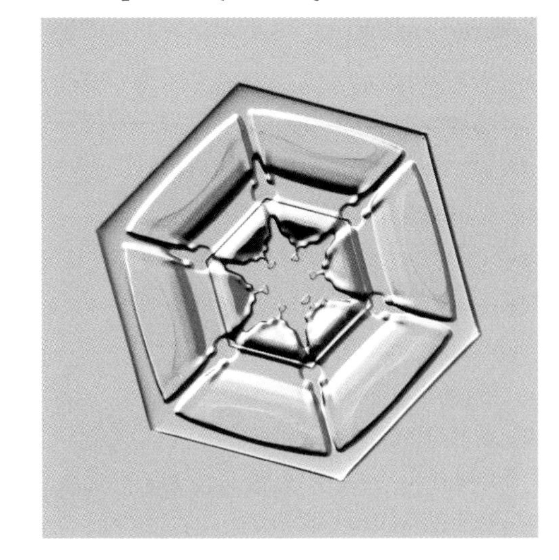

Now profile the artist-creator of these unique masterpieces: CONVENTIONAL or UNCONVENTIONAL?

With such consistency, it seems CONVENTIONAL.

Each is fashioned with extreme discipline, using just six points.

So, I guess this means

we have an artist-creator who is *both* extremely CONVENTIONAL and UNCONVENTIONAL.

It seems that the only snowflakes that look alike are those that have barely formed, sort of like us when we start out as an egg and a sperm ready to unite as one.

Believe it or not, these are also snowflakes (below)...If you look down the ends, you'll see six sides, like an ice pencil, or a faceted hourglass where the middle never meets.

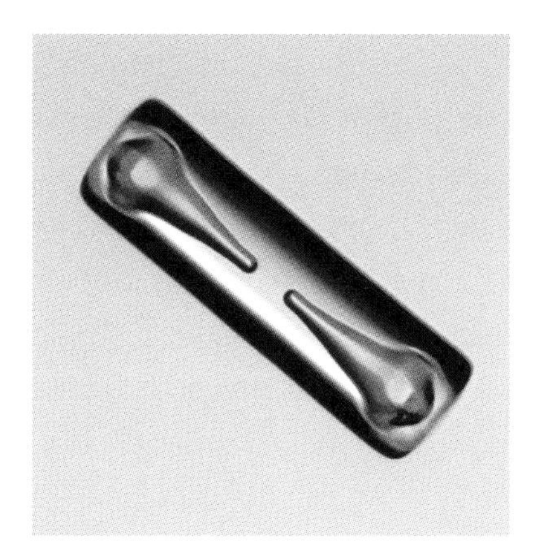

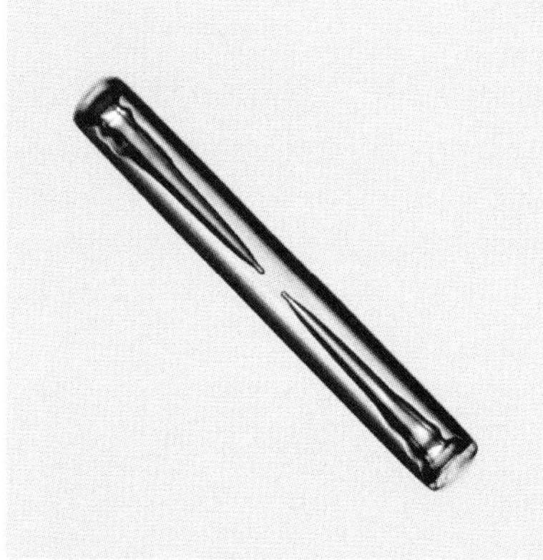

Can we agree that each snowflake is a work of art? It's self-evident, isn't it, even for those of us who aren't lovers of art?

When artists create, they usually paint, pen, carve, or chisel their name on their works of art. This artist-creator, however, doesn't leave a signature, which suggests an artist-creator without fear, as all flakes eventually melt without leaving a record behind that they even existed. Is this artist-creator CONFIDENT or CAUTIOUS/FEARFUL? Pretty easy: CONFIDENT. The absence of even the slightest creator's mark hints at an unshakable confidence that as trillions of works of art fall and melt, there is enduring confidence in a limitless imagination that ensures the next trillion will each be its own unique masterpiece.

The creative palette of infinite artistic variety expressed against six points in snowflakes is like you and me.

We all have four of the finest, thinnest threads of human behavior that we can identify with snapshot reads, yet there is infinite variety in how they are combined, making each of us unique.

Like snowflakes, we have a consistent construct, but with even greater splendor. Consider these observations I've paraphrased from the late Dr. Paul Brand, the world-renowned hand surgeon and leprosy specialist introduced in Chapter 13. They are from his book, *Fearfully and Wonderfully Made.*[3]

Our bodies each have 100 trillion cells[4] that all work in concert. As you read these words, 200 billion brain cells process the one billion messages a second that stream in from light cone images via your eyes, as your hearts pumps blood through 60,000 miles of blood vessels, as your body replenishes the 300 billion blood cells that die every day...as your fingers apply just enough pressure so you can hold this book, as your brain wanders and reflects...as you gently shift in your seat and your brain blocks out background sounds and distractions so you can concentrate, but your olfactory nerves pick up signals that freshly baked cookies are in the oven or a pizza is on the table. We have an outer covering, called skin, that flexes and folds and crinkles around joints, facial crags, gnarled toes, and fleshy buttocks ...as it protects us from millions of invading bacterium and yeast while modulating the body's temperature. A temperature increase of just 7 or 8 degrees would kill the whole body; thus, the skin is called on to act as a radiator, rushing fluids to the surface to evaporate and cool the body... and on it goes with all the other parts of the body contributing.

All simultaneously.

Added to this array of mind-boggling functionality and preservation is that we are each blessed with a unique combination of behavioral traits and how we use them. It is more than the icing on the cake. It's a work of art that profoundly declares we are human, formed under a creator's artisan eye.

Back to snowflakes....

Another constant about the crystalline wonders is there is a very specific way they like to be treated. They don't like temperatures over 32 degrees.

In this way, they're like us, as we were created to be treated uniquely, with dignity, because we are fearfully and wonderfully made.

Oh yes, the next time you take a shower or bath, look in the mirror. You won't find a signature...

CHAPTER EIGHTEEN

Building Capacity for Making Confident Decisions

[It's like lifting weights between the ears]

In a small middle-class town, a manufacturing plant that supplied several hundred jobs closed because its senior staff and employees couldn't make decisive decisions. They had known for several years that they needed to change direction, but they failed because over 30% were CAUTIOUS/FEARFUL decision makers. When competition was constant, they did well, but when decisiveness was needed from the board to the shop floor, they failed. As a group they weren't divisive or self-centered, just indecisive.

I trained the high school staff in that town after the plant closed, and you could see the same trait in many of the students. Teachers filled me in on the details of what happened at the plant, as most knew someone who lost their job.

I taught the high school staff how to use the *KPS* to increase CONFIDENT student decision-making to increase comprehension and retention. Teachers will tell you, when kids aren't CONFIDENT, it's a struggle to help them elevate. And, in this case, they emulated what they learned at home. Once the teachers were armed with new insight into how they could use snapshot reads to raise the bar, student dramatically improved. Within 60 days, high school failure rates were the lowest in school history (and only 2% of seniors failed that year), and behavioral referrals dropped 20%—this in a school system where over 50% were economically disadvantaged.

As explained in Chapter 15, destructive forces in the family have escalated FEARFUL decision making to the point where teachers will tell you that only 35–50% or fewer students in a typical classroom can make CONFIDENT decisions separate from their area of expertise, training, and giftedness. And, because this trend has continued to escalate since the late 1960s, indecisiveness is now common both for youths and adults. This needs to change.

As a life skill and social need, building increased capacity to make CONFIDENT decisions is probably the most important concept in this book that you can personally apply, and mentor someone else to learn. In this chapter you'll learn the basic construct and the common sense steps to do it. The next chapter provides the decisions adults and teens have made within 30 minutes of learning the concept.

Pulling the Trigger When It Counts

One of America's premiere football coaches told me he estimated that up to 20% of the time impact players fail to pull the trigger and make a play. I asked for his personal take on this inability to execute.

He said that about 10% of the time it was a lack of instinct. More importantly, he thought that the other 10% was behavioral—learned behavior. As we drilled down, I asked him if this might be the inability to make a confident decision in an unfamiliar situation. He said he had never thought about it in those terms, but that was probably it.

He estimated that if athletes could increase their ability to make CONFIDENT decisions, as explained in this chapter, the margin of error would probably be significantly reduced. From his perspective, that can translate into a championship season instead of just a winning season.

For the rest of us, this can mean the difference between moving forward in life or being stymied by indecisiveness when sound, resolute decisions are required. None of us can escape those pivotal moments, both large and small, which accumulate.

Here is a list of common decision-making laments. Think of those that apply to you, or people you know, and how more CONFIDENT decision making would have made a difference.

- I should have befriended ___________, who needed my help.
- She should or shouldn't have broken off a relationship.
- I should have said "no" when ___________.
- He should have said "yes" when ___________.
- She should have studied harder when ___________.
- I should or shouldn't have invested more capital.
- He should or shouldn't have taken that job.
- I should have worked harder when ___________.
- He should or shouldn't have ___________.

Imagine if the team leaders at the plant had deliberately, over time, made small decisive decisions before being faced with big ones that were needed to save the plant. As a counterpoint, when guided by their teachers, the students expanded their CONFIDENT decision-making capacity within weeks of learning how, which produced winning results.

It's Like Lifting Weights Between Your Ears

Confident decision-making is like a muscle you exercise. The more you use it, the stronger it gets. It is an act of will over which you have direct control, and you don't need permission to do it.

This means that if you're 3 CAUTIOUS/FEARFUL on a 1–5 scale, you can move to 1 when required. If you are 1 CONFIDENT, you can move to 3.

It is something you can choose to use or not use, regardless of your circumstances.

You start by making by making a small, bite-sized decision over which you have immediate control and can complete in a day or so. Then you make another one, and another. Over time you add more "weight." The decisions become more complex and require more time. At the end of the chapter, I'll give you some suggestions for a journal you'll use to track your progress.

Urgency for Building Capacity

The growing trend to CAUTIOUS/FEARFUL decision making extends beyond the condition of the economy. I first saw the trend grow in affluent communities in the 1990s, when economies were strong and unemployment was low. The common catalyst in most situations was the raging rate of family disintegration.

For students, this usually results in substandard performance. One administrator told me, "There's nothing surprising about the connection between helping kids make confident decisions and improving grades and lowering behavioral issues. The first year that I intuitively focused on this link, not only did the kids do great, but I didn't have a single behavioral issue that year."

In the private sector, the forces for change at the small-town plant are common today because of severe change in technology, markets, and other competitive factors that demand we quickly adapt, to remain healthy and competitive.

Mitigating risk caused by increased CAUTIOUS/FEARFUL decision-making using the traditional methods of providing more training and instruction won't work when change is needed—when people must make decisions *outside* their area of competency and training. This is when our core trait shows up.

When *individuals* in an organization have the CAUTIOUS/FEARFUL trait it's not an inherent negative, as they can be the ones who take that second or third or fourth look to ensure stability. But, when a group, team, or organization needs to move quickly and decisively and 40–50% have the trait, the results can be disastrous.

It's crucial to develop increased CONFIDENT decision making—*before* the day of decision arrives. Major Dick Winters, the leader of Easy Company in the classic book and movie, *Band of Brothers*, said it powerfully in his "Leadership at the Point of the Bayonet":

> Anticipate problems and prepare to overcome obstacles. Don't wait until you get to the top of the ridge and then make up your mind.[1]

Helping people increase their capacity for CONFIDENT decision making is one of the greatest gifts you can give someone, or even yourself. The inability to make confident decisions is a stymying factor that keeps millions of people from reaching their potential and leading fulfilled lives.

Five Steps to Increase Capacity to Make CONFIDENT Decisions

These themes can be learned and applied one-on-one or in group settings. If you need help, find someone who has basic insight into others for input into the best approach for each step. I've never found a well-intentioned group that couldn't find ways to apply them. At the end of the chapter a simple journal you can use to track your progress is provided.

1. Establish trust. When mentoring someone, trust must first be established. If trust has been violated in the past, patience is required along with an investment of time. For kids, establishing trust usually occurs faster than for adults—even as short as one meeting.

Be sure to clearly explain the need to develop the capacity to make CONFIDENT decisions *separate* from his or her area of competency, especially in changing times.

2. They must acknowledge the need to make more CONFIDENT decisions. Have them plot themselves on the CONFIDENT–CAUTIOUS/FEARFUL wire. This is important so that they take ownership of the process. For those who are on the CAUTIOUS/FEARFUL side of the gauge, when they show you their plot point, they are in effect making a small decision out of confidence to trust you with important information about themselves, which is a positive step forward.

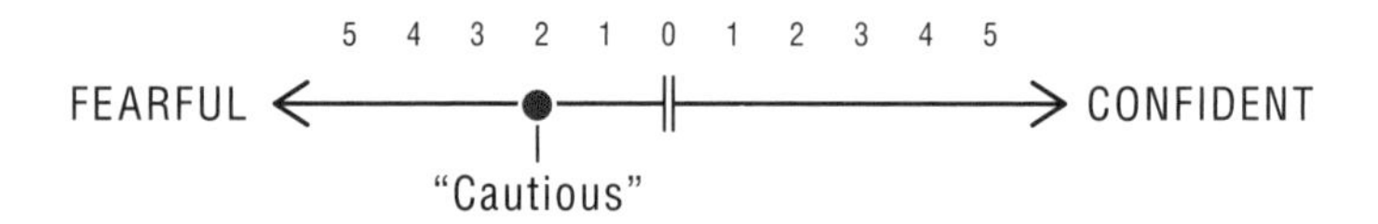

To help someone visualize how life might be different with more confidence, suggest they write a paragraph or a one-pager on how his or her day, career, life at school, personal relationships, etc. might be different if they could move just 1 or 2 points toward the CONFIDENT end of the wire.

For those who are CAUTIOUS/FEARFUL and struggle with abstract concepts and can't visualize this, have them describe someone they've observed who is CONFIDENT. Insist on specific examples. No abstractions. Be sure the example provided is someone making a decision separate from their natural talent, training, and so on. (Additional insight is provided in Chapter 22, on how to help those who are extreme FEARFUL—5 on the CAUTIOUS/FEARFUL wire—which is paranoia.)

For organizations, clearly explain that the goal is for the *team* to increase its capacity for making CONFIDENT decisions, so that it can compete when change is required. If needed, provide examples of organizations that have failed because they couldn't pull the trigger.

Increasing capacity for CONFIDENT decision-making in a group setting builds team leadership. CONFIDENT decision making pulls along those who might not otherwise participate. I watched my wife build her company around this concept.

In the early years, she had a number of team leaders who were single women, divorced from men who had significant personal issues. Most of the women were CAUTIOUS decision makers. Sandy, however, regularly placed them in situations where they had to make quick small decisions outside their area of competency. When catering major events, the unexpected often happens. Sandy's favorite saying is: *Don't panic, punt!*

She reinforced that she would protect their backside when there were unwanted or unexpected outcomes. She clearly conveyed to them that they could do it. They had the talent, the drive, and willingness to improve. They just needed to "pump some decision-making iron."

Over time, they grew.

Then, when a new staffer was struggling, the team conveyed to that person that she could do it, like they did...that as a team, they always got it done. And they did.

During a celebrity wedding, the water main for the city broke and toilets couldn't be flushed. *Don't panic, punt!* Run and buy every gallon of water within three miles.

When the electrical power went out at another event—*don't panic, punt!* Get the cars, point them toward the grills where the meat was being prepared in the parking lot, and turn on the headlights until power is restored.

A key to Sandy's team's development was increasing their capacity to make CONFIDENT decisions when circumstances demanded: *Don't panic, punt! Make a decision and move now!*

After events, decisions are reviewed and sharpened, but never criticized. This reinforces the collective mindset in which everyone is a part of the response, strengthening the decision-making muscle.

In the 1970s, USAF Colonel John Boyd innovated a legendary process for fighter pilots who must make split-second decisions during missions. It's called OODA Loop: Observe, Orient, Decide, and Act. It's an expanded version of *don't panic, punt!* and I recommend taking a look at its simple logic and how you can use it.

And, here's something organizations can leverage to accelerate *don't panic, punt!* Because our culture has shifted to the UNCONVENTIONAL, teams can leverage the inherent ability of its UNCONVENTIONAL team members to solve spontaneous situations and innovate on the fly as they apply *don't panic, punt!*

3. Make a CONFIDENT decision today. Once people you are mentoring recognize the need to make more CONFIDENT decisions, guide them toward a decision they can make, right there, on the spot. If you are doing this for yourself, don't leave this chapter until *you've* made a decision. The qualifications for a decision are:

- Concrete—not abstract
- Nugget-sized
- Time-compacted (for an immediate result)
- Specific—not expansive
- Short duration—not drawn out

The idea is to decide on an immediate CONFIDENT decision over which you or the person you are mentoring has direct control and has quick closure. Just "doing better on the job or in algebra" or "increasing sales" doesn't qualify. These are vague, general, and not time-compacted. Better options are spending 10 minutes more on a homework assignment each night for a week, or making 10% more sales calls next week.

When mentoring, it's best if they come up with the decision(s). Offering them a list of decisions doesn't make them take ownership of the process—it puts you in control, which may be part of the problem. *They need to lift the weight between their ears, not you.*

You act as a guiding, sounding board. For example, you can point them toward specific task areas, but they must wrestle with the specific decision and how it applies to their life, career, and so on. This ensures that they internalize the process and take ownership.

One starting-point option is to have them recall a confident decision that they made in the past. Have them articulate why they knew it was a good decision and if they would like to have that same kind of confidence today. If they can't think of one, have them articulate a decision they saw someone else make and explain in detail why it was CONFIDENT. (In extreme cases where someone is high FEARFUL—paranoid—postponing this type of question might be appropriate, as they might not be able to recall a CONFIDENT decision and become despondent, as explained in Chapter 22.)

Remember, we aren't looking for how a person communicates, such as talking confidently, but rather specific actions that indicate CONFIDENT decision making.

In organizational settings, a team can make decisions. If they get stuck, a team leader can present a list of suggested decisions and the team selects one of them. The idea is that the decisions are not part of the team's natural competencies, but still add value to the daily work process.

A decision may be as simple as working for just half a day with someone that's not a natural fit. Another might be assisting for a day in an area of the company where they don't have competency, but understanding of how that unit operates will help them in their responsibilities. (There are various reality business shows, such as *Undercover Boss*, that can be a source of inspiration for ideas, and many are available in various media formats.)

4. Regularly provide encouragement and guidance to make simple, time-compacted CONFIDENT decisions. New decisions must be made and acted upon monthly, weekly, or even daily (especially for kids). Remember, one is exercising a decision-making muscle—mentally pumping iron. Neglect leads to atrophy. It's one reason that leaders universally know that if they aren't moving forward, they're regressing.

5. Over time, encourage people you mentor to make decisions that are more challenging, complex, and take longer to complete. Just like athletes adding weights or increasing distances, over time, decisions should become more challenging and take longer. A simple, time-compacted decision in the beginning might be: Work with Jennifer (something he dislikes) on a project for a day. A more challenging decision a month later might be: Work with Jennifer for two weeks and find at least two ways to assist her. There is no set list of suggestions for more complex decisions—rather, just be guided by common sense, feedback, insight from others, etc.

Don't Stereotype Who Can and Can't Elevate

People often stereotype that all auditors are CAUTIOUS/FEARFUL because they check and recheck systems. That auditors are CAUTIOUS as a *unit* is a positive because it forces them to be measured and restrained when making decisions to ensure that all systems are functioning as intended. When presenting findings to boards, however, they must make decisions confidently or their findings may not be acted upon. To develop this bandwidth requires experience, training, and mentoring. Jack Welch, the former General Electric CEO, describes this process:

> The typical new hire in auditing has about three years of experience with the company.... Early on, these young auditors are tentative, holding their comments while more senior members of the team run the show. But over time, usually three to five years, I've seen these auditors develop an edge [confidence] that is razor sharp. It comes from observing their more experienced teammates, lots of coaching, and plenty of practice. They also develop an incredible knack for execution. The proof that edge [confidence] and execution can be learned is clear: several CEOs of GE's biggest businesses and vice chairmen were veterans of the audit staff development process.[2]

Snapshot Reminder: Notice that Welch uses the intuitive descriptor "edge" to describe confidence (I added the word confidence). Welch was renowned for his gift of intuition, but imagine telling someone to go into a room and identify if someone has an "edge." The success rate won't be promising, similar to the example in Chapter 9, about reading the "cowboy" (UNCONVENTIONAL trait) at Andersen.

When making snapshot reads using the CONFIDENT–CAUTIOUS/FEARFUL wire, it's better to inquire how people handled specific decisions in the past when they couldn't rely upon giftedness/competency/training. The chances of making an accurate read increases.

Get Started

Using a notebook, create a journal like this:

Date:

Decision:
Difficulty (1-10 scale):
Outcome:
What you learned, how you would improve, etc.:

Make a decision each week. Think ahead to situations you might face in the future and start making small decisions today that will increase your capacity for tomorrow.

Like Major Winters exhorted: *Anticipate problems and prepare to overcome obstacles. Don't wait until you are at the top of the ridge [when you're taking fire] and then make up your mind.* Start building capacity *now*. For more insight and inspiration, read the decisions that adults and students made within 30 minutes of learning this concept, in the next chapter.

CHAPTER NINETEEN

Adults & Kids Making Decisions Together

Pumping Decision-Making Iron

No one had any idea what to expect. Fifty or so parents and kids (ages 12–17) came together to learn how to elevate their performance. The students were all golfers and the parents came from varied professions. There was the CEO of one of the nation's leading healthcare providers, the CFO of a national sporting goods chain, the owner of a group of high-end steak houses, and on it went. The kids, well, they were just kids. Titles don't mean much. As golfers, only performance matters.

After 30 minutes of guiding them through what you learned in the last chapter, I gave them 30 minutes to each decide on a decision that would positively affect their personal life. It could be related to their profession, golf, or another facet of their life. Like you, they had to decide on one small bite-sized decision they could make *that day*. Broken out into groups, they shared their decision with others at their table to be sure it was truly a decision outside their competency and that everyone was on the same page. Each then shared the decision with the entire group and I moderated and helped sharpen it. Here were three of the decisions:

Shorten time to decide on investments. One of the dads, Nathan, the

CFO of the sporting goods stores, said, "Sometimes I tend to drag my feet when considering specific investments. I need to be more decisive and act more quickly."

"Even though you're the CFO of a major company?" I probed. "Are you sure this is an issue for you?"

"Yes, and it's something I've put off working on," he replied. "I tend to drag my feet sometimes when I should be a little quicker."

Turning to the kids, I asked, "Should he start with a large or small investment?"

"Small," they immediately called out in unison.

"And, should it be an important investment?" I asked.

"No," a 12-year-old quickly replied, "in case he makes a mistake."

"Do the rest of you agree?" I asked the kids.

"Yes," they said, again in unison.

The parents, all accomplished professionals, were amazed how quickly the kids caught on. It's powerful when kids and parents (and caregivers/mentors) learn how to increase their decision-making capacity together, gaining insight into each other that they probably wouldn't have had without this process.

●

Won't be a distraction on the next test. A 16-year-old student said, "I'm not going to goof off during my next test."

"Why?" I asked. "What does that have to do with making a confident decision?"

"Because I usually do well, but I get the other kids goofing off around me and it hurts them on their tests," he sheepishly explained.

"So your decision is for the benefit of others?" I asked.

"Right," he replied. His dad, the healthcare provider CEO, was clearly surprised—and pleased.

Get to bed earlier. "I need to get to bed earlier," a 14-year-old student explained, "so I'm going to go to bed at 8:30."

"Why is that?" I asked.

"Because I listen to too much music or text when I shouldn't, and it's hurting me on the golf team and at school," she said.

Looking to the rest of the group, I asked, "Should she do this for a week or for three months?"

"A week," one of the teens said. "And once she's done that, then decide to do it for a month!"

Kids and Adults Together

If possible, learn to increase your decision-making capacity with a young person—teen or young adult. You'll never regret your investment of time, and learning together has several benefits.

First, it will keep you on task, as most adults want to set a positive follow-through example for a teen or young adult.

Second, you learn and retain something more quickly and thoroughly when you teach it to someone else—especially if you both get stuck and need to find someone else to help.

Third, you're setting an example that we are all supposed to give our time to selflessly help others.

A friend of mine, Mark, asked me how he and his 14-year-old son could do it. After a few minutes of explanation, he got it. I suggested that maybe his son, Taylor, who was high CONTROL and NONASSERTIVE and had trouble expressing himself to others, could make a decision related to doing something positive and unexpected for someone, and use his actions to show care and concern.

When Mark explained the idea to Taylor, he decided to do something for his mother, a nurse.

She often stopped at the grocery store after work and didn't get home until 10:30 p.m. Taylor, who normally went to bed at 10:00 p.m. because he was an early riser, decided to wait up for her. As soon as she pulled into the driveway, he opened her car door and brought in the groceries.

She was stunned.

"When he brought that bundle in, there was a million-dollar smile on his face," Mark beamed. "And my wife had no idea what was going on. Taylor thought that was really cool."

I told Mark, "Now you need to explain to him that everyone, even adults, need to grow in this area. Ask him to help you figure out a couple of decisions you could work on." And, they did.

Taylor's decision points out that a CONFIDENT decision can relate to how a person chooses to *communicate*. It doesn't always have to relate to how a person *performs* tasks. One friend helped one of the hostesses at his restaurant, who had trouble making eye contact. She agreed to make eye contact with every third person for the first week, then every other person the next week, and with every customer after several weeks.

A Decision for a Little Bit of Self-Discipline

I was brought up to believe that you weren't a "man" unless you cussed. I wasn't regularly profane and I'm not a prude. In my work, I've seen just about every kind of dark scenario one can imagine, and have seen people in their rawest state. But when I had kids, cussing just didn't seem to fit, so I decided that I needed to make a change.

I told my kids, who were young at the time, that swearing was wrong. They nodded their heads as they already knew that. Sandy never used a profane word—I mean never. I told them I was making a decision to change, and anytime they heard me use a cuss word, they were to respectfully point it out—but not in front of others—and I would do 100 sit-ups.

This was something they could relate to, as we often used "aerobic" discipline for punishments. Fifty sit-ups for talking back, being disobedient, and so on. It usually worked. It applied discipline and dissipated their anger-energy if they were upset. Another benefit is that at one time or another, all the kids did the most number of sit-ups in a minute in their grade when tested in their physical education classes at school.

One day I asked the boys to quickly help me replace some shingles on our neighbor's roof. He was out of town, and I told him that some of his shingles were loose and needed to be replaced. I agreed to buy and replace them.

A couple of days later, on a weekend, I could see that a storm was blowing in off the West Texas plains to Dallas. Once the gusts kicked up, the shingles would start peeling off.

I grabbed a ladder, hammer, nails, shingles, and the boys. Once we were all on the roof and knew our assignments, I started pulling the old and hammering in the new shingles fast and furiously. Erik took the old ones and kept them in a pile while Luke gave me the new ones. I could see lightening in the distance.

Bam! I hit my thumb and out came one of those prohibited words. The boys said nothing and we plowed ahead. Crash! The lightning was getting closer. Distracted, I smashed my thumb again and again.

Finished just minutes before the storm arrived, together we saved our neighbor's roof, and quickly scrambled down.

That's when Luke, who was 6, quietly said, "Fifteen hundred sit-ups Dad."

Multitasking, he had counted each word as he fed me the shingles, never letting up on the task at hand or reminding me of my pledge.

I hadn't yet stumbled across the concept of increasing decision making capacity, but I guess I intuitively knew that I had to set the tone for my boys. *And, yes, I did all 1500 without a complaint!*

Teaching Young People How to Strengthen Their Decision-Making Muscle

Originally, this decision-making process was applied with students who had RANDOM ACTOR traits in order to prevent school massacres, as explained in Chapter 22. Within weeks, most students were guided out of harm's way.

Teachers also found that teaching *any* student this process produced stunning results. They suggested that I teach this to all parents and teachers so they could teach their kids, and I did, specifically targeting grades 7–12, as well as college students. We also started training student leaders who weren't necessarily members of the student council, but rather those who students looked up to. It was especially effective when they learned the whole *KPS* at the same time, which takes one day. Here are some of the students' comments about their decisions:

- I have made some better decisions at work.
- I decided to apply to a college that I did not think I could get into.
- I waited to do a report. I made a B, but I know I could have done the work better to make an A. Now I am mad at myself.
- I've made some better decisions in sports since I've been trained.
- I can tell I have made better decisions in the way I think.
- I am analyzing things more before I make a decision now.
- I am more confident now that I have made the right decision.
- I have used this to get along with my parents—I stay at both of their houses at different times.
- I decided to go for a role in the musical—now I am ready to commit to it.
- I decided to tell someone something very important—I didn't want to.
- I studied for a test and it was a good decision—I did well.
- I have eliminated two colleges I was thinking about.
- I've decided to work hard for my future, even if my parents don't want to help me with it.
- This has really helped me decide what school to go to.
- I decided where to go and now I am going with more confidence.
- I decided to go to a different church retreat than my own. I met new friends and am very glad I did.

The thousands of criminal and aberrant group cases I've investigated and reviewed make it clear that most roads lead back to home. If more parents loved and cared for one another and their kids, I probably would have ended up on a completely different career path. There wouldn't have been a need to focus so much of my time on dangerous trends and finding solutions to help protect and turn lives around.

That's why it's really special when we can train kids with parents, teachers, and others in their community how to make confident decisions. It's one of the most powerful deterrents to at-risk behavior and an accelerant toward a life filled with meaning, selfless contributions, and cherished relationships.

Regardless if you are learning this competency with others or by yourself, be sure to single out one youngster or young adult and help mentor them to become a more CONFIDENT decision-maker. It will be one of the most rewarding things you've ever done.

CHAPTER TWENTY

CONFIDENT–CAUTIOUS/ FEARFUL Insights

[More on getting better]

When you've used the four wires for a while, you'll gain insights into people in general. Here are some that I've observed from using the CONFIDENT–CAUTIOUS/FEARUL gauge:

The Conviction to Win Is More Compelling Than the Passion to Win

In the late 1980s, the buzzword *passion*, as it is loosely used today, entrenched itself in our vocabulary. A motivational speaker at the time made "passion" a household word. Ironically, in his private life he was high FEARFUL. Instead of using words like commitment and conviction, which were the opposite of his decision-making trait, he used "passion" because it fit his emotional pitch. He *talked* confidently about having passion, millions were attracted, and the word stuck.

Today, people talk about doing something they have a passion for. Team leaders and athletic coaches encourage players to compete with passion.

To me, the use of the word in this context seemed off because it usually implied emotional attachment. In fact, the definition of passionate is:

influenced or dominated by intense emotion or strong feeling.[1]

As you've learned, emotion has to do with how we communicate. What if a person is high CONTROL and performs, but doesn't show emotion? Does this mean they are lacking—that they should quit, even though they are committed?

I've also watched many young people quit an endeavor because they *lost their passion*. Often it was just the easy way out, a result of misguided advice that they should only do something they are *passionate about* rather than something they are *committed to*. But life just doesn't work that way.

I asked a friend who was the director of operations for a major sports franchise: "Do you want players who play with passion, which can change on a dime depending upon on how they feel...or do you want players who play with conviction and commitment, who will give it everything regardless of the circumstances and how they feel?"

He responded by changing his passion message to a commitment/conviction message.

There is nothing wrong with emotion so long as it doesn't replace conviction. In athletics, business, or personal relationships, true commitment is based upon CONFIDENT decision-making and not emotions. In short:

Do something you are committed to, not just passionate about.
Passion is about emotions, which can change.
Commitment is about sustained action regardless of how you feel.

A few years before passion crept into our daily lexicon, I wrote about this connection in the last book I authored for magicians, *Korem Without Limits* (1985). Too often, magicians I knew started with an idea for an effect, but gave up before they created a method. Some of these chaps were brilliant, but many weren't CONFIDENT decision-makers. When faced with difficulty, they quit before reaching their goal. They stopped experimenting, researching, inquiring of colleagues, and so on because they didn't *feel* that they could solve the riddle. A number of times, I would take an idea they abandoned and innovate a method—not because I was smarter, just more committed.

My attitude was that the problem—creating something that looked impossible—didn't change. It was static, a nonmoving target. However, I could change and add to my insight through research and experimentation. This was my strategic advantage over the static problem. I never thought about how I *felt*, only thankful that I could be in the hunt! I'm certain that several years of solving what was seemingly impossible, while not the most important accomplishment, did create within me a mindset for how to approach many future challenges, especially when dealing with high-stakes life and death issues.

Here is what I wrote in the introduction to my book:

> A magazine advertisement for *Sports Illustrated* depicts an athlete running up the numbered stairs of a deserted stadium. Its caption reads, "How does it feel when the road to winning is the path of most resistance?"
>
> How one feels is irrelevant. Our feelings can change due to a fluctuation in the barometric pressure. The question should be, "How do you respond when the road to winning is the path of most resistance?"
>
> It is a common error to mistake resistance for limitations. Resistance merely requires more effort, while limiting what is possible will turn a brilliant idea into a pillar of salt....
>
> The point is, don't confuse resistance in achieving the desired effect with limitations that exist only in one's mind.
>
> Our art is supposed to present the [seemingly] impossible.

Identifying True Leaders Separate From Native Ability

A frequent complaint that I hear from organization leaders and athletic coaches is that they are regularly fooled when it comes to identifying leaders. One PR exec said he always ends up focusing on someone who communicates like himself. Once he learned about rapid-fire profiling, he identified his disconnect. He was reading communication traits, an integral part of his discipline, and left out the performance traits—where action and leadership style determine who is a leader and who isn't.

The most important trait to identify in a person who you think has leadership potential is: *Can he or she make confident decisions separate from their giftedness and expertise?* You want to know who can make confident decisions after careful considerations no matter what the situation is, because that is what true leaders do.

I've witnessed organizations that were seduced by talent and placed an exceptionally gifted person in a position of leadership who wasn't CONFIDENT, with disastrous results because they failed to read the CONFIDENT–CAUTIOUS/FEARFUL wire. When this person was asked to lead in their area of competency, they did well. The moment new factors were injected into the situation, they failed to lead.

Never Confuse Talent for CONFIDENT Decision-Making. They Aren't the Same.

True leaders have competency and are CONFIDENT decision makers. They may not be the most talented, but when they need to make a decision, they can pull the trigger.

Be Careful When Using the Word Ego

Don't confuse CONFIDENT decision-making with being egotistical. The phrase "he/she has a big ego" usually implies that a CONFIDENT person is also self-directed or self-absorbed. It's stereotyping to denigrate others by saying they have a big ego because they can make CONFIDENT decisions, as if only the selfish can do that. Unfortunately, we don't have a word for confident decision-making that is others-directed. For me, the word noble is a descriptor that is close, such as *she has a noble presence.*

The best leaders are competent,
CONFIDENT decision makers, and others-directed.

A Coach's Story

Every morning, at 5:30, the coach hit the gym. A burgeoning waistline needed trimming. Someone always beat him there: Raphael. One of his players.

"Good to see you coach. I'm getting after it," he said.

This went on for two weeks. Mike saw Raphael, and Raphael always had the same greeting.

Finally, the hall of fame football coach decided he'd had enough. He could see that Raphael's time in the gym wasn't paying off.

So when Raphael greeted him with the same consistent message, Mike grabbed him, pressed him against the wall, and with ferocity said, "Don't you ever confuse routine with commitment!

A bit tough. Yes. Appropriate for all situations? Maybe not. But for Raphael, it was a life lesson that took root. He learned never to confuse consistency with CONFIDENT decisions that manifest themselves in commitment, where grit is needed. When playing for another team a couple of seasons later, the first thing he said when he saw Mike was, "Coach, I remember the lesson."

Don't ever confuse routine with commitment!

Decision Fatigue: Maybe It Can Be Thwarted

Columnist and writer John Tierney, who wrote about faith and self-control (Chapter 10), coauthored with Roy Baumeister, a foremost social psychologist and head of that department at Florida State University, a book titled *Willpower.* Here's a fascinating insight from their book that was also discussed in an article by Tierney:

Three men doing time in Israeli prisons recently appeared before a parole board consisting of a judge, a criminologist and a social worker. The three prisoners had completed at least two-thirds of their sentences, but the parole board granted freedom to only one of them. Guess which one:

Case 1 (heard at 8:50 a.m.): An Arab Israeli serving a 30-month sentence for fraud.
Case 2 (heard at 3:10 p.m.): A Jewish Israeli serving a 16-month sentence for assault.
Case 3 (heard at 4:25 p.m.): An Arab Israeli serving a 30-month sentence for fraud.

There was a pattern to the parole board's decisions, but it wasn't related to the men's ethnic backgrounds, crimes or sentences. It was all about timing, as researchers discovered by analyzing more than 1,100 decisions over the course of a year. Judges, who would hear the prisoners' appeals and then get advice from the other members of the board, approved parole in about a third of the cases, but the probability of being paroled fluctuated wildly throughout the day. Prisoners who appeared early in the morning received parole about 65% of the time, while those who appeared late in the day were paroled less than 10% of the time.

The odds favored the prisoner who appeared at 8:50 a.m. — and he did in fact receive parole. But even though the other Arab Israeli prisoner was serving the same sentence for the same crime — fraud — the odds were against him when he appeared (on a different day) at 4:25 in the afternoon. He was denied parole, as was the Jewish Israeli prisoner at 3:10 p.m, whose sentence was shorter than that of the man who was released. They were just asking for parole at the wrong time of day.[2]

Tierney said that malicious or prejudicial behavior wasn't a factor, only the judges' fatigue. Baumeister has created an entire body of research on this phenomenon and related issues, and he presents solutions as well.

Tierney and Baumeister explain how decision fatigue affects quarterbacks' decisions late in a game, executive business decisions, and reduces our resistance to junk food at the grocery checkout counter after we've made numerous decisions about what to purchase.

> Decision fatigue helps explain why ordinarily sensible people get angry at colleagues and families, splurge on clothes...and can't resist the dealer's offer to rustproof their new car.[3]

Here are two reasons you need to be aware of decision fatigue when making snapshot reads:

Misreads of others. If someone is fatigued, this can lead to a misread. You think they're operating out of caution or fear, when it's really fatigue, like the judges experienced.

When people are under pressure, we can typically read their actual trait because they usually use what comes naturally. However, if a person is simply fatigued, this can lead to a misread. So it's best to consider whether the person has made a number of decisions before you make your read. As Tierney explains:

> No matter how rational and high-minded you try to be, you can't make decision after decision without paying a biological price. It's different from ordinary physical fatigue—you're not consciously aware of being tired—but you're low on mental energy. The more choices you make throughout the day, the harder each one becomes for your brain, and eventually it looks for shortcuts, usually in either of two very different ways. One shortcut is to become reckless: to act impulsively instead of expending the energy to first think through the consequences. (Sure, tweet that photo! What could go wrong?)[4]

Regarding his last observation, perhaps those who are UNCONVENTIONAL might more easily fall into this trap.

> The other shortcut is the ultimate energy saver: do nothing. Instead of agonizing over decisions, avoid any choice. Ducking a decision often creates bigger problems in the long run, but for the moment, it eases the mental strain. You start to resist any change, any potentially risky move—like releasing a prisoner who might commit a crime. So the fatigued judge on a parole board takes the easy way out, and the prisoner keeps doing time.[5]

And, perhaps those who are CONVENTIONAL are more susceptible to fall into this trap. Something to think about.

Baumeister's research also confirms an obvious factor: Low glucose levels in the blood, like right before lunch, can induce fatigue even if a person hasn't made a lot of decisions. This can affect your accuracy for any snapshot read, regardless of a person's profile, because you may be less focused.

Reducing the effect of decision fatigue on yourself when making snapshot reads. Using the gauges helps mitigate decision fatigue as you think: *Queen Elizabeth or Jim Carrey?* If you think CONTROL or EXPRESS instead, your accuracy will drop. First, because you're not using the gauge and may be operating out of emotions and how you feel. And second, because it requires more mental firepower to compare someone to two abstract words: CONTROL or EXPRESS.

Our data shows that at the *end* of a day of training people how to profile for the first time, their accuracy continues to *increase* even though they are *more fatigued* (and yes, the clips they are profiling are more difficult than those they profiled at the beginning of the workshop). Their decision-making continues to improve because of the *KPS* methodology: Compare someone to two extremes and make your reads quickly. Don't overthink it.

Just a hunch. I bet that if people had a steady regimen that increased their capacity to make CONFIDENT decisions, their ability to resist decision fatigue would measurably increase. (Another research project just waiting to be tackled!)

Government and CONFIDENT Decision Making

I addressed the state education auditors in a major state that affects education nationally. They said they were prohibited by law from spending more than 10% of their budget on tracking *success* rates. I told them, "This is crazy. It's like a major corporation stating in its annual report to stock holders that *95% of our subsidiaries didn't declare bankruptcy last year*!"

In a nutshell, though, that's government. It is a *control.* It's not about innovation, boldly stepping forward, or treating people uniquely. It is tasked with making sure the water is drinkable, the roads are constructed to standard, the traffic lights work, flight patterns are carefully monitored to ensure safety, etc. There are exceptions, but they are rare, like innovators at NASA whom I met when I gave a speech at the Johnson Space Center.

Now profile risk-adverse government. That's right: CAUTIOUS/FEARFUL and CONVENTIONAL. This isn't inherently bad, unless change is needed. If you're tasked with applying a solution in a government context, always look for the CONFIDENT decision maker who also has political clout to pull the trigger. Otherwise the whole exercise may be a waste of time.

I think the combination of government's CAUTIOUS/FEARFUL and CONVENTIONAL traits is one reason that people are attracted to presidential campaigns that promise CONFIDENT and UNCONVENTIONAL action in the future. Many are so burned out with the negative side of the CAUTIOUS/FEARFUL and CONVENTIONAL traits that they want a change. But, that's just my opinion. What's yours? What do you see?

Bullying or Sometimes a Lack of Confidence?

A complaint I regularly hear from teachers is that many kids who are identified as being bullied aren't being bullied.

When I was in the fifth grade, I played baseball almost every day during the summer. One day, some bullies came through the yard and started tossing our bikes, pushing kids over, and we all took off. That's one type of bullying. Some bullies demand kids give them their lunch money or face the consequences on the way home. Others terrorize kids verbally.

What the teachers were talking about, though, was everyday behavior—like a student criticizing another student or making fun of a student one time.

When teachers who have been trained by us took a closer look, almost without exception, they found that the student was either a CAUTIOUS or FEARFUL decision maker. And they found that teaching these kids how to make more CONFIDENT decisions, as explained in the last chapter, mitigated most situations, and complaints of bullying dropped. Additionally, the teachers said this gave them more time to focus on truly threatening cases, rather than so many frivolous complaints.

Additionally, they've pointed out that many kids "play" in an electronic bubble—video games and the like—and don't have kinetic face-to-face activities with real kids.

"It makes them weak," one teacher told me. "They're crippled when it comes to basic everyday interactions."

So the teachers' collective advice: Mentor kids how to make CONFIDENT decisions, decrease all the "electronic" time—from media in all its forms, to texting, to video games—and increase live human interactions in all phases of their lives.

Grace and the Bridled Stallion

A final thought about CONFIDENT decisions:

For those who want to make decisions more decisively, the concepts in this chapter are a humble pathway toward that goal. It's not a magical or overnight solution, but it works with steady application. If you decide to change, you can, regardless of your circumstances. I've assisted adults and kids from many types of difficult life circumstances in moving forward—from kids threatened by gangs, to moms raising kids after husbands deserted them, and even combat veterans plagued with post-traumatic shock.

As we are fortunate enough to increase our confidence, it must be used with *prautes*. That's a Greek word Aristotle used to describe the "mean between extremes." It's a unique type of gentleness, describing people who are angry at the right time and never at the wrong time. In other words: willful and thoughtful restraint.

Jesus used the word *prautes*, which we translate as "meek," in his Sermon on the Mount, when he said, "Blessed are the meek, for they shall inherit the earth."

We think of meek—*prautes*—as being weak, but that isn't what Jesus implied. During Jesus' life, *prautes* was also used to point out a bridled stallion—suggesting enormous power that is harnessed and restrained... bridled strength.

So as you or those you mentor increase their capacity to make CONFIDENT decisions, do so with an attitude of being harnessed and focused for the benefit of *others first*, restrained from arrogance and self-centeredness.

CHAPTER TWENTY-ONE

The Cautious Innovator

[Leading and guiding the world's fastest-growing profile]

Barry hired a new associate for his law firm, Elise, who was UNCONVENTIONAL.

"She's extremely intelligent, UNCONVENTIONAL, easily engages others in conversation, and is open to new ideas, which is why I hired her," Barry explains.

"What's frustrating is that she can't make decisive decisions. If she's open to new ideas, why can't she just act on them? It just doesn't make sense," he lamented.

In Barry's profession, time is critical and decision making must often be decisive. He called me for help after a friend introduced him to the *KPS*.

"So what have you tried?" I asked.

"I've used my ASSERTIVE trait to reassure her, and invested more time in educating her for the task at hand," he said.

"Did it work?"

"No, and I can't figure it out," he said. "She adapts to new concepts quickly until she needs to pull the trigger and make a decision."

Barry isn't alone in his frustration. It is shared by countless others, especially in fields that require innovation. He was stumped because Elise has the CAUTIOUS INNOVATOR traits—the world's fastest-growing profile, which few understand. You probably know a number of people like Elise and have experienced Barry's confusion. So let's learn about who they are and how to successfully interact with and lead adults and kids with this profile.

Why the Profile Appeared

Barry found Elise contradictory. She gravitated to and was energized by new ideas and innovation, yet when called upon to make a decision based on those ideas, she often hesitated. In past generations there have always been people with this profile, but very few—maybe 5% or less of the population.

As you learned in Chapter 8, the planet has shifted in recent years to the UNCONVENTIONAL trait. This is the seminal thread for innovation. Simultaneously, though, unprecedented numbers have been pressed to the CAUTIOUS/FEARFUL trait (Chapter 15). The merging of these two traits, which I first identified in schools in the mid-1990s, has resulted in up to 30% of those under 40 now having this profile. Together, these two traits have fostered the rise of the CAUTIOUS INNOVATOR profile: people who are 0–3 on the CAUTIOUS/FEARFUL wire and 0–5 on the UNCONVENTIONAL wire.

To get a picture of how many youths and adults have this profile, remember that up to 75% of every class of students currently has the UNCONVENTIONAL trait. Then, add those who are 0–3 CAUTIOUS/FEARFUL, which can be as high as 40% (another 10% or so are the extreme, 4–5 on the wire).[1] The result is a large number of adults and kids with the CAUTIOUS INNOVATOR traits.

A graphic illustrating the CAUTIOUS INNOVATOR performance type is shown on the next page.

People like Elise like to venture out and explore new and different ideas, experiences, and more—the UNCONVENTIONAL trait. But, her CAUTIOUS

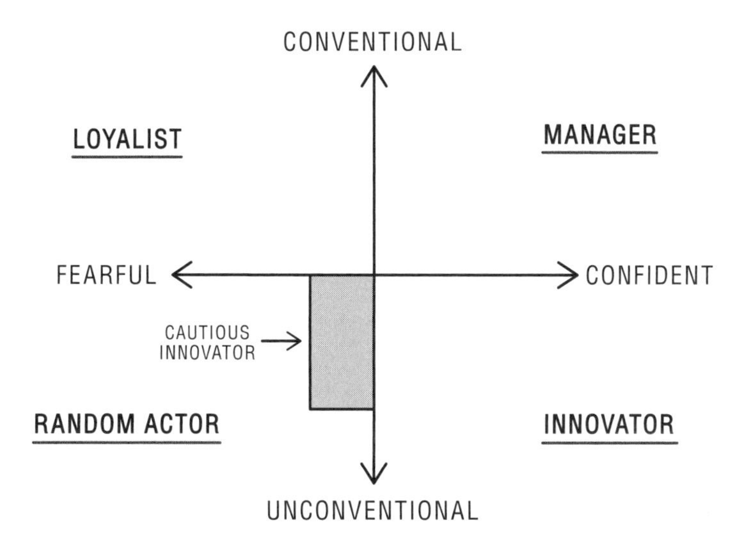

decision making tends to build tension in her. She wants to move forward, but her CAUTIOUS trait causes second thoughts. This can occur even with CAUTIOUS INNOVATORS who are just 1 or 2 on the CAUTIOUS/FEARFUL wire.

Unless you recognize and respect this dynamic, all kinds of misreads and crossed signals can creep in, like:

- She says she wants to do something different, so why doesn't she just do it?
- I thought he liked the idea/project/initiative, so why the hesitation?
- I thought he was a team player. Why can't he just move forward?
- Why is she resistant to our leadership?

In 1997, the trend appeared on my radar when thousands of teachers we trained described this phenomenon and the large number of students they struggled to instruct. A few years later, corporate team leaders described the same issue as more young people entered the workforce with the traits.

Today, the number of CAUTIOUS INNOVATORS in organizations is significant, and the disconnect when trying to lead them is sometimes incorrectly attributed to different values and generation gaps—Generation X and Y, Millennial, etc.—which is why few get it right. Any profile can appear in any "generation," while a trait disconnect is specifically related to a person's behavioral traits and requires a different leadership response.[2]

Leading CAUTIOUS INNOVATORS

The desire to explore new ideas and ventures, only to be restrained by CAUTIOUS decision-making, can be frustrating for anyone unless some simple themes are applied. That someone has the CAUTIOUS INNOVATOR profile doesn't mean they will be difficult to work with and lead. You simply must respect who they are.

CAUTIOUS INNOVATORS can be invaluable on a team where change is occurring. They can act as a check on whether or not the change/innovation is a positive, should be pursued, or reexamined, etc. INNOVATORS usually just charge forward (especially if high CONFIDENT). In innovative environments it's healthy to have team members who embrace innovation but are also comfortable taking another look.

While there is nothing inherently problematic with the CAUTIOUS INNOVATOR traits, some simple proven themes must be recognized and applied (which is what we do with any profile—treat them uniquely):

1. Don't confuse their desire to try something new—their UNCONVENTIONAL trait—with the fact they won't move forward quickly—their CAUTIOUS/FEARFUL trait.
2. They may require additional time to process a decision outside their area of competency. Build this into your plan and provide extra time to process decisions. (Remember, though, that they may be able to make CONFIDENT decisions in their area of competency, as explained in Chapter 15.)
3. As with anyone with the UNCONVENTIONAL trait, provide change, variability, flexibility while emphasizing innovating between the lines

with discipline (Chapter 12).

4. Build capacity to make CONFIDENT decisions separate from area of competency (Chapter 18).

If you have the CAUTIOUS INNOVATORS traits, the two best things you can do for yourself are to first increase your capacity to make CONFIDENT decisions (Chapter 18) and second, as necessary, review with others the first three suggestions listed and, together, develop a transparent strategy to enhance your productivity.

(If you decide to learn the entire *KPS*, be sure to take into consideration the communication part of the profile, which is briefly presented in Chapter 16 and detailed in *The Art of Profiling, 2nd ed.* to increase your effectiveness in working with any TYPE.)

CHAPTER TWENTY-TWO

Preventing Random Actor Attacks

Proven Solutions

> Don't be overcome by evil,
> but overcome evil with good.
> Romans 12:1

Two terrifying RANDOM ACTOR massacres stunned America in 2012. The first was in Aurora, Colorado, on July 12, when James Holmes, 24, dressed as the Joker from Batman comic lore, launched an assault on a movie theater, killing 12 and wounding 70, as they were watching the midnight premiere of *Dark Knight Rises,* the new Batman movie. One of those slain, Jessica Ghawi, a 22-year-old aspiring journalist, survived another rampage a month before while on vacation in Toronto, where 2 were killed and 5 wounded at the upscale Eaton Centre mall.

I immediately called the executive director of one of the nation's leading education associations and warned that the Aurora attack would probably trigger the worst year ever for school massacre threats and unprecedented lethality. My prediction was based on 20 years of tracking this trend.

You never want to get this type of prediction right, but it was.

Rampage threats by students with malevolent intent directed at schools jumped 50%, to 150 per day. (It was 50 per day at the time of the 1999 Columbine High School attack and had increased to 100 by the time of the Aurora attack.)[1]

Then, the second unprecedented attack descended on Sandy Hook Elementary, in Newtown, Conn., where Adam Lanza, 20, killed 20 students, 6 staff, and wounded 2 before turning his gun on himself. In the immediate aftermath, RANDOM ACTOR school assaults and threats spread across the country and continued through 2014. The 2013–2014 school year was the worst in U.S. history for the combined number of attacks and threats, and a 2014 Associated Press study found that school security measures had virtually no effect on the increase.[2] In the midst of all this, there were cries for increased gun control and even from some communities to ban all guns. Never mind all the bomb threats and devices found for years, or that the Columbine attack was supposed to be a bombing attack.

The Columbine killers made IEDs out of propane tanks and smuggled them into the school cafeteria disguised as bowling balls in bags. The teens had built and successfully detonated the bombs in a test run. The only reason that the bombs didn't explode, which would have killed 400–500 students and staff, was the manufacturer had changed the hands on the timer clocks to plastic, so the timers didn't make contact. When the bombs didn't detonate, the killers entered the school and committed the assault with guns and pipe bombs, which were originally intended to kill students and staff as they fled from the bombing.

For years, I've warned in countless speeches that if you take away guns, they'll use knives, like they do in China. The day of the horrific Newtown elementary school attack, there was another of the dozens of school attacks in China with knives, butchering over 20.

So what do we do—ban tableware?

If you do, RANDOM ACTOR attackers will turn to explosives (Holmes's apartment was trip-wired with explosives) or gas in air ducts (like one case I investigated). In reaction, one prominent school district budgeted $55 million to pay for panic buttons and bomb-resistant film for all windows. What good will that do you when you can build explosives with what is *inside* the school?

The most important issue is to find out what's is going on *inside* a person's mind and to reach that person before he or she (but typically males) attacks.[3]

Since the early 1980s, I've tracked the steady building of this trend, and in 2005, my book *Rage of the Random Actor—Disarming Catastrophic Acts and Restoring Lives* was published. In 2014, the FBI released its study quantifying the increase in the attacks.[4] Notable RANDOM ACTOR attacks include:

- 1997, Pearl High School, Pearl, Miss., 1997, school attack that started the global trend
- 1999, Columbine High School, Littleton, Colo.
- 9–11 attacks on America, 2001; 19 terrorists armed with box knives, cunning, and hand-to-hand combat techniques killed nearly 3,000 using passenger jets
- 2002, "DC Snipers," former vet and a teenager, launched attacks terrorizing an entire region of the U.S. for weeks; 17 slain and 10 wounded
- 2007, Virginia Tech, Blacksburg, Va.; 32 students and staff slain and 17 wounded by a student
- 2009, Virginia Tech, first beheading on U.S. campus, by doctoral student
- 2013, Boston Marathon bombing; 3 dead, more than 260 injured
- 2012, Aurora, Colo., and Newton, Conn., attacks
- 2014, Murrysville, Pa., school stabbing rampage, injures 22 (inspired by numerous school rampages with knives in China)
- 2014, Santa Barbara City College, student slays 6 and injures 13 with knife, gun, and his car
- 2014, summer, ISIL terrorist beheadings
- 2014, September, first U.S. beheading by an American at terrorist urgings

Note: Killers' names aren't provided out of respect for victims and their families.

Many more attacks will likely occur in the future because approximately 6% of all K–12 students have the RANDOM ACTOR traits, which will continue to feed the pipeline for incidents and threats (more on this later). If an incident occurred once every few years, I wouldn't have included this chapter. But, it's because of the *combination* of the statistically significant number of students with the RANDOM ACTOR traits, the chronic number of threats with malevolent intent, and regularity of the attacks, that this chapter is included.

Obviously, not all students or adults who have the traits will commit violent acts, but virtually all perpetrators of these attacks do possess the traits, and those who aren't violent still need our help. It's for this reason that I've spent most of my time helping K–12 schools fish upstream and reach kids before they ever hatch a plot, to guide them out of the destructive traits.

In this chapter, you will learn the RANDOM ACTOR traits; who people with the traits inherently like and don't like and why; the 3-point intervention that stop attacks, threats, and building evacuations, and what guides most people with the traits out of the destructive profile, without stereotyping or false positives. Together, these concepts have saved many lives in the workplace, schools, and military environs here and abroad.

Identifying the Traits and the Lethal Pattern

What do the following have in common: suicide bombers, U.S. post office shooters going "postal," company mass shooters, school rampage shooter/bombers, and most serial killers?

Answer: Most have the RANDOM ACTOR profile that I identified in the early 1990s. (My first case was in the early 1980s, but the term RANDOM ACTOR hadn't yet been applied.)

You identify the RANDOM ACTOR traits. As you've learned, the *KPS* helps you identify a person's *talk* separate from the *walk*—how people prefer to communicate separate from how they perform and make decisions.

Question: Logically, which part of a person's profile, like the Columbine killers, will kill: the talk or the walk? Which part of the profile should you focus on? His talk—how he communicates—or his walk—how he operates and make decisions?

Answer: Obviously it's the walk. People kill with actions and decisions.

Most news accounts immediately after an attack, though, focus on communication actions like *he was very polite* or *he seemed like such a nice guy*. Unfortunately, these observations don't tell us anything about how someone will perform...how he will act. For example, on September 26, 2014, a RANDOM ACTOR homegrown terrorist, who professed the Islamic faith, beheaded an employee he worked with in the Oklahoma City suburb of Moore. It was the first such beheading in U.S. history. On September 28, before details about the killer were released, I gave a presentation at the annual conference of school administrators and school board members of a major state. I told them to watch for news reports that focused on the killer's communication actions. The next day, a superintendent texted me this excerpt from a news account in his hometown newspaper (left).

for an Oklahoma City Islamic group said Saturday that Nolen was a frequent worshipper at a mosque the group maintains and that he remembers the suspect as "a little weird."
"He was a nice, quiet, low-key guy," said Saad Mohammed, director of information for the Islamic Society of Greater Oklahoma City. "He acted a little odd," Mohammed said,

So let's profile the two walk traits using the CONVENTIONAL–UNCONVENTIONAL and CONFIDENT–CAUTIOUS/FEARFUL gauges.

First trait. When someone commits a mass attack and commits suicide in the process, is this a CONVENTIONAL or UNCONVENTIONAL act? The answer is UNCONVENTIONAL—and it's always *extremely* UNCONVENTIONAL—4 or higher on the gauge. As you've learned, there is nothing inherently destructive about the UNCONVENTIONAL trait, but those who act out destructively or violently usually show the dark side of the trait, such as anarchistic and reckless.

Second trait. When attackers commit homicidal-suicidal attacks and lament that the world is against them, there's no hope, they're isolated and in despair, or they were always being bullied, from which side of the CONFIDENT–CAUTIOUS/FEARFUL gauge are they making decisions? The obvious answer is extreme FEARFUL or paranoia, which, as you learned in Chapter 15, may be a diagnosable condition like paranoid schizophrenia, or just plain fearful.

The toxic mix. People who are UNCONVENTIONAL usually prefer to do things that are different, but their high FEARFUL trait holds them back from moving forward outside their areas of competency. This is a constant tension in their lives. Then, when you add stressors—like rejection, loss of employment, marital discord, family disintegration—troubled and severely irrational behavior can be triggered.

Different ways the traits present. As you've also learned, there are several ways a person can use his or her traits, which is a reason why "warning lists" of what to look for to determine if someone is escalating often fail. However, no matter how a person displays being high FEARFUL when making decisions, when you make a read based upon the extremes of your gauge, you can read that they are FEARFUL.

Why the RANDOM ACTOR identifier was chosen. I originally designated the RANDOM ACTOR profile in the *KPS* to advise an executive to think twice before negotiating with this person as he or she may be unstable and unreliable. The identifier was selected because during negotiations, this person will often "random act" and do whatever it takes to appear CONFIDENT. It wasn't originally developed to spot mass killers who commit "random acts of murder."

How the lethal pattern was identified. In the early 1990s, leaders in the Society for Human Resource Management, the largest North American HR association, asked me if it was possible to use the *KPS* to identify a mass company shooter, as the trend had just appeared a few years before. The trend actually started in the post office which is how the pop phrase *going postal* was coined in 1993.[5]

When they provided me case studies to review, a pattern became clear that took me by surprise: Virtually every killer had the two RANDOM ACTOR traits. More importantly, by asking one question, I found a critical pattern that has saved many lives. My question was this: Who else in the delivery business doesn't have massacres?

Answer: FedEx and UPS.

These two companies have personnel working for them who have the RANDOM ACTOR profile, but they weren't committing attacks (with the exception of a FedEx pilot in 1995 who tried, but failed, to fly a plane into corporate headquarters).[6]

I discovered another pattern in other companies: There were mass shooters on assembly lines and in accounting departments, but never the art department.

With more digging, I found three themes at FedEx and in art departments that were part of their culture that deterred the rage of a potentially violent person with the RANDOM ACTOR traits.

At the same time, I was doing research for my 1995 book, *Suburban Gangs—The Affluent Rebels*. That's when I noticed a statistically significant number of students in schools with the RANDOM ACTOR traits. Concerned, I gave many speeches and interviews to major education and law enforcement groups, and wrote journal articles and a section in *Suburban Gangs* on what I believed was going to be a new terrorist trend.

In a 1996 op-ed published in the *Dallas Morning News* and more than 200 other newspapers, I wrote: *The choice is taking preemptive action now or engaging a new form of terrorism in the future—the very near future.*[7] In 1997, I included additional observations in the first edition of

The Art of Profiling, and three months after its release, the school attack in Pearl, Miss., a suburb of Jackson, started the global trend,[8] followed by others, including the 1999 massacre at Columbine High School.

How difficult is it to identify someone with the two RANDOM ACTOR traits? You've learned that people who have extreme traits, like Jim Carrey or Queen Elizabeth II, are easy to read because their behavior is *extreme*. Virtually no one profiles Jim Carrey as CONTROL or Queen Elizabeth II as EXPRESS. The good news is, it is the same for people with the two extreme RANDOM ACTORS traits.

Because the traits are extreme, since 1997, I have never received a call from someone who was professionally trained to use our system who misidentified someone as a potentially dangerous RANDOM ACTOR who wasn't—that's from a population of more than 25,000 professionals. False positives are possible, but unlikely.

Regarding RANDOM ACTORS who kill, they *always* display the two RANDOM ACTOR traits to the extreme, and there is almost always a visible behavioral paper trail long before they commit a crime. This observation is based upon the review of hundreds of cases, from workplace and school killers to suicide terrorists. The reason some dangerous RANDOM ACTORS aren't on anyone's radar is that they may have pleasing communication actions that mask their rage and intent.

Go back and reread the Steven Kazmierczak case at the beginning of Chapter 3. It's a typical example that fooled a 20-year veteran campus police chief, a leading criminal justice scholar, and the Associated Press; none were trained and tested to make accurate snapshot reads, nor did they know the RANDOM ACTOR traits.

Notice that the criminal justice scholar made the common mistake of focusing on Kazmierczak's communication actions and how he performed *in his area of competency*, which is the wrong part of the equation. Like the photos shown on the next page, Kazmierczak could *talk* pleasantly.

The police chief said Kazmierczak was "fairly normal.... There were no red flags. He was an outstanding student. He was someone who was revered by the faculty and staff and students alike."[9]

The Associated Press wrote: "If there is such a thing as a profile of a mass murderer, Steven Kazmierczak didn't fit it."

For years before the attack, Kazmierczak displayed the RANDOM ACTOR traits—going back to his high school days when he mutilated himself and was treated at a psychiatric center. He wore a large tattoo that displayed self-mutilation, revealing both his high UNCONVENTIONAL and FEARFUL traits. In college, he wrote a paper, entitled "Self-Injury in Correctional Settings: 'Pathology' of Prisons or Prisoners?" which examined why inmates self-injure themselves, like cutters.

If you tried to make a read on him by just his smile, how he talked to you, or his interest in his studies, you might never see his paranoia. But if a professor looked at his tattoo and paper, he or she could have inquisitively asked: "This is an interesting topic. How did you come up with the idea?" This exact type of thoughtful attention, coupled with using the prevention strategies, was used by another professor to deter a serious situation on another major campus.

2013 Boston Marathon attacker. Another case completely missed was the teen who, with his brother, committed the Boston Marathon bombing attack, and whose traits were in plain view for months. An engineering student, his grades plummeted, and on his social media page, read by many, he displayed paranoia and wrote about nightmares, "zombie apocalypse" dreams, and the end of the world. Two months before the attack, he wrote: "I killed Abe Lincoln during my two hour nap. #intensedream."

How many people have the RANDOM ACTOR traits, and are they all violent and mentally ill? Regarding violence, the short answer is, thankfully most people who have the traits are not violent, although they usually lead troubled personal lives because of their high FEARFUL trait. Presently, the best estimate is that up to 6% of all students have the RANDOM ACTOR traits. In the adult population, it's probably around 4%. This is based upon numerous studies I've reviewed, and the estimates of education and corporate team leaders and counselors we've trained.[10]

Regarding mental illness, most adults and students who have the traits, including many who commit attacks, do *not* have a DSM-V diagnostic disorder like paranoid schizophrenia. This was true of one of the Columbine killers, and is one reason those who kill are often missed by mental health practitioners.

How many threats? Currently during the school year, up to 250 times a day or more, students with the RANDOM ACTOR traits make threats with malevolent intent and are caught with plots, weapons, or explosives to take out their schools.[11] At the time of the 1999 Columbine attack, the number of threats per day was about 50, steadily increased to 100 by the July 2012 Batman movie attack, and immediately jumped to 250–400 after the December 2012 Newtown attack at Sandy Hook Elementary. It remains at that level in 2015. For a number of reasons, only a small fraction of the threats are reported in the media.[12] In companies/organizations, the number of threats overall can range from 25–100 times a day. In foreign lands, homicide-suicide attacks are an everyday occurrence and virtually all who commit them have the RANDOM ACTOR profile.

Who They Inherently Like and Don't Like and Why

In 1998, I found a distinct pattern in which schools did and didn't have mass shooting or bombing threats, and why. In fact, it turned out that they unknowingly used the same three themes as FedEx and art departments (explained a little bit later).

And here's the odd part: globally, most attacks occur in the safest locales—suburbs and small towns and rarely, if ever, in poor, inner-city communities. If you look at the grid below that shows the two PERFORMANCE traits, which quadrant do you think a person with the RANDOM ACTOR traits will inherently dislike and why?

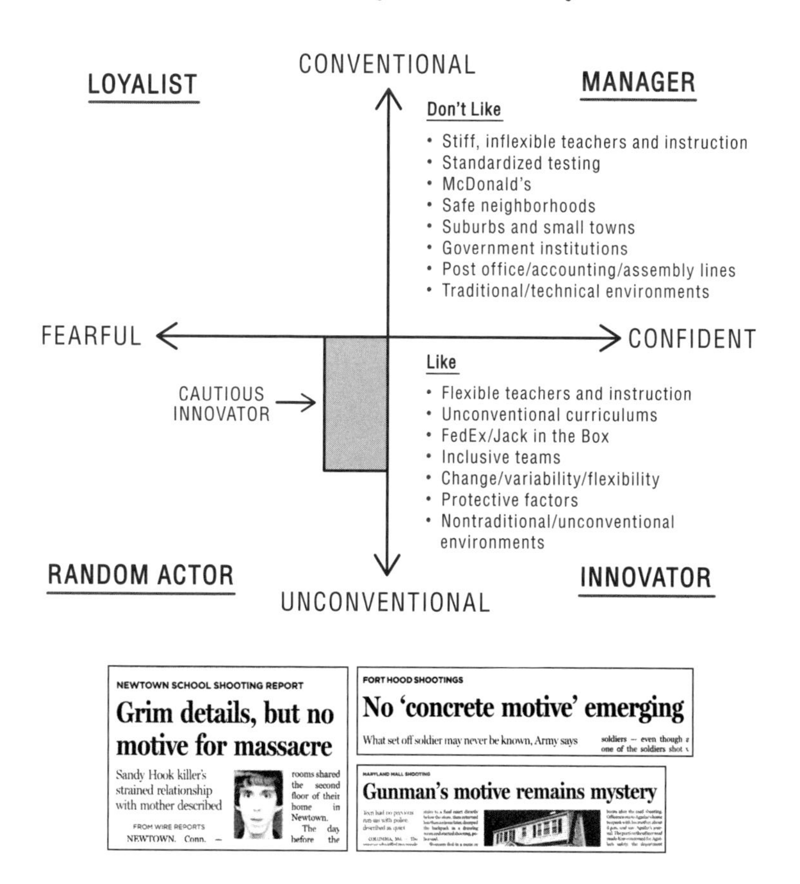

The answer is anyone or anything that represents the MANAGER quadrant because it has the polar-opposite traits of the RANDOM ACTOR—CONFIDENT and CONVENTIONAL. If you look at the issue through this lens, who they attack isn't a mystery. They typically attack their behavioral opposite. What is persistently irrational, though, is the absence of a rational motive, which is what causes difficulty for law enforcement and panic in the public psyche. Police chiefs are almost always quick to point out if an attack is or isn't random, to quell public panic when it isn't a RANDOM ACTOR attack.

Here's a little more detail on the suburbs and small towns, which are the locations of most school and company attacks, and where suicide attackers are typically recruited:

> **Suburbs:** neatly cut lawns; people confident that they have money in their pocket; sedate shopping malls; safe neighborhoods
> **Small Towns:** little change or variability; people are confident and secure—don't lock their doors; traditional; few distractions from one's troubles

It should be clearer now why historically the post office has incidents but rarely FedEx or UPS. Or American Airlines, but not Virgin Airlines. Or the assembly line and accounting, but not the art department. If, however, a UPS or FedEx station operates like a poorly run post office, risk goes up.[13] Think of it this way: McDonald's has had attacks, but not Jack in the Box because it's *out of the box.*

In 1998, following the behavioral paper trail pattern in schools, I identified an entire population of thousands of schools that rarely, if ever, has RANDOM ACTOR threats, let alone attacks. In fact, not one of these schools has had an attack. And here is the shocker: This is a specific type of school that only serves at-risk students! They are called alternative education campuses.

In most states, these campuses educate students who have been in fights, arrested, used drugs, and have engaged in other at-risk behavior. In other words, the safest campuses in North America are alternative campuses that by definition only have troubled students. More importantly, these campuses, like FedEx and specific areas in other organizations, were intuitively deploying three themes that deters the rage of a person with the RANDOM ACTOR traits!

The most important Columbine story rarely told: Why they didn't kill Brooks Brown. Brooks ran with the Columbine killers before the attack, but he didn't subscribe to their plots of terrorism—even turning them in for making threats.

The day of the attack, Brooks, a senior, was outside the school having a smoke. When the bombs failed to detonate at 11:17 a.m, the teen killers got out of their car in the parking lot, walked up to the school, saw Brooks and said, "Brooks, I like you now. Get out of here. Go home."[14]

Left: Class picture with the killers on top and Brooks in the bottom left. It's a remarkable contrast that shows the difference between Brooks who is an INNOVATOR, and the killers, who were RANDOM ACTORS. **Lower Right:** Another photo of Brooks.

They didn't kill Brooks—the first person they encountered.

OK, you profile Brooks. What was his profile? Right. He was an INNOVATOR. He *wasn't* their opposite. His profile, coupled with the fact that he never personally denigrated the teen killers, was a major factor that saved his life. He only turned them in for their actions and never attacked them personally.

Psych Ward Effect

One of the most troubling and terrifying by-products of the growing RANDOM ACTOR trend is what I dubbed the Psych Ward Effect. Here is an excerpt from *Rage of the Random Actor* that puts it in context:

> Over 3,000 people died at the hands of terrorists on 9–11, and then the unexpected happened: As if on command, thousands of American citizens over the next several weeks physically and psychologically attacked and threatened their own country. Some phoned in bomb threats. Others tried to hijack or commandeer Greyhound buses and passenger jets. Anthrax-laden letters killed or put in harm's way postal workers, media personnel, and members of Congress, forcing the US Post Office to respond to over 10,000 anthrax threats and pranks. Every local, state, and federal law enforcement agency was stretched to the breaking point. In Dallas, a few weeks after 9–11, I was nearly hit by a drunk driver in a new Cadillac. When I called 911, I was told that law enforcement was so overwhelmed with threats that it was unlikely they would be able to respond.
>
> What has gone largely unnoticed by most North Americans is that this period was one of three major and unparalleled outbreaks of irrational threats and attacks in just three years—1999–2002, totaling in the tens of thousands.[15]

The second outbreak of threats and attacks occurred after the Columbine attack, when an estimated 5,000–7,500 North American schools were closed because of RANDOM ACTOR threats, and the majority were student threats. The third outbreak appeared in both North America and Europe during the "DC Sniper" attacks in Washington, DC, Maryland, and Virginia—and many similar flurries have occurred on a smaller scale since then. Nothing like this happened during the immediate aftermath of the 1941 Pearl Harbor attack because only a fractional portion of the population had the RANDOM ACTOR traits. But that has changed. Briefly, here is what happens:

Imagine if a destabilized patient is placed in the middle of a stabilized psychiatric ward. What can happen? Others around the patient become destabilized and start acting out, as portrayed in the movie *One Flew Over the Cuckoo's Nest.* It's *not* a copycat effect, as patients act out in their own way.

After a RANDOM ACTOR attack, it is common for some people with the

RANDOM ACTOR traits to act out in irrational ways, and most can't tell you why they are doing it. It's a unique type of contagion of fear that severely agitates their FEARFUL trait.

Before the Columbine attack, I stated in speeches that when the first really big school attack occurred, it would set off the paranoia of students with the RANDOM ACTOR traits. *Why* they act out isn't a copycat effect, but the *specific way* they act out might be influenced by other attacks. For example, on the heels of many Chinese knife rampages, in 2014, a Murrysville, Pa., high school student went on a rampage, slashing 20 other students.

Only one North American region didn't have school threats. Here is what is stunning: During the weeks after 9–11, only one region in the United States *didn't* have students making rampage bombing/shooting threats directed at their schools. It was an entire region in a major state where over 2,500 educators deployed the RANDOM ACTOR violence prevention strategies and the 3-point intervention that follows. In addition, since 1997, virtually every school system that has deployed these themes experienced the following outcomes for 3–5 years: severe reduction of threats with malevolent intent; severe reduction in school evacuations; severe reduction in behavioral referrals; significant increase in academic performance.[16]

In essence, they deployed the themes I first uncovered at FedEx and alternative education schools. If I hadn't identified a proven strategy to stop these threats and guide adults and kids out of the destructive traits, I never would have written *Rage of the Random Actor*. Identifying the trend without any hope of preventing attacks is terrifying in light of all the threats facing us here and abroad.

The Three-Point Intervention

The three themes can be deployed anywhere—from schools to neighborhoods to organizations of all types. Schools are the first priority, to reach students before they journey out into life. Organizations, both private and public, are the second priority because you can reach large groups of people with resources and personnel. The third priority is individual efforts, where we can help someone in need. Additionally, many who have read *Rage of the Random Actor* and self-identified that they had the traits, have applied the interventions and guided themselves out of the destructive traits.

Remember, it isn't determinate that a person with the RANDOM ACTOR traits will ever commit an act of violence. Most don't, but they *all* need help because of their high FEARFUL trait. In schools, for example, if we help our 6%, we will *also* mitigate risk for student-led RANDOM ACTOR incidents by default.

If you know someone with the traits, consider how you or someone you trust can assist them. It's extraordinary how such simple themes can have such a profound effect on someone's life. Additional resource suggestions are provided at the end of the chapter.

1. Change, Variability, and Flexibility (CVF). Remember this theme from Chapter 12 and how it's applied with people who are UNCONVENTIONAL? It has an especially positive effect for people with the RANDOM ACTOR traits.

Unlike most accounting departments and assembly lines, art departments have lots of variety and they usually work as an inclusive team. Stiff, autocratic, and poorly run post offices, assembly lines, and accounting offices are just the opposite. This is significant because CVF accommodates the UNCONVENTIONAL trait, which people with this trait appreciate.

As you'll recall, it was teachers who applied CVF first with students with the RANDOM ACTOR traits, and then with all their students who were UNCONVENTIONAL. In a group environment, such as schools or the workplace, people with RANDOM ACTOR traits receive CVF often without their even knowing how it's helping them.

When applying CVF, teachers have learned *not* to recruit a high CONVENTIONAL student to sit next to and assist a student with the RANDOM

ACTOR traits—usually a teacher's natural tendency. Teachers tend to recruit the most organized students to provide assistance to others. This can inadvertently cause fireworks, especially if the student is also CONFIDENT—which is the MANAGER PERFORMANCE type and the *opposite* of the RANDOM ACTOR type. A student with the MANAGER traits might be able to assist a little further down the road, but it's typically not the best option at the front end. Teachers have found it's best to use a student who is UNCONVENTIONAL and CONFIDENT, but who is disciplined to assist.

2. Protective factors are provided. In companies, this means inclusive team leadership rather than exclusive, dismissive leadership. In schools, this means no student gets isolated, which is often an even greater risk factor than bullying.

While bullying can be a tipping point—a trigger—for an attack, like the Pearl, Miss. case, many school attackers and kids who threaten attacks haven't been bullied, contrary to the popular myth. A major 2014 German study of 136 cases across 13 countries found it was a factor in 30% of the RANDOM ACTOR school rampages. An even greater factor was *ineffective teacher interactions* like conflicts with teachers—a factor in 43% of the attacks.[17] (Additionally, there are no known rampages where a student who was bullied, but *didn't* have the RANDOM ACTOR traits, committed an attack. None.)

Student isolation combined with ineffective teacher interactions, and then troubled peer interactions piled on, increases the risk of an attack. This is especially exaggerated in small towns where there aren't a lot of options to redirect a troubled mind.

Protective factors in a school can include inclusive team leadership, mentors, students befriending a student, and so on.

If someone steps in and befriends a troubled person, irrational rage almost always dissipates over time. Protective factors diminish the irrational behavior of the high FEARFUL trait.

3. Mentor how to make CONFIDENT decisions outside area of expertise/giftedness. Remember this theme from Chapter 15? This not only minimizes fear, but over time a person moves out of the RANDOM ACTOR profile into the CAUTIOUS INNOVATOR or INNOVATOR profiles. The idea is to help someone in small, bite-sized steps learn to make decisions out of confidence.

Most students will move out to about 3 or 4 FEARFUL in weeks when mentored how to make CONFIDENT decisions and this is applied as part of their everyday experience at school and in the classroom. Extreme cases may take months, but violent acts or other severely at-risk behavior rarely, if ever, occur during the intervention efforts.

In companies and other organizations, it usually requires longer for someone to move to at least 3 or 4 FEARFUL, but again, severe destructive behaviors usually don't appear during intervention efforts.

Think about it. Imagine that you are extremely UNCONVENTIONAL and you were given more CVF, and someone personally helps you learn to make CONFIDENT decisions that help diminish your fear. Wouldn't it make you more stable and feel validated as a person who has worth and a place in this world? That's why you never get complaints from people who receive the interventions.

For those who have been severely traumatized and can't conceptualize making a CONFIDENT decision, have them make observations of those they know or those they have observed who have made CONFIDENT decisions. Have them write them down and articulate their observations in their own words. And, in the most extreme cases, guidance may be needed to point out people who make CONFIDENT decisions.

Can you now see why the concept of making CONFIDENT decisions separate from one's area of expertise was placed high on the priority list to help organizations and schools? It was first applied to help prevent attacks. Then, teachers and organization team leaders realized that schools and organizations improved as a whole when this became a part of the culture.

A big-picture concept to remember is that the first two themes, CVF and protective factors, can make a person feel safer, more valued, and included with everyone else. But unless that person learns to make CONFIDENT decisions, he or she will still have the RANDOM ACTOR traits. The first two themes will earn you their immediate respect. Helping them with the third theme will earn you respect for a lifetime.

There isn't any perfect solution to any pervasive problem, but the 3-point intervention has proven its mettle. On a personal note, I have worked directly with a number of students and none reverted to any high risk behavior. With some reflection, I realized something else. Over 25,000 educators and several thousand law enforcement professionals have been trained to deploy the research and they have touched hundreds of thousands of students, if not many multiples more, since 1997. While not a scientific survey, none of their students, to my knowledge, has ever committed a RANDOM ACTOR attack. What is certain, though, is that almost none of the schools in which those educators served had an evacuation or a threat with malevolent intent for three years after they deployed the interventions. My prayer is that many more professionals will reach kids while they can still be reached—and before they reach adulthood.

No Suicides on Five U.S. Bases in Warrior Transition Units

A version of the intervention strategy was deployed by Major Steve Munson across five major bases in the Warrior Transition Units from 2007–2009, when military suicides were at their peak during deployments to Afghanistan and Iraq. These units were created for wounded and injured military personnel who often had the highest suicide rates because of severe despondency and uncertainty. They were the only bases that didn't have suicides in their units for almost three years.[18]

Final Thoughts and Additional Resources

This short "public service announcement" chapter was included because I've found that when even a small amount of information has been provided in a short journal article or speech, attacks were averted because someone connected the dots or someone knew someone who was troubled and was able to get them help that worked.

If a person with the RANDOM ACTOR traits is talented, he or she may make a valuable contribution, as is common in the arts, but will still have extreme difficulty in his or her personal life. For this reason, resist the temptation to turn away when you have the opportunity to help. I have personally helped many people directly over the years, and I have never regretted the investment of time in another person's life.

If you've self-identified that you have the two traits, don't despair. Most people who work on making CONFIDENT decisions find that they experience relief in many areas of their life. Examples of people who have done this are provided in *Rage of the Random Actor.* That book covers the full spectrum of the issue, from neighborhoods to schools to organizations to combat. It details the many cases where attacks have been averted and, more importantly, lives have been restored through the application of this research.

Another helpful book that's like the "Cliff's Notes" on the student intervention side of the issue is *If Only I Had Known—The Life-Saving Solution That Thousands Have Used to Stop School Massacres*, by Dr. William Dodson. It is a short book that covers the basics for applying these strategies in schools. Dr. Dodson was the superintendent of Pearl Public Schools, where the RANDOM ACTOR attack occurred that triggered the global trend. Regarding the attack by 16-year-old Luke Woodham at Pearl High School, Dr. Dodson wrote: "I am certain that if our counselor and Luke's teachers had known this profile and the intervention, Luke would have received assistance, he would have responded, and young lives would have been saved." It was for this reason that he chose the title for the book, *If Only I Had Known.*

Postscript

On the right is the cover of the workshop notes provided to educators I trained just before the 9–11 attacks in the only region that didn't have RANDOM ACTOR threats, as already noted. I titled the second day of the training: "Ground Zero, The Student Response." I was trying to convey what I envisioned if we didn't get this right—that students and young people would be recruited to commit horrific attacks. At the time the average age of a suicide attacker was 17–24. I had no idea that the location of the later destroyed World Trade Center in New York City would be called "Ground Zero."

To provide a visual of what I saw coming, I showed the educators a front-page story about teens and young adults who descended on Seattle during the November 1999 World Trade Organization talks. The ensuing riots shut down the downtown area. Many of these young people had the RANDOM ACTOR traits. I met the mother of one of the rioters by chance on a flight. The vice president of a major company, she expressed horror at her son's actions, whom she confirmed had the RANDOM ACTOR traits as did others in his group whom she later met. Additionally, someone stole a propane truck, which was a factor in Seattle's decision not to hold a downtown Millennial celebration.

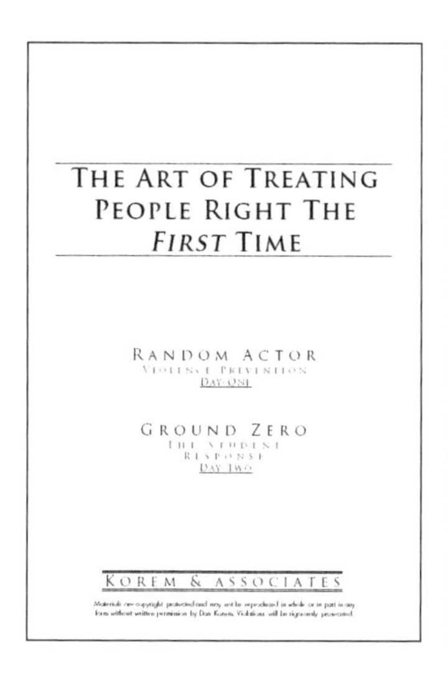

THE ART OF TREATING PEOPLE RIGHT THE *FIRST* TIME

RANDOM ACTOR
VIOLENCE PREVENTION
DAY ONE

GROUND ZERO
THE STUDENT RESPONSE
DAY TWO

KOREM & ASSOCIATES

Materials are copyright protected and may not be reproduced in whole or in part in any form without written permission by Dan Korem. Violations will be rigorously prosecuted.

Violent protests disrupt trade talks

Associated Press: Eric Draper

Seattle police use tear gas to push back protesters downtown. City officials declared an emergency and imposed an overnight curfew, but some protesters were still marauding through downtown late into the night.

National Guard called in after Seattle ceremonies are halted

CHAPTER TWENTY-THREE

Cross-Cultural Profiling

[Color-blind, but culturally astute]

Traveling abroad on vacation? Negotiations or meeting new partners in a foreign country? Or, maybe you want to better understand new neighbors who have an accent. It's a certainty, based upon our data, that most people (up to 80%) will stereotype those from another culture if they can't rapid-fire profile. This often results in the inability to interact with someone based upon who they really are.

The purpose of this short chapter is to help you quickly profile and understand someone in the context of his or her culture by making three distinct reads:

1. Identify the cultural behavioral profile—how people prefer to act (the traits they are expected to use) in public.
2. Identify customs that can create the appearance of a trait.
3. After making the first two reads, make snapshot reads to identify the person's actual traits (which may be different from the cultural traits they use in public).

Keeping these reads distinct and separate is what reduces stereotyping while allowing you to interact with someone based upon their actual profile and/or how they prefer to conduct themselves in a public setting. We'll also look at cultural door-openers that are useful in most cultures.

Americans are often inept when traveling abroad. First, we are isolated from the rest of the world by water on two sides. Second, we never get to use the foreign language we learned in school with any regularity. An exception is Spanish, but you usually have to live in a state like Texas or California, where there are many first-generation immigrants from Mexico and Central America. Thankfully, as we bumble our way around the world, we also smile a lot, which in America is a positive, but can be annoying to those on the receiving end in some cultures until they get to know us.

To begin, let's look at a case where correcting a cultural misread turned into a world championship performance.

One Read Accelerates Capture of World Championship

I received a call from a budding athletic coach, Lawrence. A graduate assistant at a major university with a storied track program, he had also been trained to profile using the KPS. One of his track stars, Bobby, was an Olympic champion and was training to win a gold in another event.

"Dan, my coach is one of the best in the country. He's teaching Bobby the right techniques, but he's misprofiled Bobby. Coach thinks he's getting push-back from Bobby. I don't think that's it, and Bobby isn't progressing," he explained.

"What do you think it is?" I asked.

"Bobby is from a Caribbean country and, as you taught us, they are usually very easygoing in public, especially in a group setting. So when Bobby is coached in a group, he appears very relaxed and NONASSERTIVE.

"Even though Coach is ASSERTIVE, there isn't a disconnect in this context," he continued to explain.

"Coach thinks Bobby is cooperative and NONASSERTIVE. Bobby's actual trait, though, is ASSERTIVE—and he uses it positively. But, when Coach works with Bobby on the track in a one-on-one environment, he senses Bobby's assertiveness and misinterprets it as push-back. Coach has stereotyped Bobby, they aren't connecting, and Bobby isn't improving as quickly as he could."

"So what's the solution?" I asked.

"I'm going to ask the coach if I can work with Bobby for three weeks. I won't change any of the mechanical techniques or how we interact with Bobby in a group, but I will give Bobby more space to process my instruction when we're one-on-one on the track," Lawrence explained.

He said that instead of standing square-on in front of Bobby, like Coach did, he'd stand by Lawrence's side, the same technique we show teachers when instructing students. This usually elicits more cooperation because it's a NONASSERTIVE stance and gives ASSERTIVE students mental breathing space. Lawrence said he'd also pull back a notch on the ASSERTIVE tone of his voice and choice of words. In other words, he'd be a little more NONASSERTIVE, like the example of Urs, the journalist, in Chapter 4.

Combined together, the result was predictable: Bobby quickly learned the techniques, turned in his fastest time in the event in several months, and won at the world championship. Would Bobby eventually have elevated his performance under the elder coach? Probably, but it might have taken months longer, which is too long in the life of an elite athlete.

What Lawrence did is the first step for successful cross-cultural interactions: He identified the profile of a culture—what people prefer to do in *public*—so it isn't confused with a person's *actual* profile.

Identify the Cultural Profile

This is what I like to refer to as being color-blind but culturally astute. You set aside all stereotypes and observe how people prefer to act in public—the cultural profile. All countries have one. For example, listed below are several countries and the CONTROL–EXPRESS trait one typically observes in each. Obviously there are differences in regions in a country and there is a difference between big cities (more EXPRESS) and small towns (more CONTROL). And different big cities take on their own personality. For example, in China, the on-the-street façade in exotic Shanghai is EXPRESS while in traditional Beijing it's more CONTROL. But just think of the big picture trait for each country.

- United States (EXPRESS: think of our media)
- Mexico (EXPRESS: warm and expressive)
- China (CONTROL: more reserved)
- Italy (EXPRESS: think of how they communicate)
- France (EXPRESS: think of their art)
- Switzerland (CONTROL: banks and clocks)

The best rule of thumb is to start with the big-picture country or region profile, and then a specific city/town and then, if necessary, the specific area of that city/town.

In Bobby's Caribbean country, people publicly tend to be more NONASSERTIVE and EXPRESS—easy-breezy, easygoing. This is true in communities large and small. Bobby's coach observed that when Bobby was in a group, he was easygoing, and his ASSERTIVE coaching style didn't intrude on Bobby's progress.

The disconnect occurred during one-on-one sessions. The coach stereotyped Bobby and didn't distinguish between Bobby's cultural profile and his actual profile. That's why he misinterpreted Bobby's ASSERTIVE trait with resistance to instruction.

Lawrence, on the other hand, learned that you may have to use more than one approach with an athlete from another culture, and when he did, positive results were produced.

Culture meets actual traits tempered by training.

I was on vacation in San Gimignano, Italy when I photographed a confrontation between an older, infirm gentleman, who needed to get medication from his local pharmacy, and a very patient police officer. There was no parking in the square, and he was too weak to walk. So he parked his bright red car in the middle of the square. The officer, who looked strikingly like Sophia Loren, gave him a ticket. Clearly NONASSERTIVE (note his open palms and body position), the more frustrated the man became, the higher he raised his left arm. Trained to be restrained, she kept her body position open, as this is less confrontational, and she used her hand in a palm-up position for emphasis, but with a very expressive Italian gesture, curling her forefinger and thumb together. Finally, after 10 minutes, she had enough. Exasperated, she squared her shoulders, lowered her chin, used a commanding gesture with her right hand, and gave him his citation. He was still persistent, so she lowered her arm, opened her body as she was trained to do, and departed.

Know Your Cultural Profile and the Stereotypes About Your Culture

Americans, for example, are known internationally for smiling. Nothing wrong with that, but when first meeting people in cultures where they are more CONTROL, it's better to restrain the frequency and the size of one's smile. It can help put others at ease.

Americans are also known for being more open and ASSERTIVE when they communicate. In some cultures this is stereotyped as being arrogant, even if a person isn't. That's why it's better to restrain your ASSERTIVE trait if you are ASSERTIVE, or operate more towards the NONASSERTIVE side of your range (Chapter 4). If you are naturally NONASSERTIVE, use your range and be just a notch more NONASSERTIVE.

British eyes were smiling. During an address to British industry leaders in London, I deliberately opened with a short remark that sounded ASSERTIVE in both tone and content. I stopped, took two steps to the left of the podium, looked at the spot where I had been standing, and in a softer tone I said, "That sounded a bit American, don't you agree? Let's start again." The response was appreciative, with wry smiles, nodding chins, and genteel laughter. I conveyed that I understood, and they expressed appreciation that I recognized and accommodated the cultural gap.

Photos that make us blush. I experienced a humorous stereotype of Americans when working with a Japanese publishing company that had a plant in China. The cover shot for a new book our press was releasing, *Deliciously Organic*, featured a picture of the author, Carrie Vitt, who is also my daughter.[1] The first time the color proofs came back, the author's face was too "red." We asked for a correction. It came back again with too much red. We asked again and got the same result—*four more times.* Now it was becoming expensive and affecting our production schedule. I talked with my print rep, and we finally realized that the people in this specific area of China always assume that Americans have blushier red complexions than Asians. He said he even noticed that the software in some Japanese cameras are tweaked to compensate for this if it "thinks" an American/European is in the photo. So what did he do? He told them to make it look more Asian! In effect, this was a situational read about the appearance of Americans. The plant politely and pleasantly corrected the error (their cultural profile was NONASSERTIVE and accommodating).

Be careful before telling someone he or she is your friend. In Poland, where relationships are greatly cherished, a friend is a very special relationship—someone for whom you'd even sacrifice your life. Most Poles would say they have two or maybe three friends. I learned to be careful not to call someone a friend without an explanation of the American meaning of that word. Otherwise, it comes off a bit shallow.

When *The Art of Profiling* was published in Poland, I included an introduction that explained the difference between the American and Polish use of this word, because the whole purpose of profiling someone is to treat them right the first time, without needless stumbles.

I explained that in America, all our ancestors came from foreign countries. In our diverse melting pot, getting along was a priority, and we used the word "friend" to signify good intent, even for a new acquaintance. To distinguish levels of friendship we say someone is a friend (for a casual or new relationship), a good friend (where there is some history), and our best friend (which is like the Polish meaning).

So, if you find yourself in a culture where people use the word friend like they do in Poland, use a little restraint before calling someone a friend. Or, as I prefer to do, explain how we use the word in America and the roots of its usage, which not only promotes better understanding of our culture, but also shows respect for others' customs.

Identify Customs That Might Appear to Be A Trait

Now we are looking for specific customs that can create the illusion of a cultural trait. For example, in Japan, a Japanese manager is asked by a salesman: Would you like to purchase this machinery? In response, the manager politely bows low at the waist and says, *Yes*. In fact, what he means is: *Yes, I will consider your request*. It is simply a courteous response. To the uninitiated, one might mistakenly believe that this potential Japanese customer is NONASSERTIVE, because of his agreeable style of communicating, when in fact the manager might be strong ASSERTIVE who is displaying a well-honed cultural custom.

An example of a communication trait custom is found in Hungary. It is common for many Hungarians to use emphatic and emotive hand gestures when they communicate, like the Italians. Even those with a strong CONTROL trait often communicate in this manner. It is the cultural façade. The uninitiated might conclude that most Hungarians are EXPRESS, similar to Italy, where most people use their hands when they communicate. The key, in Italy, is *how* do they use their hands when they communicate? Tight, controlled use of the hands kept close to the body, for example, is usually CONTROL, while a looser more free-flowing use of the hands that extends away from the body is usually EXPRESS.

Remember in Chapter 5 how Helena, the flight attendant, stereotyped a passenger and assumed a passenger was dissatisfied with her service because the passenger didn't show emotion? Her misread could have just as easily happened if the passenger was from a culture where people don't publicly show emotion until they know someone, as showing emotion is regarded as being too personal too quickly. In either case, if Helena profiled the person's culture first to understand the public norm, as well as the passenger's actual trait, she could do a better job assessing how to interact.

Lastly, there are customs that don't relate to our traits, but are still significant. I was taught by a Japanese parent that when a parent disciplines a child, the child isn't told to go to their room, because it is considered an honor to have your own room in a country where real estate is precious. Instead a child might be told to wait out in the hallway for their punishment! I guess that's the difference between a situational and a behavioral read...or maybe it's a combination of both!

Invest A Day or Two Before Your Trip or On Location

Ideally, it's best to identify cultural customs, expressions, and façades that can be confused for traits *before* entering a new culture. Many companies offer training for staff members who travel internationally. Additionally, independent workshops are taught on this subject. Other places to find recommendations for source information are the major international airlines and embassy offices. If you do your research online, be careful, as there is a lot of misinformation out there.

I prefer to ask around and find a real person I can talk to face-to-face with; someone who is known to have insight and who lives or lived in that culture. I ask about the 6 must-do and 6 must-never-do insights. This minimizes the potential of making a horrible bobble. Also, if you are returning to a country you haven't visited in a few years, renew and replenish your knowledge, as cultures are rarely static.

When asking someone directly for insight, request examples of what people prefer to do in public that might appear to be one of the traits. In Italy, for example, they'll tell you about how they don't mind showing their feelings. In Switzerland, people will share that they prefer to be a bit reserved. Most people have never been asked this type of question, but once you convey your sincerity with patience and an attentive ear, you will be amazed at what you will learn and how much more productive or enjoyable your experience will be. In Poland, after the fall of communism, for example, I found that in public, people were still extremely CONTROL, a holdover from not wanting to draw any attention. They mirrored the dismal apartment structures which they called Polski-in-a-box. However, when I was invited over for dinner, the apartments were alive with color and the people more freely expressed their emotions.

If you have to make your observations impromptu because you've decided on a lark to hop a train from Italy to the south of France, go a little bit slow the first few hours.

If you have the time, observe and confirm the most important cultural traits or customs that are relevant to your stay. If you're on vacation, for example, confirm the communication traits. If on business, also identify the performance traits. Reliable sources to confirm your observations—or provide insight—include hotel concierges, teachers and professors, professional translators, and any other profession that has a natural interest in people within the culture.

Be Prepared to Interact in More than One Way

Once you have identified the culture profile and customs that can appear to be a trait, you can then focus on identifying the person's actual profile, like Lawrence did. Then, if necessary, be prepared to interact with someone in two different ways. In a public setting, you might interact based upon the cultural profile, while in one-on-one or small and familiar settings, you may interact based upon their actual profile.

Be Careful of Making Assumptions if People Speak English

In the U.S. are distinctive cultures in which people speak English, but with additional phrases and expressions from their native languages and cultures, including Cajun, Chinese, Mexican, Polish, etc. In these communities people speak English, but, because they have a unique cultural/language background, they also have unique turns-of-phrase, pronunciations, and customs that may confuse us. This can also occur in other English-speaking countries, sometimes causing a bit of embarrassment.

When in England giving a speech to a group of professionals, I spoke about a nearby affluent community. I pronounced the word, as do many Americans—e-fluent—with the accent on the second syllable. Everyone started chuckling. I asked what I had said that caused the merriment. I was informed that effluence, which sounded nearly the same as my American pronunciation of affluent, is a word that is used in England to describe that which comes out of a sewer, while affluence is what emanates out of one's pocket book!

I was embarrassed. They were entertained.

Strangely, I have observed Americans having more communication snafus in England than in countries in which English isn't the native tongue. People mistakenly and complacently assume that clear dialogue is taking place because English is being spoken. In countries where English isn't the primary language spoken, people tend to pay closer attention.

Therefore, an important rule when in a different culture in which English is spoken is: Don't assume that you understand all that is being communicated. It's easy to be lulled into complacency when speaking in or listening to your native tongue. Stay alert and be sure that everyone is tracking with the same level of understanding. Be curious and vigilant. Be curious about unique expressions and pronunciations. Be vigilant in your efforts to thwart miscommunication and avoid stereotyping.

What Do You Cherish or Honor About Your Heritage/Culture So I Can Honor That?

Although not the best English, this simple question can unlock doors to hearts and minds and put you in someone else's shoes. If someone asked an American this question, a common response might be our freedom. In Japan, it might be honoring family relationships. In Kenya, it might be one's community as related to past or current tribal roots.

While working in a ministry at our church with low income youths whose families recently moved to Texas, the kids told me they didn't want to be called "Hispanic" but Mexican-Americans. When I asked why, they said they were proud of Mexico, and besides, there's no country called Hispania!

You can't stereotype what is important to people, so it is always best to ask in a way that shows thoughtful intent. Here's another thoughtful question:

How Do You Say Thank You and I Love You?

There is an electronics and computer store near my home where many of the employees are Ethiopian. Whenever I make a purchase, I always say thank you in their language, *amesgnalehu* (ah-mi-si-gi-nah-lu). Yes, it's difficult, but they really appreciate it.

More than 60 languages are spoken in our suburb, and when my children were growing up, I taught them to ask how to say "thank you" in the language of the person they were talking to. I instructed them to ask their new friend or acquaintance to write it out phonetically, and then to practice saying it to get the accent right. This is a thoughtful way to let people know you care about them and their heritage.

If I see someone regularly, I might also ask them to tell me how to say "I love you" in their language. I explain that I will share this with my wife when I go home—really. (Whenever Sandy hears a new phrase, she wags her finger and says, "You've been to the computer store again!")

It is a simple gesture, but it tells people that you care about and respect others. And, that you want to take a little of their culture into your home.

Amesgnalehu - Thank you

"Thank you" written out phonetically by a new friend, so I could pronounce it, and my English next to it. It also helps to pay attention to how letters are written, as there can be subtle differences that can lead to misreading a letter.

How to Start a Speech

I wish someone had explained this to me before I went on my first European speaking tours for professional and university audiences: You can't always start speeches the way you do for American audiences.

Starting a speech culturally correctly in another country is something few Americans have been taught. In part, this is because we are separated by oceans on our western and eastern shores, unlike Europe, where travel to other countries is like going from Florida to Alabama. Here are two examples:

When you start a speech in a country that has a *cultural* profile of CONTROL, it's usually best you start your speech with your theory or concept. You don't start with a personal anecdote or joke, like we're accustomed to in the U.S. Switzerland is a country where I quickly learned this. If you don't start formally, they will think of you as "the American," and you start a point or two behind. Jokes are considered a bit too informal for most Swiss professional and university audiences.

Romania, however, is a very different story. The cultural profile is EXPRESS. When you give a speech, you must start with a personal story about yourself. When I asked why, I was told by my Romanian translator: *If you don't, they won't trust you.* In other words, if you won't reveal a little bit about yourself, you obviously have something to hide and can't be trusted.

In March of 2001, I was tasked to address about 7,000 students at the five major universities in Romania and convince them that deception was no longer an acceptable way of life. You see, under communism, only those who paid bribes had their own businesses. The students and professors, even those who were honest without blemish, believed that deception was still a necessity.

My presentation, *Lies, Cons, and the Truth* started off with a singular question: *If you could only choose one, which would you choose? Would you choose to become an expert at detecting lying or detecting the truth?* I followed this with a short sleight-of-hand demonstration while explaining that I was not only proficient in profiling, but since I was a boy, I was also a professional magician, which gave me more insight into deception. I sometimes do this because magic is an entertaining reminder that *anyone can be deceived.* Immediately, the students were on board. (I actually fudged a bit, integrating what I was going to talk about *with* my personal anecdote and a demonstration—all in just a couple of minutes. This hybrid approach worked because of the entertaining demonstration and the tone of my opening was personal.)

People's Palace, Bucharest, Romania, March 2001. My high EXPRESS and extremely helpful translator, Daniel Popa, instructed me to start every speech with a personal story so I could reach student hearts and minds with a life-changing concept.

As explained in Chapter 5, those who are the best at detecting lying are *first* expert at detecting truthfulness, and I presented compelling evidence to the students to back this up. Imagine their response if I *hadn't* started with a personal anecdote that also related to my presentation? Immediately, I would be considered suspect. A critical message intended to help guide their future would have been needlessly derailed. But, I did, they took ownership of the message, and over two-thirds of the students signed up for study groups to learn how to detect truthfulness.

So when you give your first speech in a new culture, ask, "what is appropriate and why." Often the *why* part of the equation will provide insight into your audience so you won't stereotype and you'll start off on the right foot.

Closing Thoughts

Obviously, an entire book could be dedicated to just this subject. What's extraordinary is the notion of identifying the cultural profile and customs separate from a person's actual profile isn't even taught as a benchmarkable competency in the diplomatic community. Some can do it intuitively, but not as a discipline where they are tested for their accuracy. No wonder there are so many needless international disconnects. But you now have this insight and can apply it. For your convenience, here's a summation of what we covered.

1. Identify the behavioral profile (cultural profile) of the country/region/town/city. Example: Do people smile or show emotion in public in daily interactions?

2. Identify customs that might appear to be a trait (as well as those you must respect). Examples: What is the best way to start a speech—personal story or theory? Should I call someone a friend without some explanation?

3. Now, separately identify a person's actual profile as needed.

4. Identify which cultural traits are most important for you to understand based upon what you will be doing. Are they the communication traits, the performance traits, or both?

5. Be prepared to interact with someone in two different ways—in a group, where the cultural profile is more important, and in a one-on-one situation when they use their actual profile.

6. Ask people what they cherish about their heritage so you can honor and respect it.

7. If you meet someone here in North America from another country, ask them to teach you how to say "thank you" and "I love you" in his or her language.

8. Know the stereotypes people have of your culture. Example: Americans can be stereotyped as being ASSERTIVE, EXPRESS, and CONFIDENT. Be certain that you deliberately, and with some forethought, show some restraint and demonstrate the positive side of a trait as appropriate.

SNAPSHOT REMINDER
Snapshot reads are the *opposite* of racial and ethnic stereotyping, which government officials incorrectly call racial and ethnic "profiling" as explained in Chapter 2.

CHAPTER TWENTY-FOUR

Snapshot Reads on Holiday

Have you ever traveled to a distant land, seen something that caught your eye, didn't stop to take a second look, and wished you had?

Normandy, 2013. It was the last destination of our 40th anniversary trip across Israel, Italy, and France. No tour guides, even in Israel, our first stop. We just launched out. Then on to Italy, where we lumbered through the vineyards in Cinque Terre and other magnificent locales for nine more days. Then Normandy.

It was in our hearts for years to visit the D-Day beaches and small towns where over 10,000 young lives were sacrificed to free France and the rest of Europe—without asking for anything in return.

Sandy and I always look for places off the beaten path. Away from tourists, but where there are hidden stories just beneath the surface—if you'll just look around and make some polite inquiries. We often start with Karen Brown's bed-and-breakfast books. She and Rick Steves, another gem of a travel writer, have pointed us to some of the most remarkable and off-the-beaten-path locales and sights.

In Karen's Normandy guide, what caught my eye was the Château de Vouilly, 20 minutes from the Utah and Omaha beaches. It was used as the headquarters for the U.S. press corps during Operation Overlord, what we call D-Day. Walter Cronkite, Andy Rooney, George Capa, and Ernest

Hemingway were all there. Even General Omar Bradley, the invasion ground commander, set up his headquarters there so he could be close to the messaging of the corps. I couldn't believe what a find I was reading. So we booked our stay, and it was one of the most extraordinary experiences in all our travels to dozens of countries.

Surrounded by a magnificent moat, it is a working manor with over 200 cows. Magnificently maintained, its roots date back to when William the Conqueror gave the plot of land to one of his faithful knights, circa 1190. The James Hamel family has owned and cared for the manor since 1800. James was our host—and soon became my pal.

Even on the overcast day we arrived, Vouilly had a presence that made you feel at home. Like the Normandy region itself, it was *magnifique* without self-important posturing. For the working stiffs of the press corps, it was a respite from the terrors of war.

The Hamel family generously allows folks like us to stay at their "bed and breakfast" which is truly frozen in time—not just the manor itself, which is appointed just as it was on D-Day, but also the rich historical artifacts from the press corps that they leave out on display. And then there are all the hand-carved furniture pieces, crafted by James's father, and compelling works of art—paintings, busts, carvings, and more. In so many manors in Europe, you often see giant and even pompous portraits of family members adorning halls and stairways. There was none of that here. It was all *authentique* and earthy.

Thankfully, the morning after we arrived, the sun warmed up the

breakfast room. After breakfast, I started studying all the artifacts, then moved on to the works of art. My instinct told me that one painting, a portrait of a woman, high on a wall in the breakfast room told a tale. The subject looked resolute and fiercely determined, probably CONVENTIONAL, CONFIDENT, and with a steely vision for the future. Oddly, what was missing, though, for such a fine work, was the artist's signature. I asked James who she was. His hospitable and warm expression changed to reverent admiration.

"Ah, that's my grand-mére, Alexandrina."

"Is she the one I heard tricked a Nazi commander?" I asked, remembering a tale I briefly read.

"Yes, that's her."

"Please tell me what happened," I asked.

The French Resistance that stood up to Hitler was small, but its heart was like Alexandrina's countenance. I noticed the artist didn't sign his work, no doubt so as not to diminish the essence of who Alexandrina was and her heroic act.

Enlivened, James's countenance morphed to that of an engaged storyteller. Together, we navigated our French and English. (Although I studied French for five years and a book I published on sleight-of-hand card magic was translated into French, I rarely get to use this beautiful and lyrical language.) So onward, we plunged into the tale.

Born in 1880, Alexandrina and her husband, Nederic, who was four years older, were married in January of 1902. Their only child, Dumilly, James's father, was born later that year in November. Nederic died in an accident in 1937.

Dumilly, circa 1924

Three years later, war descended on France. Dumilly, the male stalwart of the family who previously served his country, was captured by the Germans in 1940. He was imprisoned for three years at Stalag 6, the northernmost POW camp, near the old Prussian town of Heydekrug (now Šilutė, Lithuania). James's mother, Marie Legendre, married Dumilly in 1934, but they hadn't yet been blessed with children.

With Dumilly gone, life on the manor was difficult for the Hamels, but at least they were alive and could sustain themselves.

One day, a Nazi commandant came to the manor with his officers in tow. They entered through the archway where Alexandrina parked her car.

He said he was considering using the manor house as his headquarters and wanted to be shown its interior.

Deftly, Alexandrina guided them to a door off the kitchen to view the upstairs. As Sandy and I learned more about Alexandrina, Sandy was convinced that Alexandrina's demeanor was probably *deceptively* accommodating.

"I'm certain she was polite and even gracious without overdoing it as she gave them a tour. I like her!" Sandy said, beaming a smile. I could see a bit of Alexandrina in Sandy, who, if you'll remember, played the part of five different men's wives for me during one undercover investigation—but that's another tale.

Alexandrina led the broad-shouldered German officers up an extremely narrow and steep staircase. They had to turn slightly sideways to mount the steps and there wasn't a railing to guide them. They struggled to keep their balance. Chalky powder from the walls rubbed off on their uniforms as they were forced to lean against the walls for stability to keep from falling. This was a time when plaster-covered walls often weren't painted.

Once at the top, the stern and pompous officers slapped with frustration at the powdery substance sullying the legs, arms, and shoulders of their uniforms.

"*Nein*," this wasn't for him, the commandant arrogantly announced, and he left. He was looking for French *élégance*. Château du Vouilly didn't match his expectations—a place where grandiose opinions of one's self are self-exposed.

Alexandrina could have taken the officer up the wide spiraling main staircase at the other end of the main house, which is stunning, but she didn't.

I told James he should name the narrow stairway the "Stairs of Resistance!"—*Escaliers de Résistance!*—and the spiraling stairs the "Stairs of Victory!"— *Escaliers de la Victoire!*

Later, James explained that the portrait of Alexandrina was painted by one of France's great artists, Maurice Delavier. And, that's when the rest of the tale unfolded.

Escaliers de Résistance! James demonstrating how narrow and steep were the "Stairs to Resistance" Alexandrina used to cleverly discourage the Nazi commandant—now lined with paneling and wallpaper. (Dan Korem, 2013)

Plaster chalk still rubs off the attic walls at the very top of the stairs. (Dan Korem, 2013)

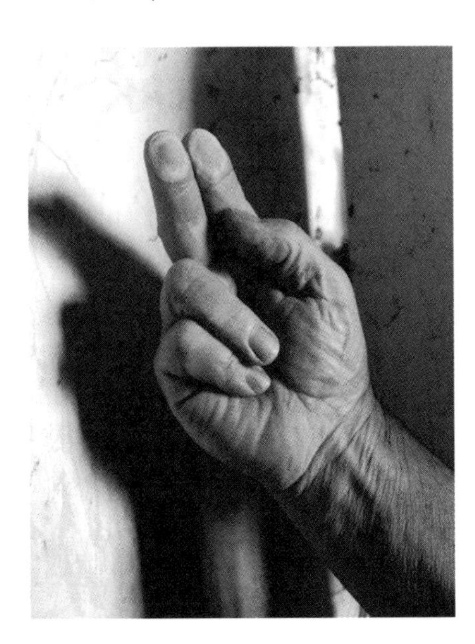

Above: The nondescript door to the stairs, now in the back corner of the kitchen.

Right: *Escaliers de la Victoire!* The "Stairs to Victory" (Dan Korem, 2013)

I asked James about his father's time as a POW at Stalag 6. It was intriguing that he was released by the Germans in 1943, before the war ended—presumably to help produce food on his manor for the invaders, and because he wasn't considered an active combatant.

Spurred on by my question about the camp, James rummaged through one of the drawers in the breakfast room and brought out a loose-leaf book/portfolio entitled *Stalag 6–A* filled with drawings of his father's comrades rendered by the esteemed French painter Maurice Delavier, who was a POW with Dumilly. They were extraordinary. Not artistic abstractions with fanciful interpretations, but so real in their expressions and deportment, you could see their traits.

Delavier used a mixture of techniques and whatever materials he could find in the camp—small splinters of wood, ink, pencil, and charcoal—probably remnants of what they burned for heat. The 60 prints were all hand-pressed in a limited edition of 500. (When I returned home, I located and purchased through an antiquarian book dealer a mint copy of *Stalag 6–A*, Number 145,

Left: Delavier self-portrait.
Right: Dumilly before his capture, drawn by another comrade.

the only one available.)

I carefully laid the drawings out on the embroidered French linen table cloth and photographed many. James also showed me a pencil drawing of his father rendered by another one of his comrades, from May of 1940, before he was captured.

The collection of Delavier's includes intensely poignant drawings which also reveal the traits of WWII POWs. When faced with severe uncertainty, except for the certainty of one's mortality, the POWs' communication and performance traits are timelessly and clearly etched in each face.

As you look through this small sample gallery from Delavier's 1946 loose-leaf book, view them through the lens of your new ability to make snapshot reads. Put yourself in their shoes, in their time and space, and consider what they might have experienced, and how you might help each one uniquely endure life as a POW—how you would give cheer, encouragement, or comfort. Can you see glimpses of their actual traits separate from the facade imposed by wretched camp conditions?

POWs from France and West Africa observed by curious town folks from nearby Heydekrug on the old Prussian border, the northernmost German POW camp.

Top: Mac Némi, Delavier's somber comrade, November 12, 1940. Probably dated to remind him of something important.

Bottom: At first glance, this looks like Némi, but he's a British sailor. Of the two, who is probably more FEARFUL or UNCONVENTIONAL? More CONTROL or EXPRESS?

Top: POW Boyer, a British pilot with unusually deep-sunken eyes. Perhaps he has the CONTROL trait?

Bottom: The caption reads: Representative of the *Massif Central*. Probably a representative of the local community. When a friend, a military officer who I trained to profile, was looking through the collection and saw this drawing, he picked it up and instantly said, "He isn't a POW." "How do you know that?" I asked, as he hadn't read the description at the bottom of the drawing. "Because he has too many layers of clothes and his cheeks are full."

Many of Delavier's drawings reveal the heart of soul of his comrades and one or more of their traits.

Left: Titled, "The Philosopher," captures his comrade's NONASSERTIVE trait—the soft, inquisitive tilt of the head.

Bottom: Poignant hope humbly portrayed in a fellow prisoner, who catches a glimpse of the first English daytime air sortie.

Top: French POW from the Landes "department" of Southern France.

Bottom: African POW who is a marabout—a Muslim religious leader. Maybe ASSERTIVE?

Upon returning from the war, Dumilly restored the manor's productivity. If you saw him tending to the cows at 4 a.m., repairing a roof, or negotiating the best price for his cheese, you might have stereotyped him as CONVENTIONAL, like many disciplined farmers. Unless you profiled his UNCONVENTIONAL trait by asking him about his interests, you might never imagine him as a disciplined artisan, creating works of art like his UNCONVENTIONAL chum Delavier, with whom he easily connected. Above is one of his wooden sculptures (his wife's portrait hangs in the background).

Top: James and Sandy in the breakfast room. The curtains are the same that hung when famed journalist Walter Cronkite came to Vouilly on June 6, 1994 to commemorate the 50th anniversary of D–Day and his time there. A bronze plaque, presented by the Overseas Press Club of America as a reminder of that day, hangs on the face of the chateau.

Bottom: View of the moat around Vouilly.

It's easy to be transported to distant places in our imagination when we view works like Delavier's or even black-and-white photographs.

When we return to the time of "now," which is real and in color, it's even more important that we take the time to engage one another based on who we really are.

James and I became overnight pals. Both UNCONVENTIONAL and EXPRESS, we were a match. He even lent me his super wide-angle lens for shots I took of Vouilly.

What amazed me is that none of America's iconic journalists, who were all mothered by Alexandrina—Mama Hamel—and all knew the story with the commandant, ever reported or wrote about her heroic effort. And, to think, that it might never have been told in these pages if I hadn't been drawn to one snapshot read of Mme. Hamel in Delavier's masterpiece which reveals her immovable CONFIDENT trait and courage—defying Hitler with her only weapon—the essence of who she was. I hope one day someone will reprint Delavier's drawings for future generations.

Bon chance mon ami!

CHAPTER TWENTY-FIVE

Digital Profiling? No! Look Up!

[I mean it. Look up!]

"Can I profile someone online?"

It's one of the most common questions I'm asked since we've changed overnight how we communicate.

The answer is maybe—*if you look up!*

The intrusion of self-serving electronic devices in our lives is a blessing and a curse when reading and treating people right the first time. It's a blessing when we use them to take someone's photo so we can remember what they look like in that moment. I do this often, to the surprise of new clients. I explain that I want those who work with me to have a visual of who they are working with by phone. It's more humane.

Our digital machines are a curse when we let them dictate when and to whom we pay attention.

Today, from my perspective of training tens of thousands how to read and treat people right the first time, I believe people are far *less* insightful in their understanding of others and how to interact than they once were. They may know the facts about a person or culture, but their understanding of the person in front of them has diminished.

I can teach people how to *read someone's trait in just hours of practice,* but most need far more help when it comes to using that insight for the benefit of others or themselves. Our kids, for example, can type like lightning with their thumbs and access information at warp speed, but understand humans? Rarely.

One of the most remarkable things about my friend, Shawn Humphries, whom you met in Chapter 7, is that he daily sets the right example that is then emulated by his kids. Rarely, if ever, will you find him distracted by digital intrusions. When his kids leave a training session with their golf bags slung over their shoulder, they are making eye contact with each other as they engage in real dialogue. Nothing artificial. It was what so attracted me to Shawn and his style of leading kids. And they get it.

Digital shortcuts? Don't think so. This book started with an example of an entrepreneur trying to close a deal via email. The read of the executive, though, was made based on history with the exec. It's also possible to profile traits by researching someone's background using articles, video recordings, eyewitness accounts, etc. (For more on using background reads for rapid-fire profiling see *The Art of Profiling*).

What most people mean, though, when they ask about profiling people online is, *can I profile them from their social media pages?* The short answer is maybe or maybe not, because so many create fantasy worlds that don't resemble who they are or, at best, exhibit unintentional distortions. They present themselves a certain way because it's fashionable.

It's too easy with a stroke of a key to appear EXPRESS by typing *Thanks!* at the end of an email or text—a common expression of the day which will no doubt change tomorrow. Or the illusion can be created that one is UNCONVENTIONAL with the insertion of a clever picture or design element on a social networking page.

Then there is another challenge we all encounter daily.

Millions of people seem to have their chins glued to their sternums as they text other humans—even as you are speaking to them and without

"Dave, are you really the man you say you are, or do I need to go on LinkedIn and find out?"

an *excuse me*. It's not only a cultural rudeness, it profoundly affects the ability to read another person's traits and treat them uniquely as they deserve to be treated.

At one Dallas ad firm, young guns in a strategic meeting texted each other instead of talking to one another, even though they were sitting across the table from each other. The president was livid and banned those "little communication machines" from all future meetings.

And then there are all the various visual and audio media tearing us away from human interaction.

If you communicate digitally with others, here are some suggestions to avoid stereotyping and improve your ability to read and treat someone right the first time:

Communication traits. Never trust punctuation marks or the adjective of the day. It's too easy to insert an exclamation mark or a cute smiley face. It will not tell you whether a person is CONTROL or EXPRESS or has compassion or empathy for others. A better read is the content and choice of words that aren't just the adjective or adverb currently in vogue. This also applies to trying to read ASSERTIVE or NONASSERTIVE. Some have learned to be less or more ASSERTIVE with a written voice that absolutely doesn't match their actual trait.

CONFIDENT–CAUTIOUS/FEARFUL. It's easy to misread people who are CONFIDENT in their area of expertise but are actually CAUTIOUS or high FEARFUL. They can present a CONFIDENT decision-making face because they have expertise, but you can't identify their core trait. *Always rely upon background research and preferably face-to-face meetings to confirm.*

Phone conversations can help somewhat, but a face-to-face meeting is more likely to reveal the actual trait.

CONVENTIONAL–UNCONVENTIONAL. This is a little bit easier to read online as you are looking at what a person prefers to do and why. For example, if someone is an accountant, your first hunch may be CONVENTIONAL. If you test the hunch and find they are attracted to the newest trends and creative approaches and most of their other interests are UNCONVENTIONAL, then you need to correct your read. It's best, though, to base your final read on face-to-face reads or background research. One of the most brilliant UNCONVENTIONAL inventors I've ever met has a very dry, uninteresting website. When asked about it, he says that it doesn't interest him and it's simply a portal for people to find him.

Look up! Reduce your digital intrusions by 30% *today*. I almost always keep my cell phone in my pocket when talking to someone. The person in front of me is the priority. Like everyone else, I do text and check emails, but *not* when having meaningful dialogue with another human being. Our little machines we carry are not the priority. There are, of course, exceptions, like when my wife is at a catering event and must constantly check for messages from staff or clients. But, when she is sitting with a client for the first time, gathering data and learning the unique needs of her client, her cell phone is out of sight.

If you'll keep your "machine" in your pocket 30% more often than at present, you'll make a good start.

Then reduce digital time-consumption in *all* forms. It's unhealthy for promoting human interaction and insight.

Mrs. Irena Koźmińska, wife of the former Polish ambassador to the U.S. (Chapter 6), drew an illustration for me that shows her impression of how fast we have moved away from human face-to-face communication, especially as it relates to our most intimate relationships—what she calls the family university.

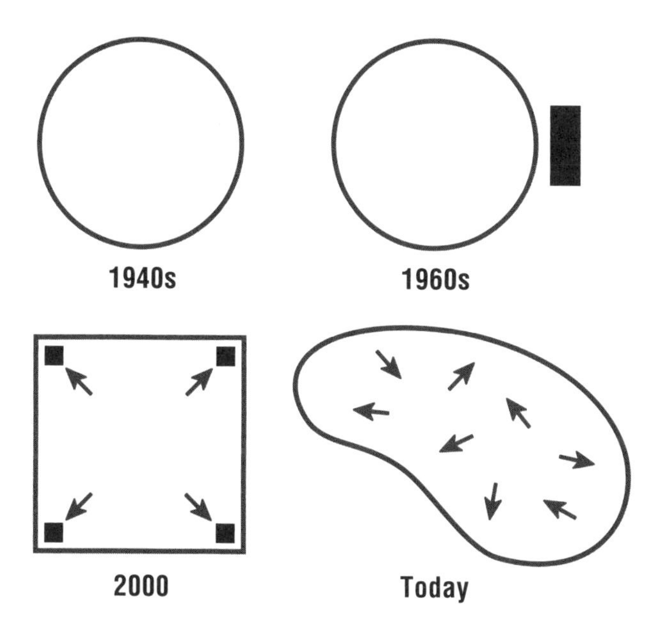

1940s: Families sat around a table and engaged one another as they ate dinner.

1960s: Television intruded, becoming the distractor at the dinner table.

2000: We all started to get our own stationary computer.

Today: We walk around with tiny machines that contain our correspondence, instant communications, music, photos, cameras, unlimited data, and more in our pockets. It is a wonderful tool, but people are looking down and not *up* at others.

Remember Delavier? Do you think that Delavier would have painted with near the force he did if he were constantly distracted by digital intrusions? His insight was shaped by real events, with real people, and without apology. Do you think I would have noticed his portrait of Mme. Hamel if I were constantly checking my email while on vacation, as so many do?

When people hear the Mme. Hamel–Dumilly–Delavier story, they always commit to going just a little bit slower on their next vacation, looking up and at those around them, and making snapshot reads along the way. Others also commit to walking a little bit differently *every day.*

Put the digital world in its place.

Let it serve us rather than turn us into mindless Pavlovian dogs mentally salivating every time we hear a ding or feel a slight vibration.

When we traveled through Israel without tour guides, my little device helped us in so many ways: GPS locations; software that translated words; a website posted by a generous tour guide allowed us to find the exact location of the Valley of Elah where David fought Goliath; a currency exchanger; still camera and video recorder; texting to share a spontaneous moment with our family back home replete with a photo; and more.

But...

We never allowed that little device the slightest crack of an opportunity to intrude in one conversation or distract us for a moment as we explored ancient ruins, witnessed sunrise on the Sea of Galilee where Jesus walked on water, or gave comfort to a motorcyclist who had just crashed near the ancient city of Kursi.

We have friends that now have device-free zones in their homes—dens, kitchens, and other places where they are most likely to converse—and times of day and night when they are turned off altogether. We don't need hard rules to tell us how to limit intrusions, rather the will to do it as it matches how we live.

Moral of the story? Look up! You can't make accurate rapid-fire reads staring at your navel or with earbuds sealing you off from human contact. Real people require real interactions.

We can do *things* fast, but *treating people thoughtfully takes time.* The digital injection into our lives, while providing us with more knowledge, is so distracting that it's creating an even greater need to make snapshot reads of real people so we can *treat them right the first time.*

Marketing and governmental forces are simultaneously reducing us to digital bits of information to be prodded or ignored as their preprogrammed matrixes demand. And their pressure will continue to increase, adding to our own missteps.

Resist!

Look up!

Remember my friend, Richard Turner, the world's greatest card mechanic/magician who is blind (Chapter 11)?

He complained to me that, "It's terrible that people are constantly looking down at their devices and not at the person in front of them. Their attention span is poor and so is their people insight. It's just plain rude."

How does he know people are looking down and are disconnected from live human beings? He's blind.

Richard is acutely attuned to anyone he meets. He knows when you aren't paying attention and when you're digitally distracted. That's because he's focused on your voice, the direction from which it's coming, and what you are saying—the content, tone, and rhythm—just as he was with Chris, the hesitant teenager. Richard may be physically blind, but his insight into others is extraordinarily elevated because he cares. And, we should do the same.

The final story and chapter that follows not only encourages us to look up, but also to look *back* and make snapshot reads of those who have impacted our personal history—both those in our family and those who have affected our nation and world. By looking back with snapshot reads and reading the essence of who they were, we can better understand who we are and the influences that shape how we think and what we value.

CHAPTER TWENTY-SIX

Two Men, Two Profiles, and the Destiny of a Nation

[History talks to us,
but with greater clarity]

It was one of the most important friendships in American history. Together, two me shaped our nation's destiny.

One man was called an enigma. If he were a monument, he would be the Sphinx. If he were a painting, he would be the *Mona Lisa*. His best friend called him a "shadow man."[1]

The other man was a farmer and a lawyer, fascinated with the newest ideas, and a reluctant statesman. His traits are easy to identify: CONFIDENT, UNCONVENTIONAL, ASSERTIVE, and EXPRESS.

His friend, the "shadow man," was difficult to size up, even for his closest friends. They knew he was brilliant, but his voice was barely audible if asked by his peers to speak on perilously important matters.

Both men shared a common destiny. Both were patriots. Both were scholars. Both were willing to die for their country. Both became presidents.

The shadow man didn't consider becoming president among his most important accomplishments.

He was NONASSERTIVE when he spoke and always controlled his emotion, except with his pen. He was UNCONVENTIONAL in his pursuits *and* he was FEARFUL—extremely fearful. In fact, he had the RANDOM ACTOR traits.

Yet, he penned one the most quoted passages in our history:

> We hold these truths to be self-evident, that all men were created equal, that they are endowed by their Creator with certain unalienable Rights, that among these are Life, Liberty and the pursuit of Happiness...And for the support of this Declaration, with a firm reliance on the protection of divine Providence, we mutually pledge to each other our Lives, our Fortunes and our sacred Honor.

The "shadow man" who became our third American president was Thomas Jefferson.

His dear friend, the CONFIDENT INNOVATOR, was John Adams, the second president of the new republic.

Adams was the vocal and vigorous voice of the Continental Congress, the verbal coals of logic on the fire that compelled all to debate *and* act. He refined the arguments with ASSERTIVE force, the passion of his emotions, confidence in what was right and necessary, and the willingness to risk all to do something the world had never seen. On July 1, 1776, he one last time rallied the hearts and minds of those assembled to vote to separate from England, and he wrote to a friend:

> Objects of the most stupendous magnitude, measures in which the lives and liberties of millions, born and unborn are the more essentially interested, are now before us. We are in the very midst of revolution, the most complete, unexpected, and remarkable of any in the history of the world.[2]

Jefferson, while shy and retiring, was confident in his moral conviction and, emboldened by Adams's urgings, that with his pen he could shape the moral voice of those assembled.

Both men were UNCONVENTIONAL, living in extremely UNCONVENTIONAL times that were, in Adams's words, "the most honorable" to human nature, despite errors and vices. He wrote:

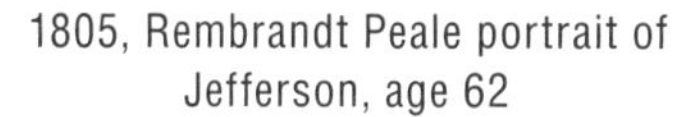
1805, Rembrandt Peale portrait of Jefferson, age 62

c. 1791–1794, Charles Willson Peale portrait of Adams, age 56 (approx.)

> Knowledge and virtues were increased and diffused; arts, sciences useful to man, ameliorating their condition, were improved, more than in any period.[3]

In the midst of great change, both men were intensely stimulated by new ideas, voracious readers, and students of all manner of disciplines, but there was a difference—Adams was CONFIDENT, and Jefferson was high FEARFUL.

If left to stereotypes, one would assume that Jefferson, the FEARFUL one, would flee when asked to give his life. Moral decisions, however, as you've learned, can override our actual trait and how we make daily decisions. Perhaps this is one reason why Jefferson and virtually all the other signers of the Declaration of Independence openly wrote about and discussed the need for two "indispensable supports," faith and morality, to bolster their convictions.[4]

Jefferson, and the rest of the world, had watched the counterpoint in France, when the UNCONVENTIONAL trait combined with paranoia, produced the guillotine mobs of the 1789 French Revolution. No moral or spiritual imperative there.

Jefferson's moral convictions demanded that he be willing to give his life for his country; here he didn't hesitate. When called upon to write the most important document in our history, something that was a deep-rooted part of his competency—his ability to reason and articulate through the written word—he penned the Declaration of Independence.

Extraordinary.

A man with the RANDOM ACTOR traits was at the epicenter of one of the greatest changes for good in the history of the world.

Yet, Jefferson's day-to-day decision-making *was* shackled to his FEARFUL trait, which chained him to slavery. Jefferson owned more than 200 human beings. He desired their labor without cost to support his massive estate, his constant modifications to Monticello, to pay for his library, and his ever-present debts. Adams, his CONFIDENT friend, openly abhorred slavery and debts and at his death left an estate worth $100,000. His friend, Jefferson, died with over $100,000 of debt, greater than the value of Monticello.

Eventually, though, Jefferson acknowledged that the institution of slavery itself was immoral, and requested that Congress pass the Act Prohibiting Importation of Slaves in 1807. Yet he still owned slaves when he died. In effect, he had the moral conviction to abolish slavery, but lacked the confidence to earn a living without them and pay a fair wage.

The ball and chain of his FEARFUL trait plagued him all his life, even affecting his health by regularly stinging him with bouts of deep depression and illness.

Like most people, I knew little of Jefferson. History teachers, professors, and their books diminished his humanity, grinding him down to a thin stereotype on the face of a nickel. It was while reading *John Adams* by David McCullough, whom I believe is America's greatest historian, that I stumbled across the fact that Jefferson had the RANDOM ACTOR traits.

To tell the Adams story, McCullough used more than 1,000 letters between Adams and his wife, Abigail, as well as their diaries. It is the largest collection of letters between a president and his wife.

In their letters and other accounts provided by McCullough, one could plainly see Jefferson's RANDOM ACTOR traits—if you could profile. Otherwise, as most historians do, you'd rely upon metaphors—like the Sphynx and the *Mona Lisa*—to describe Jefferson.

How many of us were ever taught in school that Jefferson had the extreme FEARFUL trait, let alone that he was a RANDOM ACTOR? He was so afflicted with paranoia that he holed himself up in Monticello, his estate portrayed on the back of our nickels, which he relentlessly modified and remodeled. He'd build a wing, tear it down, only to rebuild it again with innovative new design twists. It was puzzling to most, but not if you understood that it was his distraction from his FEARFUL trait.

Often described as detached and not interested in deep, personal relationships, Jefferson used Monticello as one of many escapes where he applied his UNCONVENTIONAL trait in an area of competency, all at the expense of those working for him whom he didn't pay an honest wage for their labor.

The Adamses were very different.

They had strong views against slavery. At the time, 1 in 5 inhabitants of the colonies were slaves: 500,000 slaves amidst a total colonial population of 2.5 million.

Abigail, like her husband, was a CONFIDENT decision maker and a resolute and deep thinker. In 1774, when the colonies were struck by the "bloody flux"—epidemic dysentery—killing Adams's youngest brother, her mother, and many she loved and knew, she "pondered whether the agonies of pestilence and war could be God's punishment for the sin of slavery."[5] She and her husband believed slavery would doom the future of their new country, if not corrected.

Like Abigail, Jefferson also suffered great loss. His wife, Martha Wayles Skelton, died several months after giving birth to her sixth child, presumably from diabetes and other infirmities. She was 33 years old and made her husband promise not to remarry. She herself was raised by several stepmothers, due to untimely deaths, and she didn't want the same fate for her children. Jefferson agreed, although only one of his six children lived past the age of 25—four died before the age of 4.

While Abigail battled depression at various stages of her life, due to so many untimely deaths and being isolated on their farm while her husband often was away, her trait was still CONFIDENT. She took comfort in her Creator, which she learned from her father, a Congregational minister. Jefferson, however, regularly succumbed to ever-deepening bouts of fear.

Still, Jefferson and Adams, two UNCONVENTIONAL men, were drawn to each other and were willing to die for the price of freedom, no matter how imperfect their personal lives. In this way, they are like us: drawn to others like themselves.

When he was president, Jefferson selected another UNCONVENTIONAL man to be his personal aide, the brilliant Merriwether Lewis. We know Lewis for his last name. Jefferson chose him to lead the Corps of Discovery, a team of 33, on the famous Lewis and Clark expedition (1804–1806). It was the greatest exploratory adventure in our history—even greater than our landing on the moon, which we had already had photographed. We knew what was there and the extreme conditions. As for the West, we knew nothing.

UNCONVENTIONAL Lewis was the right fit for the *discovery* objectives, such as chronicling new plant and animal life, geography, and more.

Lewis, though, had something else in common with Jefferson.

He also had the high FEARFUL trait. He had the RANDOM ACTOR traits, which are powerfully shown in the 1997 documentaries, *Thomas Jefferson* and *Lewis and Clark: The Journey of the Corps of Discovery*. Both were produced by Ken Burns, our visual historian emeritus, from which I quoted observations about Jefferson in the opening of this chapter.

Similar to when I read *John Adams*, I was stunned as Burns recounted the tale of the UNCONVENTIONAL yet extremely FEARFUL Lewis, who, like Jefferson, battled severe depression throughout his life, often turning to snake-oil cures for his hypochondria. Like Jefferson, who used his

Monticello building and remodeling projects as a distraction from his fear, the expedition to find a western water passage across the continent to Asia was Lewis's distraction from his anguish.

While Jefferson admired his friend, who on paper seemed right for the task, he complained of Lewis's lackadaisical efforts and lack of discipline to chronicle the Corps of Discovery's expedition—negative actions of the UNCONVENTIONAL trait which UNCONVENTIONAL Jefferson didn't have.

c. 1807, Charles Willson Peale portrait of Lewis, age 33

Tragically, three years after returning from the unprecedented expedition, Lewis accepted the post as the governor of the Louisiana Territory, but he became distraught with life. If you couldn't profile, you'd say it was just a lack of adventure. The real story, though, was something else.

Without an outlet to create and innovate, and criticized for a lack of CONVENTIONAL administrative skills, which didn't fit his UNCONVENTIONAL trait, his FEARFUL trait and bouts with depression overwhelmed him.

While traveling to Washington to report on matters of disagreement, he stopped at Grinder's Stand, about 70 miles outside of Nashville on the Natchez Trace. In the middle of the night, shots rang out. Lewis was dead. William Clark, Jefferson, and Lewis's family assumed it was suicide, in the absence of contradictory evidence. Recently, some historians have asked for an exhumation of his grave, as they believe he was murdered. It is clear, though, that he had the RANDOM ACTOR traits, and he battled depression to the end.

If you reflect, you can't help wonder how Lewis's and Jefferson's lives might have been different if they had realized how to serve one another through mutual encouragement to make small, bite-sized decisions out of confidence. But that didn't happen.

So there it is in history.

At the inception of our UNCONVENTIONAL and CONFIDENT country, two UNCONVENTIONAL yet FEARFUL men made momentous contributions. Jefferson penned the Declaration of Independence and Lewis led the greatest exploratory expedition in American history. While both had the RANDOM ACTOR traits, you can't stereotype their lives. Jefferson fought through his bouts of depression, while Lewis apparently succumbed. Jefferson was a fastidious chronicler, but Lewis wasn't.

A common, dark pattern. Turning back to the CONFIDENT Adams and the FEARFUL Jefferson, what can you predict is likely to happen over time if they work side-by-side? Severe conflict is often common, as the FEARFUL person silently or overtly resents the CONFIDENT trait of the other. This doesn't mean they can't be reconciled, but you can usually predict conflict. And that's what happened.

When Adams ran for a second term as president, this time against Jefferson, it turned into the most contentious and demeaning political battle in presidential history. It was ugly, and both men in the end were ashamed of what happened.

One wonders how our early history might have been different if Adams or Abigail had known how to help their friend—or perhaps a teacher who may have guided a young Jefferson.

Imagine what might have been if Jefferson had been mentored how to make small decisions out of confidence apart from his native genius, then had moved forward in life unshackled by fear, enabling him to help his friend Lewis do the same.

Reconciliation. In the end, it was Benjamin Rush, an UNCONVENTIONAL physician, one of the signers of the Declaration of Independence, and a devout Christian man, who appealed to the two men of faith to reconcile. This culminated in 1812, and the country took note. Rush relayed to Adams that he had a dream in which future history recorded their reconciliation.

While chronicling cases of people who self-identified that they had the RANDOM ACTOR traits after they read *The Art of Profiling*, I found that the most common reason they decide to apply interventions to reverse their FEARFUL trait is that they made a new or renewed spiritual commitment. I recorded some of these cases in *Rage of the Random Actor.* In one remarkable unpublished case, a young man, tormented by his past and having thoughts of terrorist acts, wrote me for three years how his newfound faith gave him hope and the power to resist evil.

This same thread of hope also surrounded Jefferson and Adams, evidenced in the writings, letters, and speeches of the founders—that what they were creating was only sustainable with selfless moral and spiritual restraint.

Washington, our first president, in his farewell address to the nation wrote: *Reason and experience both forbid us to expect that national morality can prevail in exclusion of religious principle.*

Adams, the lawyer-farmer turned president, wrote: *Our Constitution was made only for a moral and religious people. It is wholly inadequate to the government of any other.*[6] As McCullough records, when Rush asked Adams if America could succeed in the struggle, "Yes," Adams replied, "if we fear God and repent of our sins."[7]

Jefferson, who also stated he was a man of faith, wrote that it was immoral for a person to force another to follow a faith. Jefferson never suggested that faith and morality be removed from sight, rather that specific denominations should never be mandated by the state. He had observed malevolent RANDOM ACTOR coercion in France, where royalty and the mob forced others to believe out of fear rather than letting individuals make up their own minds and thereby express faith. Freedom beckons to faith, tyranny beckons to forcible worship. Jefferson made it clear in his Statute of Virginia for Religious Freedom that how a person worships the

Lord is between the individual and the Creator and there is no stereotypical denomination for how it should be done.[8]

For his tombstone, Jefferson gave explicit instructions that the following be engraved:

> Here was buried Thomas Jefferson, Author of the Declaration of American Independence, of the Statute of Virginia for Religious Freedom, and Father of the University of Virginia.

He considered the seeds of noble thought planted more important than becoming the third president of the United States or obtaining 828,800 square miles of the continent from France for only $15 million—what is known as the Louisiana Purchase.

Upon reflection, it still seems preposterous, doesn't it, that Thomas Jefferson had the RANDOM ACTOR traits—the same traits as the leader of the 9-11 attackers and the two Columbine killers? But, Jefferson's history—the facts of how he lived out his life—tells us he did.

But we know that *anyone* can make right and just moral decisions—and Jefferson did that.

Think of it: A man with the RANDOM ACTOR traits helped change the course of history bringing more freedom, not less, to the Earth on which we live. Was Jefferson troubled? Yes. Did he make momentous contributions that directly affect our lives today? Yes.

Considering the significant number of young people in our country who today have the RANDOM ACTOR traits, don't you think they should be told this story? Shouldn't they be taught the pathway to CONFIDENT decision-making?

Jefferson's life is a reminder that we can *never* stereotype anyone, *ever.*

This isn't wishful thinking. It *is* our history.

July 4, 1826. In the end, the two men exited history in a way that caused the new country to ponder the spiritual depth of all that had happened. It's a fact few in America today know or have been taught.

July 4, 1826 was the fiftieth anniversary of the signing of the UNCONVENTIONAL and CONFIDENT Declaration of Independence. It was a time of profound rejoicing. On that day, only three of the original 56 signers were still alive—Charles Carroll, 88; Jefferson, 83; and Adams, 91. Jefferson and Adams were the only two who served as presidents. Both men died that day within hours of each other...and the country reflected on the greater meaning of their lives and what it meant for the future.

If you want to sit in the seat of history, read *John Adams*, watch the two documentaries by Ken Burns, and make snapshot reads of each player. As you do, ask yourself who you know that has the traits of Adams, Jefferson, and others, like John Dickinson, who wrote *Letters from a Pennsylvania Farmer*, a pamphlet that lamented the evils of British policy and for which he became a hero. Dickinson opposed separation from England, however, in part, because he knew good people in England who recognized that their country was in severe moral decline. He knew the forerunners of Robert Raikes, a catalyst for the Sunday School movement, and William Wilberforce, who worked for the "reformation of the manners" and the abolition of slavery. Separation from England, for Dickinson and other colonialists, was like separating from family. Although Dickinson was a CAUTIOUS decision maker, he was driven by a moral and spiritual compass to do what was right. In his case, rather than divide the colonies and their mission, he abstained from the final vote on the Declaration. Adams wrote in his diary that Dickinson, "has an excellent heart, and the cause of his country lies near it."[9]

As you read and watch their stories, picture their faces with current hairstyles and attire. Put them in time and space in your neighborhood. Reflect on how they showed their traits. Then dig into the history and profile one of your relatives who made a positive contribution in the lives of others. See if you find any linkage in how you think and carry yourself.

Or, perhaps someone who didn't make the right turn and could have if they had possessed the moral and spiritual courage to do so.

Today, we are an UNCONVENTIONAL nation, and we were established through the leadership of two UNCONVENTIONAL Americans—one CONFIDENT and one FEARFUL. In their younger days united, then separated by human sin, and later united by the spirit.

Reading and treating people right the first time is a part of our blood. It's a sacred duty summed up by Adams in a single sentence:

> He who loves the Workman and his work, and does what he can to preserve and improve it, shall be accepted of Him.[10]

Regardless of our individual profile, we can still do the right thing and nobly make choices for the benefit of others.

The word *grace*, as you have learned, is derived from the Greek and means freedom to fail. And grace extends beyond our inherent traits. Noble deeds can transcend our profile, strengths, infirmities, and misdeeds.

The path has been charted for our planet, and it is UNCONVENTIONAL with unyielding, constant change. The concepts in this book and the others I have written are only intended for a people who genuinely care about others. Please consider what this uniquely means for you as you apply what you have learned for the benefit of others.

SOURCE NOTES

CHAPTER 2

[1] Our data shows that 5–15% of people can rapid-fire profile with 75% accuracy or higher without instruction. When asked, these people usually they say it's something they could always do or a knack they picked up from a parent. Others said it was something they learned as a self-defense mechanism as a child. I've found, though, that most people who think they have the knack don't, and this shows up when they're tested. The reasons for their misreads are consistent with those who don't think they have an innate ability.

[2] Since 1983, it has aired in dozens of countries and still airs today. Many found it intriguing, as it was also the first time someone who claimed to have powers "confessed" on camera how his tricks worked.

More importantly, though, the U.S. Department of Health and Human Services contacted me and said it was the first documentary that traced the effects of child abuse through the eyes of an adult, and asked me to produce a version of the documentary that could be used for training on that issue, which I did.

[3] For a detailed discussion on the differences between behavioral profiling and racial and ethnic stereotyping, see *Rage of the Random Actor*, Chapter 3.

[4] In addition to these limitations, in order to effectively interpret a written test, extensive training is necessary. Also, there is no way to correct misreads on the spot, as is possible with rapid-fire profiling.

CHAPTER 3

[1] "Ill. gunman's rampage baffles friends," Associated Press, Deanna Bellandi, February 16, 2008.

[2] "NIU gunman's baffling trail reveals no motive," *Chicago Tribune*, David Heinzmann, Gerry Smith, and Eric Zorn, February 16, 2008.

[3] "Police investigate NIU shooter's 2 sides," Associated Press, February 16, 2008.

[4] "Older bombing suspect 'was up to no good,' cousin says," *Boston Globe*, April 19, 2013.

[5] For the details of how the four behavioral gauges were modified, see *The Art of Profiling, 2nd ed.*

[6] We've tracked this with tens of thousands of people by showing video clips of real people in real situations. They enter their read on interactive keypads and our software tracks responses. When we started pressing people we trained to make decisions faster, rather than taking one or two minutes, accuracy jumped as much as 20%. Similarly, when we allowed people to take a minute or two after viewing a clip, their accuracy was typically 20% or more lower than those who made 10-second reads.

CHAPTER 4

[1] More on the concept of range and people plotted near the middle of a gauge in *The Art of Profiling, 2nd ed.*, Chapter 4.

CHAPTER 5

[1] The research on this is still in its infancy and will no doubt be refined in the future. It can be argued that the brain actually has "thought through" its response due to a previous experience or a piece of information, which is the reason there is a protection reaction when we see something threatening. Another theory is that we are born with certain pieces of protective data already imbedded in us.

[2] Joe was awarded the Frederick Douglas National Man of the Year award for empowering youth to prevent rape and other forms of male violence. *Parade Magazine* heralded him as "The most important coach in America" for his work to transform the culture of sports. He and his wife, Paula, cofounded Building Men and Women for Others, an organization that addresses issues of masculinity and femininity, and seeking to redefine and reframe the social responsibility of sports, coaches, parent and players.

[3] *InSideOut Coaching*, Joe Ehrmann, (Simon and Schuster: NY, 2011), p. 5 & 7.

CHAPTER 6

[1] I only found this balance and quality of leadership in about 15% of the 200-plus school systems we've assisted since 1997 (predominantly suburban and small town school districts across North America). Most were driven to meet state and federal testing demands.

[2] The research of Dr. Helen Fisher, an anthropologist and expert on gender differences at Rutgers University, and others are highlighted in the 2002 documentary, *Science of the Sexes*, and includes fascinating video recorded studies related to gender differences, like multitasking. This is a good place to start if you want an overview before reviewing current studies.

[3] During the five years I was writing this book, research theories and data points continued to grow and change, so I refrain from making any declarative statements regarding cause and effect in this arena. But, it is a statistical fact that women as a group are better multitaskers than men.

[4] Research seems to point to testosterone as the key factor. As noted in *Welcome to Your Brain* (2008) by Sandra Aamodt, Ph.D. and Sam Wang, Ph.D., when women are given injections of testosterone, their ability to solve spatial problems significantly improves, although the authors also point out that additional facial and chest hair from the injections aren't acceptable for most women!

CHAPTER 8

[1] I replaced the PREDICTABLE–UNPREDICTABLE gauge because it was sometimes mistakenly used, even by behavioral professionals, to determine whether a person's actions are easy or difficult to *predict*. After presenting alternative descriptors to thousands of professionals across diverse cultures, CONVENTIONAL and UNCONVENTIONAL were found to be practical replacements. Like other terms, though, if the meaning of specific identifiers becomes intrusively weighted, they will be modified in future editions.

[2] My estimate is based upon my study of history, popular books, advertising (in popular magazines), etc. We've always tilted toward the CONVENTIONAL trait. Even though many of our founding fathers and key leaders were UNCONVENTIONAL, the messaging directed at the majority was CONVENTIONAL.

[3] There are also other factors such as increased self-centeredness as media and advertising messages bombard us with an expectation that we should get everything our way. The new opportunities selflessly applied are good. The addictive expectation that it should all serve us personally, right now, isn't.

[4] Members of the medical community, including a number of graduate students, regularly ask about conducting a study. Hopefully, one day, this will happen. (The profile of most academic "institutions" is usually CONVENTIONAL and risk-averse so things take a while.)

[5] This is a severely complex issue that affected me personally during undercover investigations. Most people automatically think that all deception is inherently harmful, but this isn't the case. For example: There is camouflage, trick plays in sports, mirages, etc. For me, it was critical to have my bearings on this issue. I adopted a three-part question used in various law enforcement environments to decide when to use deception. The question was: What is the motive, method, and consequence for using the deception? If any of the three was a negative, then deception wasn't used and another tactic would be employed. While not perfect, this allowed for quick decisions to be made when required with a foundational respect for morals and ethics. Applying this process, though, is only relevant in a moral society, contrary to what one finds in gangs, cults, terrorist groups, etc.

CHAPTER 9

[1] I addressed the Houston chapter of the Institute of Internal Auditors (IIA) the month after Andersen closed its doors as the scandal unfolded. The speech was scheduled months in advance. I had keynoted at many IIA conferences and had discussed the shift to the UNCONVENTIONAL trait. The Houston speech, however, was the first time that auditors in the trenches grasped the full impact of the shift.

[2] *Winning*, Jack Welch, (Harper Business; New York, 2005), p. 22.

[3] Hunter S. Thompson, noted for his irreverent "gonzo" approach, where objectivity was sidelined and he often became a part of his story.

CHAPTER 10

[1] The attack occurred in October 1997 in Pearl, an upscale suburb of Jackson, Miss. The superintendent, William H. Dodson, Ph.D., wrote a book, *If Only I Had Known—The life-saving solution that thousands have used to stop school massacres* (2009), that explains this trend in detail and how the application of research I developed has prevented attacks and mitigated risk in many North American schools.

A major focus of my time from 1997–2002 was teaching school systems how to prevent school rampages, and many were averted. Thousands of educators during these trainings and keynote addresses complained about the ineffectiveness of standardized testing and how it was ruining education with a primary emphasis on teaching kids how to take a standardized test. One school superintendent noted the horrific rise in suicide attempts across dozens of suburban and small-town school districts in his state. He asked the university where he was getting his Ph.D. if he could do a validation study on this trend. The request was denied because of political implications.

[2] T. M. Luhrmann, an anthropologist at Stanford University, conveyed similar findings in another April 20, 2013, *New York Times* article, "The Benefits of Church," adding that she similarly found that, as a group, everyday churchgoers experience a boost to the immune system, a decrease in blood pressure, and have "more contact with, more affection for,

and more kinds of social support from those people than their unchurched counterparts... drink less, smoke less, use fewer recreational drugs and are less sexually promiscuous than others."

[3] *Willpower*, Roy F. Baumeister and John Tierney (The Penguin Press: New York, 2011), p. 182.

[4] From a November 25, 1783, letter from Raikes to Colonel Townley, a "gentleman of Lancashire," which was later printed in 1784 in the *Gentleman's Magazine*, Vol. 54, #6, p. 410–412. The publication, which endured from 1733–1922, was the first to use the French term, *magazine*, which meant storehouse or arsenal.

[5] Like other movements, others were similarly engaged with troubled youth, and it was William Fox, a deacon, who wrote and asked Raikes if he could organize the Sunday School society in England, which he did. Several free archival books on Raikes are available through Google books.

[6] Gloucester has an extraordinary history of inspiring others to launch unprecedented social and spiritual movements. In 1791, Sir George Onesiphorus Paul, a philanthropist, built the first prison with more humane treatment as its goal, inspiring a global movement. The influential church leader George Whitefield was born in Gloucester and began his ministry there before taking his brand of evangelism to the American colonies and igniting what became known as the Great Awakening.

[7] I chronicled this case in *Suburban Gangs—The Affluent Rebels* (1995). At the time, it was an unprecedented case in North America. Approximately 75% were African American, 20% were Mexican American (1/3 couldn't speak English), and the balance were Asian and Anglo. It was the first large-scale deployment of the *Missing Protector Strategy* also detailed in *Rage of the Random Actor* (a brief overview is on the Korem & Associates website).

CHAPTER 11

[1] Luke's company was producing another documentary when Richard and I finally connected. On a later trip, he and his wife, Kim, stayed with Sandy and me for a weekend. As I learned more about Richard's extraordinary life beyond what he could do with cards, I called Luke and told him Richard would be a terrific subject for his next documentary. Absorbed in his current documentary, Luke thanked me and quickly forgot about our conversation. Then, in 2012, the brother of one of Luke's producers told him about Richard and said he found the subject for their next project. Luke called me and asked if I had ever heard of Richard. I thought it was a joke. "Don't you remember me calling you about Richard?" Luke remembered nothing, and then I remembered that I'm just the dad trying to do his part! Profiling, shmofiling, some things never change!

CHAPTER 12

[1] "Office Mess," *New York Times*, Lisa Belkin, July 18, 2004.

[2] "A Natural Fix for ADHD," *New York Times*, Richard A. Friedman, October 31, 2013.

[3] "The Not-So-Hidden-Cause Behind the ADHD Epidemic," *New York Times*, Maggie Koerth-Baker, October 15, 2013.

[4] "Why French Kids Don't Have ADHD," *Psychology Today*, Marilyn Wedge, Ph.D., March 2012.

[5] My experience is that higher-education institutions (which are extremely CONVENTIONAL) are resistant to research related to new instructional techniques, even in the face of hard numbers. I watched educators and administrators, who had successfully applied these strategies, lobby to bring them to the university/college table, but all were turned down. I didn't initiate their efforts, they did it on their own. The UNCONVENTIONAL trait was originally a point of focus for providing assistance to students with the RANDOM ACTOR traits, described in Chapter 12. Although most of these students performed better in the classroom and most schools experienced an extreme drop in threats, evacuations, and behavioral referrals, regrettably schools didn't keep rigorous data on the improvement for 2 reasons. First, their goal was to reach these students before they ever acted out violently. Second, the number of these students was small, about 2%, and their improved academic performance didn't affect the overall academic performance of the school.

[6] "The No-So-Hidden-Cause Behind the ADHD Epidemic." Another excellent source of current research is the book, *The ADHD Explosion*, by Stephen P. Hinshaw and Richard M. Sheffler. (Hinshaw is referenced in the *New York Times* article.)

[7] Ibid. 1) incorporation of ADHD under the Individuals With Disabilities Education Act in 1991 2) a subsequent overhaul of the Food and Drug Administration in 1997 that allowed drug companies to more easily market directly to the public.

[8] "A.D.H.D. Seen in 11% of U.S. Children as Diagnoses Rise," *New York Times*, Alan Schwartz and Sarah Cohen, March 31, 2013; citing research from IMS Health, a healthcare information company.

[9] Keith Bryant did this originally as part of the 3-point intervention strategy to prevent RANDOM ACTOR school incidents described in Chapter 22. He has deployed this research longer than any superintendent in the U.S.—more than 12 years—and never had to evacuate a building because of a student threat, although school districts around him did. He is also the first superintendent that saw the benefit of the concepts described in this chapter. He is currently the superintendent at Lubbock-Coopers Independent School District, an upscale suburban-type community in Lubbock Texas, where Texas Tech University is located. He hopes to participate in a study demonstrating outcomes at his district.

[10] "Exercising the Mind to Treat Attention Deficits," *New York Times*, Daniel Goleman, May 12, 2014.

[11] "For Therapy, a New Guide With a Touch of Personality," Benedict Carey, *New York Times*, January 26, 2006. Additionally, with the recent release of the DSM-V, even more controversy surrounds this manual, especially regarding issues like ADHD, autism, and others.

[12] "Office Mess."

[13] Ibid.

[14] "TV Linked to Kids' Attention Problems," Associated Press, April 5, 2004.

[15] I first wrote about the *Missing Protector Strategy (MPS)* in my book, *Suburban Gangs*. I went to 11 countries over 7 years to uncover why gangs were forming in affluent communities in significant numbers for the first time in history. I also looked for a pattern...a profile...of who was most likely to be recruited, why youths disengaged from a gang, and an antidote that stopped gang formation. I found all three, wrote about it, and that research was then successfully applied across North American schools.

In 1992, while I was lecturing in universities in Budapest, Hungary, I met Dr. Maria Koop, who had just finished a landmark study on what drives suicide. At the time, Hungary, a country of 10 million, had the highest suicide rate in the world; 1 in 7 youths had attempted suicide, according to medical reports. Her study of 22,000 identified what I dubbed the *Missing Protector Factor* (*MPF*). The *MPF* becomes operative when a youth 1) is faced with a crisis 2) doesn't have an adult to turn to for help who lives in their neighborhood/area. Koop also found the *MPF* was the number one factor that contributed to gang recruitment and chronic drug use. We agreed that I would publish her research in *Suburban Gangs*. I then developed the *MPS*, which was deployed in many school systems across North America, and produced the outcomes detailed in *Suburban Gangs*.

The *MPS* was deployed as follows: 1) Students who didn't have a Protector were provided one from the neighborhood 2) The Protector checked in with the student by phone once a week and saw the student in person for an hour or so (location was determined by the campus) 3) If a student was confronted with any type of crisis, they called their Protector who was provided with a short-list of professionals who could assist as needed.

MPS Results: For every 100 students who received a Protector, only 5% ever made a call for a crisis due to an unforeseen consequence of receiving a Protector: *The students removed themselves from risky situations*. In a Canadian case study, none of the approximately 50 students had a crisis for an entire year.

Stopped Suicides in Military—Another variation of the *MPS*, combined with RANDOM ACTOR violence prevention strategies (Chapter 22), was developed for the military (2008–2010). It was deployed across five major U.S. Army bases in their Warrior Transition Units (WTU): Fort Benning, Fort Campbell, Fort Stewart, Fort Gordon, and Fort Jackson. The WTUs were established to help wounded vets transition to their next assignment, out of the military, etc. Because of soldier despondency, the WTUs had some of the military's highest rates of suicides, attempts, and ideation. When the strategies and training were deployed, they were the only WTUs that didn't have a suicide for almost 3 years, from July 2009 to early 2012. On the heels of the initiative's success, the southeastern commander told Major Steve Munson, who spearheaded the deployment of the research/training, that he would have it to deployed across all bases. The commander transferred to another assignment, and the initiative that proved its mettle, fell into another federal black hole. Major Munson, who counseled thousands of wounded soldiers and is recognized as one of our lead subject-matter experts on counseling these soldiers, was devastated. When he was transferred to another assignment, the deployment of the strategies stopped, and suicides started 6 months later. This has been my consistent experience with government agencies that are charged with taking care of people, but I'm thankful for the lives that were saved and restored. Munson retired from active duty in 2013 and is currently working on his Ph.D. studies on the effectiveness of the *MPS* and Random Actor Violence Prevention strategies.

For more details and outcomes regarding the *MPS*, see *Rage of the Random Actor*, *Suburban Gangs*, or the Korem Associates website.

16 "Can Pesticides Cause ADHD?" *ABC News*, Andrea Canning and Jennifer Pereira, May 17, 2010.

17 "Some Food Additives Raise Hyperactivity, Study Finds," *New York Times*, Elisabeth Rosenthal, September 6, 2007.

18 "Diagnosing the Wrong Deficit," *New York Times*, Vatsal G. Thakkar, April 27, 2013. Here is more from that article (I recommend reading the article in its entirety): "As it happens, 'moves about excessively during sleep' was once listed as a symptom of attention-deficit disorder in the Diagnostic and Statistical Manual of Mental Disorders. That version of the manual, published in 1980, was the first to name the disorder. When the term ADHD, reflecting the addition of hyperactivity, appeared in 1987, the diagnostic criteria no lon-

ger included trouble sleeping. The authors said there was not enough evidence to support keeping it in.

"A 2006 study in the journal *Pediatrics* showed something similar, from the perspective of a surgery clinic. This study included 105 children between ages 5 and 12. 78 of them were scheduled to have their tonsils removed because they had problems breathing in their sleep, while 27 children scheduled for other operations served as a control group. Researchers measured the participants' sleep patterns and tested for hyperactivity and inattentiveness, consistent with standard protocols for validating an ADHD diagnosis. Of the 78 children getting the tonsillectomies, 28% were found to have ADHD, compared with only 7% of the control group. Even more stunning was what the study's authors found a year after the surgeries, when they followed up with the children: A full half of the original ADHD group who received tonsillectomies—11 of 22 children—no longer met the criteria for the condition. In other words, what had appeared to be ADHD had been resolved by treating a sleeping problem.

"I don't doubt that many people do, in fact, have ADHD; I regularly diagnose and treat it in adults. But what if a substantial proportion of cases are really sleep disorders in disguise?"

CHAPTER 13

1 *Fix the Yips Forever*, Hank Haney, (Gotham Books: New York, 2006), p. 22.

2 Once I solved the riddle about what caused yips, I looked at other sports that might be affected and eventually assisted other athletes and coaches in those sports. In each case, the two-point solution stopped the yips and they never returned.

3 *Fix the Yips*, p. 5.

4 *Fix the Yips*, p. 13.

5 *Fix the Yips*, p. 6.

6 *The Only Golf Lesson You'll Ever Need*, Hank Haney, (Harper Resource Books: New York, 1999), p. 3 & 7.

7 *Fix the Yips*, p. 14. Hank tested 3,000 people and only three yipped during a practice stroke.

8 *Fix the Yips*, p. 21 and 22.

9 *In His Image*, Dr. Paul Brand, (Grand Rapids, MI: Zondervan, 1984) p. 353–356. This was reprinted under the title *In the Likeness of God*. Brand was responsible for ground breaking procedures that saved tens of thousands of limbs of those afflicted with leprosy, was the recipient of the Albert Lasker Award, and was the only Westerner to serve on the Mahatma Gandhi Foundation.

10 *Golf Digest*, August 2004.

11 The following is provided by high performance coach Erik Korem: Briefly, this concept revolves around the principle: Specific Adaptations to Imposed Demands (SAIDS). One never introduces variability for variability sake, which is the sign of an inexperienced coach. The process is to stimulate the athlete, and the athlete then adapts. After adaptation you then allow the athlete to stabilize their new level of performance. The final step is to allow the athlete to actualize that performance in any environment at any time under any kind of stress. Dan Pfaff deserves credit for this thought process (see speedendurance.com/2012/08/14/dan-pfaff-on-the-importance-of-rest-and-recovery/).

[12] Ballesteros was also high FEARFUL, a trait described in Chapter 15. He had a devastating fear of not being able to perform which accelerated his demise, and also manifested itself in a very troubled personal life. My estimate is that about 10% of the golfers who have the yips have it because of an extreme FEARFUL trait.

[13] Other terms used in baseball were Steve Sax Syndrome, named after the Los Angeles Dodgers second baseman who inexplicably couldn't throw to first base in 1983 and committed 30 errors. Another term was Steve Blass Disease, named for the Pittsburgh Pirates pitcher who suddenly couldn't throw the ball over the plate in 1973—this after winning 2 games in the 1972 World Series. Blass never recovered his skill, while Sax did with guidance from Dr. Richard Crowley, author of *Mentalball.*

[14] Short list of "More and Less Likely to Yip": (I also recommend reading Hank's book on the yips for practical insight on other grips you can try which are mechanically more sound and yield less errant hits for some golfers.)

More: Golfers with CONVENTIONAL trait.

Less: Golfers with the UNCONVENTIONAL trait.

More: Golfers older than 45, because as we age, we tend to move toward the CONVENTIONAL side of our range. This marker may *decrease*, though, as those who are 3 or higher UNCONVENTIONAL reach this age.

Less: Golfers under 40, especially teens and young adults, because the hard-wiring in the brain that increases impulse control hasn't fully developed, which is one reason those who are young as a group tilt toward the UNCONVENTIONAL trait.

More: Repetitive shots on the course: putting, driving, chipping. Severely CONVENTIONAL instruction that doesn't build tolerance for variability.

Less: Approach shots with irons when the distance is over 100 yards. Why? There is a lot of variation required for approach shots that require a lot of choices. Do I open or close my stance? Should I open or close the club face? Put the ball further up or back in my stance? Use a steeper or flatter swing plane? How much spin should be put on the ball, and so on.

Less: Those who are more social *on the course*, which relieves the intense focus on a shot and provides more variability to the round. One might be less competitive, but you have more enjoyment from your round.

CHAPTER 15

[1] "Census: Divorces Decline But 7-Year Itch Persists," Associated Press, May 18, 2011.

[2] In *Suburban Gangs*, I documented that globally over 90% of gang members come from homes where there is separation, divorce, physical or sexual abuse, or one of the parents is severely dysfunctional. The number of U.S. youth who have one or more of these risk factors is over 40 million out of 64 million—more than the entire population of Canada.

CHAPTER 16

[1] An example is when someone deliberately learns an action *separate* from their natural inventory. For example, when I was a young investigative journalist, one of my profiling / interviewing mentors, Dr. Margaret Singer, instructed me on techniques on how to restrain my natural ASSERTIVE trait and be NONASSERTIVE during interviews to allow those I interviewed a chance to explain and finish their thoughts. Urs, the Swiss journalist in Chapter 4 is a similar example.

CHAPTER 17

[1] Libbrecht posts the following on his website, SnowCrystals.com, in an article "Is it really true that no two snowflakes are alike?": "Now there's a question I hear a lot....The short answer to the question is yes—it is indeed extremely unlikely that two complex snowflakes will look *exactly* alike....The number of possible ways of making a complex snowflake is staggeringly large. To see just how much so, consider a simpler question: *how many ways can you arrange 15 books on your bookshelf?* Well, there's 15 choices for the first book, 14 for the second, 13 for the third, etc. Multiply it out and there are over a trillion ways to arrange just 15 books. With a hundred books, the number of possible arrangements goes up to just under 10^{158} (that's a 1 followed by 158 zeros). That number is about 10^{70} times larger than the total number of atoms in the entire universe!

"Now when you look at a complex snow crystal, you can often pick out a hundred separate features if you look closely. Since all those features could have grown differently, or ended up in a slightly different places, the math is similar to that with the books. Thus, the number of ways to make a complex snow crystal is absolutely huge.

"And thus it's unlikely that any two complex snow crystals, out of all those made over the entire history of the planet, have ever looked completely alike." (For more, be sure to read the rest of his fascinating article.)

[2] According to cloud physicist Jon Nelson at Ritsumekan University in Kyoto, Japan, (quoted in livescience.com). Whatever the real number is, it's more than we'll ever be able to count—about a million billion kilograms a year.

[3] This book and its companion, *In His Image*, are two of the 10 most cherished books I've ever read—and periodically reread. Dr. Brand saved thousands of limbs for those afflicted with leprosy, mostly in India. Later in life, regarded as one of the individuals responsible for ridding the Earth of this scourge, he was the chief of rehabilitation at America's only leprosarium, in Carville, La., the president of the Leprosy Mission International, and the only Westerner to serve on the Mahatma Gandhi Foundation. His life, and the lives of his mother and father, are some of the most extraordinary I've ever encountered.

[4] Regarding the number of cells in our body, current estimates are over 37 trillion which have DNA and over 65 million microbes that don't.

CHAPTER 18

[1] Major Dick Winters, *Beyond Band of Brothers, The War Memoirs of Major Dick Winters*, (Berkley Caliber: New York, 2006) p. 293. This is principle #6 of his "Ten Principles of Success." I keep all 10 posted in my office and regularly share them with others.

[2] *Winning*, p. 93.

CHAPTER 20

[1] *Webster's Unabridged Dictionary of the English Language.*

[2] "Do You Suffer from Decision Fatigue?" John Tierney, *New York Times*, April 17, 2011. I don't recommend many books, but I highly recommend reading *Willpower*, which provides insights that will stimulate and lead you to ways to uniquely counteract the reasons for your decision fatigue and apply specific concepts based upon your own profile. There are also other fascinating insights related to the broader subject of willpower. And, because you can now make snapshot reads, you'll gain even more insight into their other findings,

such as magician David Blaine's ability to endure stunts like being encased in a solid block of ice for 63 hours, with the ice only one-half inch from his body; fasting in a Plexiglas box above the Thames River in London for 44 days. And, how he completely changes his lifestyle for weeks while preparing for one of these feats, only to revert to completely undisciplined behavior when he isn't.

[3] Ibid.

[4] Ibid.

[5] Ibid.

CHAPTER 21

[1] Precise numbers vary by geographical location such as small town versus large city, industrial versus agrarian, etc. Originally this trend surfaced in Western nations, but it's now a common trend in the East.

[2] Generation X is usually applied to those born between 1966–1976, who experienced the first devastation of the American broken home. Generation Y, born between 1976–1994, experienced the continuing family deterioration and simultaneously became technology/ media savvy as the advent of computers, cell phones, and the Internet became an integral part of their lives. Millennials are about 80 million, graduating from college between 2003 and 2018. You can't minimize generational factors, as they do affect trait formation, but trait disconnect related to the CAUTIOUS INNOVATOR traits, as discussed in this chapter, is a separate factor from generational issues.

CHAPTER 22

[1] My data is based upon thousands of surveys of educators and law enforcement professionals across North America, at state and national conferences since 1997. By "threats," we're talking about threats where there is malevolent intent, and does not include prank threats. Few states track this data and when they do, it's usually chronically low. Low state reportage and by media occurs for many reasons, including no reporting mechanisms; school administrators failing to report for fear of creating a panic or an unfavorable impression of the community; small towns without newspapers to report incidents; incidents reported but buried in crime blotter sections of local newspapers and not perceived as a trend.

In the absence of hard data, I found that a more reliable method is to survey professionals directly and to have closed-door discussions with law enforcement and education administrators who will provide real numbers. This provides a much better picture of how many threats occur that are never reported. In one case, for example, the local impression was that there was one threat by a student, when in fact over a dozen area school districts had independent threats by different students. In another case, 6 different students in one large suburban high school were simultaneously plotting independent attacks, and each was not aware that other students were doing the same. None were reported on crime reports or in the media. This is very common. In another case, I met with the assistant attorney general of a major state who was unaware of how many schools were being evacuated because of threats.

Presently, I use various Internet search engine alerts and take the national number reported and multiply by 10–15 depending upon on other factors, to get a more accurate picture. I use this variance because that is about the number I've found that go unreported across the US.

[2] Associated Press study, February 2, 2014.

[3] Teenage women have never committed an attack, and participate in approximately 10–15% of threats with malevolent intent. This correlates with young women convicted of violent crimes and female suicide bombers. In the latter case, it usually requires that a significant event occurs in their personal life, like divorce, death of a male member of the family, etc. For more, see *Rage of the Random Actor*, "The African-American and Female Factor" chapter.

[4] September 2013, "A Study of Active Shooter Incidents in the United Sates Between 2000 and 2013. The FBI's report focused on rampage shooting incidents in any locale, including companies, schools, malls, military, etc. It reported that between 2000–2013, there were 160 incidents, 486 deaths, and 557 wounded.

[5] Karl Vick, first used this phrase in a *St. Petersburg Times* article, "Violence at Work Tied to Loss of Esteem," December 17, 1993.

[6] In 2014, both FedEx and UPS had RANDOM ACTOR attacks, but not as part of a sustained trend when compared to the sustained number of postal incidents. I included observations in *Rage of the Random Actor* of increased risk factors at UPS that I have observed. It still isn't clear, though, if those risk factors will trigger a trend. Also see Source Note #13.

[7] "Youth Gangs: Problem no longer limited to poor, inner-city areas," *Dallas Morning News*, Dan Korem, January 14, 1996. I had begun to track small gangs of RANDOM ACTOR students, like the Columbine killers. I redefined a gang as follows: *two or more youths gathered together in a specific context that commit crimes.* State and federal agencies usually defined gangs related to "street" or "drug gangs" as most gangs were in the inner-cities. I uncovered, however, many gangs in affluent communities and small towns that didn't fit this descriptor, but did share the same profile for vulnerability for being recruited, as detailed in *Suburban Gangs—The Affluent Rebels.*

[8] While there were attacks before Pearl, none triggered a trend in their immediate aftermath. The Pearl attack did because of the extensive coverage it received. An attack in Alaska several months before, for example, received little media attention and didn't result in a jump in threats and attacks in its aftermath. Pearl was the first where this occurred.

[9] "Police Search for Motive in N. Illinois Campus Shootings," Chris Dolmetsch and Andrew Harris, Blomberg.net, February 15, 2008.

[10] From 1997–2002, I quoted that 1–2% of all students had the RANDOM ACTOR traits. This was based upon surveys of school districts we trained, especially from counselors and mental-health professionals. They believed that the number was much higher, based on students for whom they had provided the intervention themes, but in the absence of hard data, we quoted the above rate. Then, in 2009, the United States Preventive Services Task Force, which sets guidelines for doctors on health issues, reported in the April issue of *Pediatrics*, that 6% of all students are clinically depressed, which means that at least 6% of all students have the FEARFUL trait. In addition to their report, there are many students who have the FEARFUL trait and don't have a diagnosable DSMV condition. This 2009 report, combined with the interventions observations by school districts we trained, seems to indicate that 6% is about an average number that is consistent across the U.S.

[11] See Source Note #1 in this chapter.

[12] See Source Note #1 in this chapter.

[13] As already noted, in 2014, both UPS and FedEx had RANDOM ACTOR attacks, but there isn't enough data currently available to confirm if poor management practices were a

contributing factor. It was the first such attack in many years for both organizations. For more detailed history, see *Rage of the Random Actor.*

[14] *No Easy Answers*, Brooks Brown and Rob Merritt, (Lantern Books: NY, 2002), p. 14.

[15] *Rage of the Random Actor—Disarming Catastrophic Acts and Restoring Lives*, Dan Korem (International Focus Press: Richardson, TX) 2005, p. 163. Officially, California reported 548 bomb threats during the 1998–1999 school year, with 80% after Columbine. My experience, however, with official state and federal statistics is that there is significant under-reporting—due to lack of effective/timely reporting mechanisms, unwillingness to report actual data, etc. One study group, the national School Safety Center, estimated that approximately 5,000 schools had threats, but based upon interviews I did with educators and available samplings I took across North America with educators, who revealed many cases never reported, the more accurate estimate is probably 7,500 or more North American schools.

[16] Particularly frustrating is the fact that universities and colleges are slow to move to facilitate an independent study of these outcomes—even when they have reduced their own risk and incidents by applying the intervention themes. Instead, they want to bury the issue and move on. Going forward, the plan is for school districts to collect data that will be supervised by contracted Ph.D. candidates who have contacted me for journal articles.

[17] 2014 "TARGET" study by the German Federal Ministry of Education and Research at Freie Universitat, Berlin. This correlates with the observations made by thousands of educators trained by Korem & Associates.

[18] Major Munson, now retired, but every bit engaged, is doing his doctoral thesis on this case study. Like researchers interested in the school rampage trend, other researchers have also contacted me about doing their doctoral thesis on various aspects of this research to quantify intervention effectiveness. But doctoral dissertations is a slow process and can takes years. Recently, a military social worker with a masters successfully placed the first medical journal article.

CHAPTER 23

[1] When Carrie first asked me about publishing her book in 2009, I counseled her to put together a proposal, send it to top agents, and see what would happen. Because her subject was brand new at the time, I didn't expect her to have much success, but top agents were genuinely supportive. Several months later, Carrie approached me again, and I told her I'd publish her book, as I believed in the issue. There was a condition, though: Our relationship would now be publisher-author not father-daughter for the project. She agreed. Several weeks after we started, she was flooded with requests from the same agents because of a documentary related to her issue that was just nominated for an Academy Award. We published her book, which was very successful for her. Subsequently a top agent represented her for her next book, *The Grain-Free Family Table*, 2014, that secured a nearly six-figure advance in a bidding war amongst the top publishing houses. And yes, she is on the cover and her color was right! And yes, because we know each other's profile, *we treated each other right the first time*...almost every time!

CHAPTER 26

[1] As described in Ken Burns's documentary, "*Thomas Jefferson*," 1997.

[2] *John Adams*, David McCullough, (Simon & Schuster: NY, 2001), p. 127.

[3] *John Adams*, p. 650.

[4] From George Washington's farewell address, 1796. Washington also said, "Let us with caution indulge the supposition that morality can be maintained without religion. Whatever may be conceded to the influence of refined education on minds...reason and experience both forbid us to expect that national morality can prevail in exclusion of religious principle."

[5] *John Adams*, pp. 26 & 134.

[6] *John Adams*, Works, Vol. IX, p. 229, "To the Officers of the First Brigade of the third Division of the Militia of Massachusetts on October 11, 1798."

[7] *John Adams*, p. 160.

[8] Jefferson never used the words or conveyed the intent of "separation of church and state" in the Bill of Rights or any other of his writings. He did state that there shouldn't be a government-dictated denomination as was present in England, a primary reason so many left there and came to America. In 1779, he submitted the following bill in Virginia: "Statute of Virginia for Religious Freedom," to put an end to the state religion first imposed by England. What follows is his original intended draft, which was amended in 1786 when it was finally passed. Jefferson was not pleased with the modifications and preferred his original draft shown here.

"Well aware that the opinions and belief of men depend not on their own will, but follow involuntarily the evidence proposed to their minds; that Almighty God hath created the mind free, and manifested his supreme will that free it shall remain by making it altogether insusceptible of restraint; that all attempts to influence it by temporal punishments, or burthens, or by civil incapacitations, tend only to beget habits of hypocrisy and meanness, and are a departure from the plan of the holy author of our religion, who being Lord both of body and mind, yet chose not to propagate it by coercions on either, as was in his Almighty power to do, but to extend it by its influence on reason alone; that the impious presumption of legislators and rulers, civil as well as ecclesiastical, who, being themselves but fallible and uninspired men, have assumed dominion over the faith of others, setting up their own opinions and modes of thinking as the only true and infallible, and as such endeavoring to impose them on others, hath established and maintained false religions over the greatest part of the world and through all time: That to compel a man to furnish contributions of money for the propagation of opinions which he disbelieves and abhors, is sinful and tyrannical....

We the General Assembly of Virginia do enact that no man shall be compelled to frequent or support any religious worship, place, or ministry whatsoever, nor shall be enforced, restrained, molested, or burthened in his body or goods, nor shall otherwise suffer, on account of his religious opinions or belief; but that all men shall be free to profess, and by argument to maintain, their opinions in matters of religion, and that the same shall in no wise diminish, enlarge, or affect their civil capacities."

[9] *John Adams*, p. 94. Dickinson, born into wealth, was a farmer and a pacifist and didn't want bloodshed, many said because of the influence of his mother and his wife.

[10] *John Adams*, p. 650.

INDEX

Note: "n" following a page number—ex: 349n9 (ch 1) denotes the Source Note on that page.

A

B

C

G

H

N

O

P

Q

R

S

U

V

W

Y

AUTHOR

Dan Korem has worn some pretty diverse hats that together have helped people in so many situations. . .

Best known for developing the *Korem Profiling System*™, he and the Korem and Associates faculty have trained over 40,000 people how to rapid-fire profile—more than any other firm. His consulting clients globally include: professional and collegiate athletic coaches, corporate executives and professionals, entrepreneurs, educators, law enforcement, and military units. He also spends time showing people how to use profiling to enrich their personal lives and retard stereotyping. Each year he trains high school and college student leaders how to profile and use their skill to improve campus academics, lead students, reduce behavioral issues, and more.

As an investigative journalist, he produced the documentary *Psychic Confession* (1983), in which he obtained the first confession of a suicidal cult-like leader who claimed to have psychic powers—viewed by over 200 million globally. The *Los Angeles Times* wrote: "It's an altogether fascinating study..."

A frequent keynote speaker and distinguished lecturer for groups in over thirty countries, he uses these opportunities to hunt for answers to all kinds of issues and uncover the unexpected.

Before 1981, he was a professional sleight-of-hand magician who used his skills to educate and protect the public from threatening deceptions and was often called by law enforcement for assistance. It's how he transitioned to investigative journalism, and he often times uses effects he has invented in speeches and lectures.

For thirty years he has worked with at-risk youth as an expression of his Christian faith to "care for the widows and the orphans in their affliction." While researching his 1995 book, *Suburban Gangs—The Affluent Rebels*, he developed and applied the "Missing Protector Strategy" to over 400 inner-city youth. For six years, not one student joined a gang or became pregnant. The strategy has been used to stop gang formation and suicide—including suicides in the military during the wars in Iraq and Afghanistan.

An avid golfer, he has been married for forty-two years to his wife Sandy, one of America's premier caterers and owner of The Festive Kitchen®. They have three children, three grandchildren, and reside in the Dallas area.